WORLD ROLLOVER

An Economic Portrait Of The World

C.V. MYERS

WORLD ROLLOVER
An Economic Portrait Of The World

Copyright © 1985 by C. V. Myers

Library of Congress Catalog Card No. 85-90349

ISBN 0-9614883-0-1

*Published by Falcon Press, P.O. Box 18586,
Spokane, Washington 99208*

*First Printing June 1985
Second Printing August 1986*

TO MY SON, JOHN —
except for whose tireless research,
with a nose always for the "CORE" of the truth,
this sweeping title would have been impossible.

CONTENTS

TABLE OF ILLUSTRATIONS

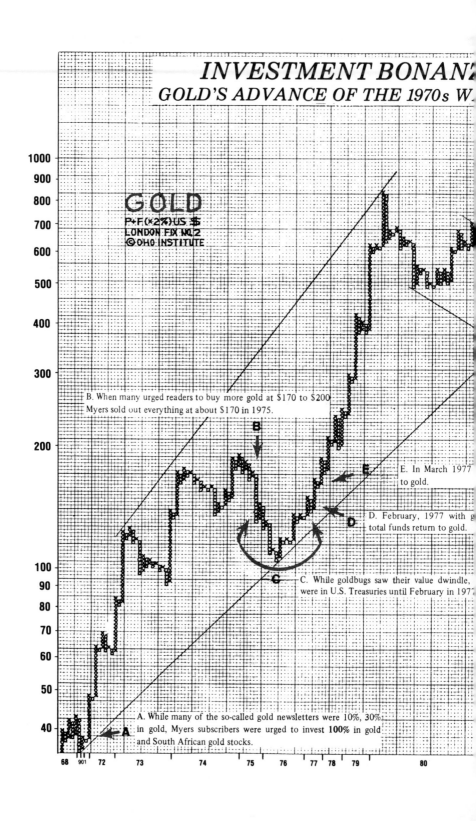

INVESTMENT BONAN
GOLD'S ADVANCE OF THE 1970s W.

GOLD
P+F(×2%)US $
LONDON FIX NO.2
© OHO INSTITUTE

B. When many urged readers to buy more gold at $170 to $200
Myers sold out everything at about $170 in 1975.

E. In March 1977
to gold.

D. February, 1977 with g
total funds return to gold.

C. While goldbugs saw their value dwindle,
were in U.S. Treasuries until February in 197

A. While many of the so-called gold newsletters were 10%, 30%:
in gold, Myers subscribers were urged to invest **100%** in gold
and South African gold stocks.

No other newsletter, no other financial adviser anywhere in the world matched the performance of *Myers Finance & Energy*. There were six big secrets. The biggest was 100% investment in **GOLD** and South African gold stocks at the start when gold was $35 an ounce. The **second** was riding the advance through.

The **third** was selling out at around $170 in 1975.

The *Myers* letter kept its subscribers in U.S. Treasuries at good interest until February, 1977.

The **fourth** secret was 50% of all investable funds in gold at $130 in February, 1977.

The **fifth** was increasing that to 100% of assets two weeks later.

The **sixth** was when Myers made a 180 degree reversal on gold at the NCMR Conference in New Orleans in November, 1980 at a sellout price of around $670. Since then, Myers' subscribers have been kept in U.S. Treasuries bought at lucrative interest rates ranging from 12% to 15%.

His advice now: "Don't do anything deflation is coming."

F. In November 1980 Myers made a 180 degree reversal on gold.

d 100% of funds be committed

Myers advised 50% of

ribers

82   83   84

Other books by C.V. Myers:

Hell to Alaska, *Exposition, Inc. Press, 1955*

Philosophy of Investment, *MFR Publications Ltd., 1968*

The Coming Deflation, *Arlington House Publishers, 1976*

Unbridled Bureaucracy in Canada, *Falcon Press, 1979*

Money & Energy, *Soundview Books, 1980*

PREFACE

Change is normal, not abnormal. It is inherent in the nature of all things that no condition remains static.

The human species has gone through a series of social revolutions, each of which was unforeseeable and, one might say, unbelievable, even unimaginable before its time.

Each of the revolutions transforms the human race profoundly. Cavemen could hardly have perceived roaming shepherds who always had their own supply of meat with them.

Ordinary people during the feudal system could not have conceived of being free, of living in plenty, of leisure, and of fun.

Each of the old modes is now regarded as backward, primitive, unenlightened.

It is only reasonable to suppose that future historians will look upon our present society as just another stage in humanity's forward movement.

Wouldn't it be strange if we did not, sooner or later, experience another complete **ROLLOVER** in human existence in all its aspects, race, education, leisure, family, the sexes and perhaps — at the base of it all — **MONEY**.

Money is the kingpin in our structure. Its use has become an inherent part of the fabric of our lives only in the last few hundred years. Today it looks like this device which worked so well is out of whack.

What gave us stability, now produces instability. What gave us security, now produces insecurity. Our system seems to be breaking down and we don't know what to do about it. Our leaders are non-plussed; like boys in the jungle, helpless.

It is not their fault; it is that the evolution of our social order has caught us unprepared, and the weakest pillars are beginning to crack.

It is safe to say that the Industrial Revolution has reached maturity; that the next transformation has begun. And it is safe to expect that it will differ from what we now know as the Industrial Revolution differed from the feudal system.

The first big fractures will come in the monetary system and, if you listen carefully, you can hear the cracking process deep underneath.

When it starts, one large adjustment will begin to follow the other until, over the course of time, the world **ROLLOVER** is complete. The first of these major fractures is visible now, already beginning in 1985.

Basically, you have to expect profound changes. And that is the subject of this book.

WORLD ROLLOVER

INTRODUCTION

When I was born, the world was populated by one and one-half billion people; China had half a billion; India had a third of a billion; the United States had a mere 44 million.

Formerly the world's largest city, New York, has grown from less than five million to over fifteen million — *a multiplier of three*; Calcutta has grown from a million to ten million — *a multiplier of ten*; Tokyo has swelled from two million to seventeen million — *a multiplier of nearly nine*. The biggest city in the world today is Mexico City, 18 million — *a multiplier of 28*.

The shifting of the population has also been a factor of, as yet, unmeasured proportions. In the United States in 1900, 42% of the population were farm families. By 1940, only 25% lived on the farm. By 1980, only 2 1/2% lived on the farm.

* * * *

These developments have been carrying a bombshell story for most of this century, but a story that seldom is thought about by growing populations. Obviously, the world has finite space and its population is on an infinite curve now, demanding infinite space. No one perceives any method which will hold the world population in check to the point where it can be contained in this shrinking globe.

When I was a boy, New York seemed millions of miles away from a homestead in Canada; Los Angeles, I thought I would never see if I lived to be 100. It took a long time to get anywhere. For instance, to go to town by horse and buggy or by team and wagon took five hours, and it took another five hours to get home. A ten-hour day was consumed if you spent no time in town. The town would get a newspaper once in awhile; otherwise news traveled by word of mouth. It must have taken some days for my parents and their neighbors to learn that the Lusitania had been sunk; and some days even to know when peace had been declared in 1918. We were six years away from generalized radio yet, and even telephones were just getting into rural districts. **THE WORLD WAS UNIMAGINABLY LARGE, INFINITELY HUGE.** It was a fantastic universe, of which you would see only a little.

Ever since, the world has been shrinking at a rate only in keeping with the shrinkage of Alice in Wonderland.

The world gets smaller and smaller by the year — the population gets larger and larger by the day.

There can never come a day when we will say, "That's enough! No more people after tomorrow!" We will never know when we have passed the limit of a sustainable population. We only know that we are getting closer to it all the time. We will indeed have passed the limit before we realize we have approached it.

The trouble lies in the backward lifestyle of the so-called "developing" nations. That really means "undeveloped" nations and that really means "backward" nations. But of course the United Nations would not like to say that, so they say the "developing" nations meaning nations that are forging ahead. But I see little forging. There have been many examples when food and supplies have failed as an answer to starving populations. Food and supplies encounter three great obstacles. One is lack of any efficient system of distribution. A second is graft and greed. A third is the undeveloped nature of communications and transportation.

It isn't just enough to produce the food and goods that the starving millions need. Someone has to produce the magic to get it to them. And among primitive populations how can these vital facilities be brought to operate?

*　　*　　*　　*

Much of the world is doomed to starvation. Much of the world is doomed to fierce uprisings and bloody revolutions. But the only answer those events are likely to lead to will be further starvation. Further suffering. And the beginning of anarchy.

Meanwhile, western civilization, the so-called "rich" countries, have risked bankruptcy and have risked a breakdown of our monetary system in order to put enough capital into these countries that can't help themselves. But alas, money that was meant to build dams to produce water to irrigate crops, to build roads, to teach horticulture, to buy productive machinery, has gone in other directions — shiny new state capitals for brutal dictators, great palaces, extravagances beyond compare in the western world; gone into bank accounts of the grafters and the crooks and the governments of these so-called "developing" countries into Switzerland and elsewhere abroad. Butchers like Idi Amin have stolen hundreds of millions of dollars meant for the people of Uganda and progress and productivity never got underway. And unless, and until, the peoples of these countries become enlightened enough to elect purposeful politicians, no such progress can be expected.

But these countries cannot pull themselves up by their bootstraps. They remain uneducated. What the western world blindly rejects is the knowledge that these countries are not ready for democracy. The difference between the blacks of the U.S. and the blacks of Africa is a few hundred years of civilization. The blacks of America were steeped in the western culture which surrounds them on all sides and at least were exposed to the educational system; whereas, a few whites in Africa, a bit of western culture, a smattering of western industry, are drops in a bucket of millions of native people unacquainted with even the meaning of the word "economy."

And the situation continues to worsen.

When I visited Portuguese South Africa in 1957 the white population in most of those countries averaged from one in a hundred to one in ten of the total population. Most native people lived in the jungle. The weather was kind to them. They didn't need to protect themselves against the cold. A grass shack would do fine for shelter. A little corn cultivated by women in the jungle could see them through for basic food. A pig here and there and some poached game looked after basic protein necessities. A witch doctor administered the remedies and the diets.

That population could survive. There was a rather high mortality in the early years from birth forward. Assisted by a fairly short life expectancy in later years, the population in general stayed in balance with the land.

Western civilization has thrown the whole living balance out of order. It has greatly reduced infant mortality and increased overall life expectancy. The result is that populations are breaking out of their britches because the western culture has not shown them how to produce the wherewithals to

15

nurture these increased populations or to motivate them to produce the necessities of a comfortable living.

All of this mess just gets worse as the populations increase but the productivity does not. (See graph, Page 18.)

*   *   *   *

Nowhere is the mess worse than on the southern border of the U.S. where hordes of the 71 million Mexicans — 17 million in Mexico City alone — are straining and pressing on the American borders. Since there really is no cost, to trying entry, this process is not likely to let up. After all, what can authorities do to you if they catch you? The authorities can bundle you up and send you back across the border. Then the next day you can try again. Meanwhile, Mexico is either starving or moving toward starvation.

Men will stop at nothing in order to get food; and they certainly won't stop at an imaginary borderline because leaders in another country say they should stop. The problem with the Mexicans has only begun. In fact, nothing but a great wall such as the Wall of China or the Berlin Wall can hold them out, eventually.

*   *   *   *

Meanwhile the western economies have been strained to the limit. The banking structure is skating on thin ice. The debt overload is pressing down with ever-increasing exponential force. In the U.S., alone, the interest on the debt is about $130 billion, which is more than the entire budget was two or three decades ago. It means $130 billion in new money must come into the economy each year just to pay interest on the government debt. But the money supply is at least ten times the government debt so it means the money supply must be increased. A trillion dollars a year in total interest — just for the purpose of spinning our wheels — getting nowhere. When you get into conditions like these, lasting over a long number of years, the result is easily foreseen. The stupendous problems inherent in all of this situation — in total — were never addressed by our leaders probably for the simple fact that the problems are too big. The leaders would rather close their eyes to them. So the problems just keep growing.

*   *   *   *

As we approach the end of the 20th century, these multi-faceted imponderables begin to come into a focal point as the rays of varied light through a glass. Sometimes those rays of light through a glass can set fire to the object of focus. The current turbulence of the many critical situations in the world is

16

beginning to produce altogether one focal point, and that focal point is what I mean as I entitle this book **WORLD ROLLOVER**.

We are facing situations of unlikely solutions in so many of our ways of life; first of all, the urban life as opposed to rural life and resulting pollution and crime. Secondly, the deepening cracks in the monetary foundation of the western world, including the whole subject of money which, in history, has involved gold, but which now can hardly be saved merely by a change to gold. The health of the way of life of a society depends mainly on a stable economic order and we will surely face a disintegration of our monetary and, therefore, economic order.

Revolutionary changes abound in science and the introduction of high technology, drastically reducing the number of available jobs, massively increasing unemployment, producing a fundamental change in our concept of what our life should be all about. The division of time between leisure and labor is a major obstacle that has to be settled. The growth of population aggravates that one. All in all, our entire way of life, our entire social order, our entire economy, our entire concept of many nations living together on this shrinking planet — all together these things predict a huge **ROLLOVER**.

This **ROLLOVER** marks the end of the Industrial Revolution and the social order it produced, just as the Industrial Revolution marked the end of the feudal system and the Middle Ages' way of life that preceded them.

World problems are dealt with efficiently in the press, but dealt with spottily, one at a time, so that the average reader never gets an overview of what the **whole** of it means.

I have put together here some of the processes at work, and dealing with these one by one I have shown how each of them is inevitably working itself to a conclusion, that many of these conclusions will bring on other conclusions which, in the end, will produce the **ROLLOVER** of the World.

We are moving very fast now and the more people who understand the **whole** situation as the various parts are related within it, the better will be the chance that we will be able to handle the changes intelligently, and for the future benefit of mankind.

To do that, we need to be fully acquainted with the problem. Study the implications of the following graph.

T. R. Malthus in *Essay on Population*, 1898, warned us of the inevitable collision between the exponentially growing

17

population of the earth and the finite limits of the earth. Not much attention was paid in any practical manner to Malthus then, and not much is paid now, but we are coming to the point of the collision and we see it in many places. China has been forced to pass inhumane laws limiting the size of families and is pressurizing abortion, even in advanced stages of pregnancy. Mushrooming populations in Latin America and Africa are bringing a myriad of problems. Even relatively advanced Russia

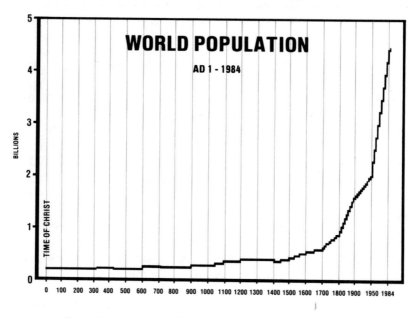

cannot feed its own people from its hundreds of millions of acres. World population is out of control and is raging like a prairie fire.

At the time of Christ, the earth's space was as large as the universe. There were 170 million people. The population grew slowly and in the next thousand years it failed to double, reaching only 265 million. In the next 500 years, it grew slowly to less than half a billion persons. But in the next 500 years, by 1800, it had more than doubled to 900 million. In the next 100 years, by **1900**, it had almost doubled — but still to little more than one-and-a-half billion people. In that 100-year span — the earth's population increased by an amount almost equal to the entire earth's population in 1800; the growth amounted to the entire population surviving after scores of millenia of the species on this earth.

18

So when I was a boy, we had a fairly thin population on earth; the globe was huge.

By 1950 we had 2.5 billion people and now in 1985 we have 4.5 billion people. Can we sustain 5 billion, 6 billion, 7 billion? That's where we're headed. Where will the finite limits of the globe collide with population growth gone wild?

Population is bound to be part of the triggering mechanism of the WORLD ROLLOVER now beginning and the focal point of it all may well be Latin America with the flash point in Mexico — on our very border.

I

A SNAKE
SHEDS ITS SKIN

"*The whole social system is going to turn over in the next decade; the guideposts of the last 40 years will be discarded; new guideposts will arise in their place; and, as a result of all this, our society will be transformed.*" From C.V. Myers' "*The Coming Deflation,* " 1976.

History may pinpoint the decade of the eighties as the time of the ROLLOVER — when in a 10-year period the whole concept of labor and capital had profoundly changed. The rule of money had changed and banking had been revolutionized.

The objectives of education had turned a somersault. Curricula in schools and universities had been revised.

Our view of ourselves, our place and purpose in the world of nations, had been revised. History will say the ROLLOVER came quite suddenly compared to other social revolutions in the history of man. But it will note that while the ROLLOVERcame as a shock and a surprise to the generation of the 1980s, there were, nevertheless, to the perceptive few, a great number of indications that a big change in man's social structure had begun much earlier.

For instance, a turbulent ROLLOVER of the monetary system was foreseeable as far back as 1967 when President Lyndon Johnson said: "*Silver is too valuable to be used for money.*"

To the astute this seemed to be saying that the president of the wealthiest country in the world had come to believe that money oughtn't to be valuable. And sure enough, that was the beginning of the greatest inflationary period in the history of the United States. It virtually galloped for 16 years. In that short time, a dollar had lost two-thirds of its power to buy.

There were many other signals along the way, but people chose not to look upon them as signals. Unanimously, including economists, politicians and professors, forecasters ignored these signs as nothing more than passing events, even including the U.S. repudiation of gold in 1973. Their projecting the future was based on outmoded criteria. When their tools no longer worked, they blinked incomprehensively, and tried to figure it again.

It was sort of like the Peter Sellers movie, "Being There," where television addict Chauncey Gardner, out on the street for the first time, tries to get rid of the scene in Harlem where two black ruffians are advancing upon him, knives drawn, by pushing the buttons of the remote control for his television set. But the scene wouldn't change. Peter Sellers blinked.

During the 1970s and the early 1980s economists blinked when they found that pushing the same old buttons no longer changed the scene. Thunderstruck, when their never-failing remedy of increasing the money supply failed miserably, their response was to send out still more money. That had always stimulated the economy before. But this time not only did inflation increase, but the economy shrank, and the unemployment rose.

Here marked the spot which began the renunciation of the Keynesians, formerly, and since the days of Franklin D. Roosevelt, high priests of monetary theory.

It didn't occur to anyone and doesn't much yet occur, that they were witnessing the first rumblings of what would become the monolithic quake that would set our social system on its ear, because it would result first in the collapse of the monetary system. Even today, economists seem still blithely unaware that the controls they are manipulating have been disconnected from the rudder so that our economic ship will miss its target by a mile, and we shall find ourselves in completely new waters without compass or any guideposts. The captain hasn't yet announced our predicament, because if he did there would be instant panic among passengers and crew. At this moment the passengers are still copacetic because the captain conducts himself with complete confidence, as if he had the situation comfortably in hand.

We are approaching the maelstrom — **the ROLLOVER** — and we still don't realize there is anything wrong.

Among the signs that we were coming to grief was the fact that old principles had to be set aside for new ones. During the Johnson era, particularly, did the basic reversal of our philosophy take place. We learned from Johnson that it is better to spend than to save. He urged the utmost spending. Credit is better than debt. He wanted people to borrow. The old beliefs we were taught — thrift is good and waste is bad — were reversed to become thrift is bad and waste is good, because it stimulates sales. Thrift is bad because it slows spending. This reversal of our old philosophy reached its peak in the second half of Johnson's elected term. The style of the time was illustrated in this satire from Myers Finance & Energy, May 5, 1967:

ONE ACT PLAY
Nothing is Better than Something
Act I: Scene 1

Vice President Hubert Humphrey enters the president's office.

L.B.J.   Hubert, Ah'm gettin' downright worried. Sit down. People have stopped borrowing. I've made lots of new money for them — but they don't seem to want to borrow. WORSE, they won't even spend what they're getting. This could ruin us.

HUMPHREY: (surprised) I didn't know that was bad. Don't you remember what they used to tell us about the grasshopper and the ant?

L.B.J.:   Humphrey, don't give me any of that old-fashioned stuff. That went out with the depression. Don't you realize that today you gotta keep spendin'? If they'll only borrow — they'll buy! That makes a big gross national product. *Borrowing is at an alarming four-year low.*

HUMPHREY: But the more a fellow owes, the poorer he is.

L.B.J.:   That is not true anymore. It used to be true, but today here is how it works: We throw a billion dollars into the bank. People borrow that and buy cars. So auto production goes up — stock market goes up. People who have stocks are now richer than they were. They can borrow more on their stocks and buy T.V. sets. Their stocks go up — and so on. Value on the New York Board increases by billions of dollars.

	Think of the security that represents for further credit. That's what I mean by *stimulating* the economy.
HUMPHREY:	I'm beginning to see it now. Yes, I see it. The more we owe the richer we are.
L.B.J.:	Exactly.
HUMPHREY:	And so logically — the less a person owns the better off he is.
L.B.J.:	Now you're talking. Follow that on and you'll see that "nothing is better than something."
HUMPHREY:	Hard to believe — but it does follow.
L.B.J.:	Course it follows. Now listen to this. When people borrow more and own less they pay more interest — savings and loan shares advance — their profits go up. The whole economy starts earning more. When they earn more we get more in taxes. Then we start to give it to the poor — NOW EVEN THE POOR START TO BUY! Away we go again, and the market goes up some more.
HUMPHREY:	Absolutely amazing — you're a genius!
L.B.J.:	My natural modesty won't let me take all the credit. I got good advisers — there's Gardner Ackley. You take Gardner — his economic forecasts are better than if I wrote them myself. Course — they're never right. But then who looks at a forecast a year after it's been made? Meantime, it's stimulatin'; CRITICAL TIME FOR FORECASTS IS RIGHT WHEN YOU MAKE THEM.
HUMPHREY:	One question — if we spend all that money — what happens when we have to pay it back?
L.B.J.:	You're still acting stupid — I swear you're just like the Republicans. When you pay back you just borrow to pay back — MEANTIME THE DOLLAR IS ALWAYS WORTH LESS so when you pay back you pay back much less than you borrowed at first. With this easy money policy, when you borrow a lot, you MADE on the deal — besides all that stimulation.

HUMPHREY:	(laughing) Those old-fashioned Republicans — did we ever leave them behind. I bet Henry Fowler helped you with that.
L.B.J.:	Now there is a genius! He has just added a brand new concept to our "New Economics." Want to hear it?
HUMPHREY:	I don't know if I can take the shock of another concept.
L.B.J.:	This one's a ringer. You know how it used to be when the creditors had all the power and the debtor was a "nobody." Why they'd even foreclose on people. That's all changed now. We got her reversed.
HUMPHREY:	You mean the fellow that owes money is coming to the top now? You don't say.
L.B.J.:	I guess we do say! You see, all those countries that collected our dollars we been makin' over here — started to get mean and wanted us to redeem them with gold. Well, we did that for a long time — until we didn't have any gold left. When they started to holler — Henry lowered the boom. He told 'em right out. *"You guys stop asking for gold or we won't pay any of you — NOTHING!"*
HUMPHREY:	Don't we have to pay? — Won't we go bankrupt?
L.B.J.:	(smiling) THEY go bankrupt. You see, they have figured those dollars like pure gold in their vaults. If we say we won't pay gold, then they got nothin' — THEY'RE BANKRUPT!
HUMPHREY:	I get you, Chief. In the "New Economics" the debtor calls the tune and the creditors dance.
L.B.J.:	You're on the beam.
HUMPHREY:	But is it really true that paper dollars are better than gold?
L.B.J.:	Certainly it's true! You take Canada. They've got quite a lot of gold up there, and we pay them 35 of our paper dollars for an ounce. Did you know that they pay an extra $5 up there to miners just to get that gold? That gold is costing them $40 an

HUMPHREY: ounce but they're turning it over to get our 35 paper dollars. They figure that our paper dollars are worth a $5 premium over gold — per ounce. Does that answer your question?

HUMPHREY: Well I'm sure sold. I'm going to call Muriel now and tell her to go shopping and spend everything we got. Then tomorrow I'm going to borrow all they will lend me. I'll set an example!

L.B.J.:   Now you're talkin' like a Democrat! If people see you do all that spendin' —maybe they'll start spendin' too. We got to get this spendin' goin'! That's the road to prosperity!

HUMPHREY: (Rises to leave — pauses at door.) But suppose it backfires — and it doesn't work?

L.B.J.:   Ah dislike that question. Anything Ah hate is a defeatist. (Pressing button.) Ah'm just orderin' another billion dollars. Get outta here!

HUMPHREY: Yes, Chief. (Exits.)

Scene Two

(Small classroom. Teacher has just finished reading play aloud).

TEACHER: Now children, I want you to study this play carefully to see if you can discover the *revolutionary new truths* developed by our president in pursuit of "THE NEW ECONOMICS."

CHILDREN: (Snapping fingers excitedly). We already see! We already see!

TEACHER: Here is a little true or false test. Read each statement carefully and write after it 'true' or 'false.'

Nothing is better than Something—

Paper is better than gold—

The more you owe the richer you are—

Debts are better than credit—

Spending is better than saving—

Bigger the debt, greater the wealth—

Debtors foreclose on Creditors—

(Children quickly begin filling in answers, and bring them to the desk.)

TEACHER:	But,children. You have put a "FALSE" after each of these statements. I don't understand.
1ST CHILD:	We discovered a *deeper* truth.
2ND CHILD:	The deeper truth is: "False is True."
3RD CHILD:	You see, if we had written 'TRUE' after the statements, that would have meant they were FALSE.
TEACHER:	That's absolutely brilliant—and it is true—no, I—I mean false— No, true—No—I don't know what I mean.
CHILDREN:	(Chanting and dancing in a circle.) False-is-true-and-true-is-false-true-is-false-and-false-is-true!
TEACHER:	Remarkable. You have qualified for the "NEW ECONOMICS." You will all grow up to be government advisers! (Exits.)

Ridiculous as it may seem, this was pretty well the philosophy of the government during the mid-1960s and the 1970s. The approaching disaster, rising straight out of inflation, seemed to pop up all at once like a black cloud in the sky. When injections of large gobs of new money only brought increasing unemployment and even more inflation, the money managers panicked. All of a sudden, they realized we were looking straight into a black hole and more inflation would push us over the brink into it. It was clear that if we went even a little further, we would spawn a disaster for the whole world. The expectations of inflation would defy every effort to stomp it out.

The expectations are still smoldering in many quarters, but those who have counted on it have lost. Disinflation brought interest rates down from 21½% in 1980 to almost 12%. Unfortunately, the suppressed interest rates also brought us to the brink of depression. In fact, many of the statistics matched those of the unforgettable 1930s.

But Federal Reserve Board Chairman Paul Volcker has convinced many, by his acts, that inflation will not get away again. Unfortunately, expectations of deflation will be a powerful propellant toward more deflation and a full-fledged depression.

You will see later why we inevitably must face inflation on the one hand or deflation on the other, and why either one of them spells economic disaster. That is why the future

26

historians will observe that the decade of the 1980s produced the ROLLOVER that transformed the monetary system of the world into a new being, unrecognizable at first as the progenitor of the new social order of the 21st century. Changes will be so great that even education aims in the system will be transformed to meet the needs of the new social order of man.

I will not be able to tell you in this book what the new order will be, but I will be able to make some general guesses, and I think I will be able to convince you that it is advancing inevitably and inexorably, and to convince you also to be alert to taking measures to prepare for it.

Generally, and in an introductory way, it is clear that a new era of science has moved in to replace smokestack America, and it is accordingly clear that unemployment will rise and will continue to rise probably throughout the rest of this century. This factor in itself would be enough to cause a rollover in our customs of business, of social reforms, of taxes, of spending, but it will slop over into the area of our liberty, to our disadvantage, I am afraid.

Before going any further, I think it is important to understand that complete rollovers are not uncommon in the history of man. Every so often we come to a period where social evolution has brought forth forces, the culmination of which result in the rejection of old customs, new reactions to meet evolving conditions, resulting then in a whole new set of concepts, leading to a social order almost unrecognizable from the world that existed before it. It's like a snake shedding its own skin. It's usually accompanied by great trauma, but in the end immense improvement for the snake, just as this will lead to an improvement in our culture and our way of life.

II

METAMORPHOSIS
OF MAN

Every social system represents an evolution of the conditions as they have developed from the former system. For the most part, the system survives, perhaps even for hundreds of years. It is decked up in new clothes but the basic components remain essentially the same. But every once in a very long while, developments, inventions, change of beliefs, strike at a system's very foundations. That is when we get the **ROLLOVER**.

We are currently at the tail end of the Industrial Revolution. By the invention of numerous labor-saving devices which were most productive under the efforts of a unified work force, the population patterns began a transformation. The people living a pastoral life all over the country began to concentrate in centers. One invention led to another. The redistribution of the population in big centers led to different patterns of consumption and marketing. As productivity increased, the standard of living began to improve. Obviously, this new system was a success. Once underway, there was no stopping it. The primitive inventions of the Industrial Revolution led to more and more, and these led to more and more productivity, more and more goods. When all of this came into place, along with the manufacture of steel and locomotives, shoe factories, clothing factories, we had been through a complete **ROLLOVER**.

By modern standards the changes were very slow, but by olden standards the Industrial Revolution consumed only a brief lapse in time in the social development of the human race. Out of 5,000 years, back to the time of the Egyptians, it took only a couple of hundred years.

Today it appears that the Industrial Revolution has about run its course. It has gone "about as 'fur' as you can go." So far, in fact, that it has become musclebound. The smokestack industries have become cumbersome, unable to meet the keen new competition. Wages have become so high that the newcomers, like the aggressive new small-scale airways, are eating at the heart of the established monsters.

I am reminded by the advent of the small flesh-eating dinosaurs as they came upon the clumsy and lumbering monsters weighing many tons, eating vegetation — unprepared for this new danger and defenseless against it.

The small, vicious, toothed dinosaur came up extremely fast. A tiny predator weighing less than a ton could bring down a 30-ton monster without any trouble at all. It amounted to a **ROLLOVER**. High technology and comparatively low wages in South Korea, Taiwan, Japan are the small carnivores. The American way of life is under attack.

What I'm working at is perspective. We must realize the changes we have been going through in the past 10 years, and especially the last couple of years, are not the ordinary evolutionary changes of the industrial society. We've always had small revolutionary changes, each an improvement on the last. But this time it's different. We should recognize that, by its very nature, the highly developed Industrial Revolution has run its course and has created the conditions which make it fit for extinction, in the face of the erosion of its fundamental base.

Energy has played a big part in this transformation, but even without the energy crisis, it would have come. The **ROLLOVER** was merely speeded up by making it necessary to introduce technologies that were already on the drawing board and ready to go. The energy shortage has speeded up the change to the efficient small cars of 1985. The energy shortage has led to lighter constructed airplanes, to more efficient use of energy, to miniaturizing the newer houses. The energy crisis of 1979-80 is being held responsible for the vast development of robots and the absolute miracles produced by the computer chips. They were coming anyway. Energy has speeded them up.

But the fact for you to bear in mind above all others is that the nature of these changes is swiftly changing the nature of our entire society complex. Tomorrow we will need new skills. Tomorrow we will need fewer workers. Tomorrow we will see smaller factories and more of them widely distributed across the land. Tomorrow we will see that the people formerly scheduled for the assembly lines have found occupations of their own in their own homes by the use of the computer and accompanying inventions, the nature of which I cannot even guess.

But this change is the big one: Reversing the population flow into great cities, out of them. It's not like the introduction of Social Security, or the invention of the income tax in the early part of the century, or the many labor laws, minimum wage acts, etc. These have all had big effects on the way our society lives, where it lives and how it operates. But this one is a different breed of cat. This one is striking at our foundations. How can we tell that? We can tell that by the impending collapse of the monetary system of this world. Each year the structure is under greater strain. And now the men at the very top of the world's monetary mechanism can no longer make it work. What's more, they admit it.

The old rules seem obsolete. We have huge new populations in countries where the rate of increase was very small due to disease. Now, with our science, the people are living longer and the birth mortality is dramatically less. We have virtually created a Frankenstein and we don't know how to handle it. And our monetary system has failed to adapt to the realities of today. It's come to the point now where either we let these teeming and increasing millions starve, or we send them the food to keep them going. That's reducing a living standard to which we've become accustomed. If we manufacture the money for them to buy their necessities, we rekindle inflation. In that case, the monetary system will also tumble because money, in time, will become valueless.

All of these things are coming into focus to produce this fast approaching **ROLLOVER**. Look around you at South and Central America and at Africa and it's clear. Look at the sea of debt around the world.

It may seem to you that these early words have little bearing on what you should do in your everyday life, or how you should plan to meet this future. But I can't emphasize enough that the breadth of your perspective will give you great additional confidence in the judgment you will arrive at by the time you have finished this book. The petty arguments about the supply of M-1 and whether the Fed will intervene in interest rates, or whether the growing deficit will kill the recovery. These will be seen as tiny ripples in a tide. The tide's furious assault on the shoreline is inevitable, unstoppable by any of our leaders, combined or separately. And it will not be influenced over the long run regardless of what they do. We are watching a wave of history and we are riding the surf.

Consider the following words by Henry Grady Weaver in *The Mainspring of Human Progress:*

"For 60 known centuries, this planet that we call Earth has been inhabited by human beings not much different from ourselves. Their desire to live has been as strong as ours. They have had at least as much physical strength as the average person of today, and among them have been men and women of great intelligence.

"But down through the ages, most human beings have gone hungry; and many have always starved. They often killed their babies because they could not feed them.

"The Roman Empire collapsed in famine. The French were dying of hunger when Thomas Jefferson was President of the United States.

"Why did men, women, and children eke out their meager existence for 6,000 years, toiling desperately from dawn to dark — barefoot, half-naked, unwashed, unshaved, uncombed, with lousy hair, mangy skins, and rotting teeth — then suddenly, in less than a hundred years, Americans have conquered the darkness of night, the weather, pain, and disease — even space and time?"

There is great significance for us in this question. It shows complete **ROLLOVERS** in the social order. It also shows us clearly that standards arising from the history of one era of man never could be used as a reliable guide to prophesying the next.

For instance, up to 4,000 years ago, a large section of humanity was comprised of shepherds, always moving their flocks. How far astray those prophets would have gone if they had tried, by their knowledge at that time, to define the future of sheep raising in coming times! Would they ever have predicted stationary agricultural population? In the later age of stationary farms and towns, could the wisest people have foreseen the crowding of millions into cities — the abundance that would be produced by the Industrial Revolution?

But in a couple of hundred years, all of the progress of the previous thousands of years was surpassed, by that revolution.

Yet, the progress of the past hundred years has outstripped, multifold, the progress of all civilization in the preceding thousands of years.

I wonder how the people of Abraham's day, of Cromwell's day, or even Abraham Lincoln's day would have viewed the future?

In each of these eons there were fashions for life.

I wonder if the people of Martin Luther's day would ever have conceived of a world of great commerce, greased by the lightning flow of the money of one country — worldwide.

And I wonder if the people of 1850 ever thought of a world dominated by a certain kind of money printed in the United States where a handful of huge banks greased the commerce of the world.

I have an idea that if there had been newsletters then, they never would have foreseen ships that cross the ocean without sails, huge bird-like monsters that fly the sky at hundreds of times the speed of an eagle, and people talking to one another across the globe and responding faster than your eye can twinkle.

And I wonder if, in the 22nd century, history readers will marvel at the naivete of financial advisers approaching the 21st century. They will say: It was silly of those so-called forecasters to use the monetary standards of the past to predict the nature of the monetary order that would arise out of the collapse of Bretton-Woods. It was as silly to believe that their monetary order would survive, any more than the manufacturer of scythes would survive.

Did people of Lincoln's time have an inkling of the transformation of transportation? Almost certainly, forecasters would have dwelt on things like the breeding of faster horses, enlarging carriages, equipping them with wheels that would turn more easily. Whatever their forecast might have been, it would never, never envision the relegation of the horse to recreation. *(No more than present seers would relegate gold to trinketing.)*

There are people these days who are forecasting what is going to happen to gold and inflation, on the basis of what they have known in the last century. And they are absolutely rigid about it. I wonder if these people have ever thought that the monetary system of today may be a complete antiquity even early in the next century. Maybe it is just impossible to foretell the monetary system that is emerging, as it was in Lincoln's day to forecast airplane transportation in the United States.

I don't believe that the past history of gold is a valid forecasting tool if our monetary system breaks down, which seems increasingly likely.

The main message is: Whole social systems disappear and are replaced by others — completely unforeseeable — and totally different.

I wonder if future history students won't be somewhat amused at what happened to the monetary system based on gold that had grown up in the short space of a few hundred years.

I wonder if the monetary system as we know it today is not going totally out of style and whether it will be transformed through traumatic economic revolution into something quite different — where gold will not be used at all, or maybe where all of us will be issued vouchers by the government? God forbid!

But I want to say that I think it is a mistake to believe that we can use standards of the short past as guides to our monetary future.

I want to emphasize that the failing liquidity of the big banks, the bankruptcy of many countries, and the breakdown of the international monetary system — that all of these are leading to a collapse of the present economic and, therefore, social framework — but that there will be a new one.

Is it possible that the time for the use of gold to grease the commerce of the world has come and gone like the flocks of Abraham, the Spinning Jenny of the Industrial Revolution, and the horse carriages and ox carts of the days of Lincoln?

It is dangerous to conclude that just because an often-mouthed saying has stood the test of time, it will always stand the test of time. Eventually what all people mistakenly thought was true — that Rome would rule the world forever — just settled like a cloud of dust, leaving no trace of the edifice of this power as the world drifted toward the Dark Ages.

I have come to mistrust many of the grand statements which find their bases in recent history. Many of these start out: *"It can't happen here,"* or *"They'll never let it happen."* We may think that a statement held true for a hundred years will hold true eternally. But really nothing in the written history of man has held eternally true except the eternal natural laws or a law like this: **"A debt is always paid, either by the one who borrowed — or the one who lent."** It is obviously a natural truth and it will never change.

And so the debts that we have in this world today will all be paid. Every cent of $100 billion now on loan to the bankrupt countries of the Third World. It is the method of payment, the identity of the losers, and the consequences thereof that concerns us here. Because these very debts and their submission to the above-stated natural law are pushing us faster and faster toward the IMMINENT ROLLOVER.

33

As we examine the metamorphosis of man, we should place all of the history of man in its proper perspective in the history of this earth on which we live. And so, at the risk of repeating something that has been explained by geologists on numerous occasions, consider where we are:

One of the main things we ought to pay attention to now is the enormous acceleration of events — the hundreds of years consumed by the Middle Ages, the Dark Ages, the Roman and Grecian Empires, and before them the Egyptians. Then consider the Industrial Revolution. Its changes have come like lightning compared with changes of previous history. And now at the end of the 20th century the changes are coming ever faster, faster!

We are the product of what we have done and results keep coming in faster all the time. We are the product of our philosophy. We have to meet the consequences of our philosophy. Man is changed by the evolution of his ideas and his

If the history of the earth be represented by a single year, the first life occurred in October and man made his appearance at 11:00 p.m., December 31. This rash newcomer is upsetting everything and it may be that he will disappear from the planet, leaving it as barren as it was when he came.

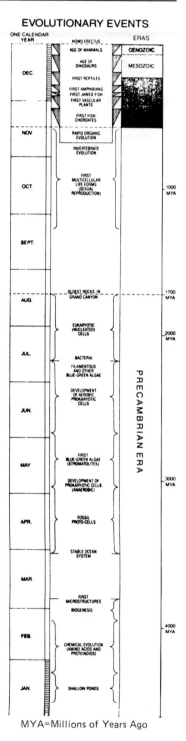

EVOLUTIONARY EVENTS

MYA=Millions of Years Ago

34

actions. Past politicians, past leaders, past dictators, have more to do with what is going to evolve over the next 10 years than the current leaders. That's because those events are seeds that were already sown, and are now growing as plants. The present events and the present leaders are limited to dealing with the inevitable harvest of these prior events and philosophies.

It is time now to move into the present, to define the circumstances in which we are encircled, and even imprisoned, rather than listen to the description given by politicians and economists, who often don't have any long-range savvy, and even if they did, wouldn't tell us. And it is time to define, once having understood the true nature of our surroundings, what we may best do to meet the upcoming consequences — not with a voice that speaks gloom and doom — but with a voice that is perceiving, real, strong, unflinching.

OUR SEARCH IS FOR THE TRUTH AND HOW TO HANDLE IT.

III

ROLLOVER IN EMPLOYMENT

Nothing could be more revolutionary in our way of life than a change in our perception of the role of "work."

Increasingly for decades, children have been born into the cocoon of a lifestyle taken as much for granted as the stars and the moon. You would go to school, you would get a job, you would get married, you would earn enough money from this job to support your family. And by and by, toward the end of your life, you would retire from the job and then have fun going boating or seeing the world.

A job has been the core of existence of men for a long, long time. Without a job a man's sense of worth is lost. He flounders in a sea of uncertainty. He loses confidence in himself. His vision of himself is badly damaged. He wonders why he is on this earth, if there is purpose to anything.

This was illustrated in millions of instances during the Great Depression. I knew these men. Yes, many of them. I never was one of them. But I was awfully close to it at $49 a month on top of a college education. But I saw many friends walking with slow, uncertain steps, heads low, to all appearances beaten.

You would not be overstating the matter by much if you said that employment had become the key to a contented life. Being blocked off from a job was the equivalent of religious excommunication.

So I'm not very happy about what I'm going to say here. You may not be happy to read it. But that doesn't mean we should shrink from the truth. And I think we are heading

36

toward a very traumatic truth which will be a part of the birth pains of a ROLLOVER in our society.

Employment is something new — very new — to the human race. The shepherds never thought about unemployment. The pastoral populations on the farms surrounding the towns of rural North America probably didn't know the terms "employment" or "unemployment." The sailors under the gold rule of Britannia never thought about unemployment. The industrialization of society brought on the terms, and gradually and relentlessly they became the biggest terms in the lifestyle of the most highly industrialized nation in the world. Until, in the end, the whole quality of life became hinged on employment.

Smokestack America and its supporting industries represented the substance of America. Only a small proportion of the people didn't have to think about employment. Those few happy souls who lived in small towns or farmed the homesteads still escaped this monster that arose out of the smokestack industries.

The movement of great chunks of the human race from the countryside into the concentrated cities amounted to a massive migration. All were caught up in the employment syndrome and all were in the same boat.

But in the progress of civilization all things, all fashions, all customs reach their apex and then decline. The migration was completed long ago. We notice that in several industries freight workers have begun to settle for wage cuts.

In 1976, I authored a book, THE COMING DEFLATION. In that book I said that we would recognize the advent of deflation when we saw labor taking less instead of constantly getting more. That would be a sharp departure from a history of decades.

I said we were at the apex of labor power, or we were nearing it.

As the events of today indicate, we have passed it. We have seen at least the following capitulations.

In 1982, employees of Republic Airlines voluntarily took a $73 million reduction in wages in the way of temporary pay cuts and deferrals and amortization of their pension fund — in order to keep their jobs.

In 1982, employees of Pan Am World Airways put up $350 million in wage concessions, taking for that 13% of the stock.

37

In 1982, employees of Western Airlines had to give up $50 million in wages — to hold their jobs.

In 1983, this process continued.

In March 1983, United Steel Workers, as militant a union as you will find, agreed to a four-year contract with seven major steel companies, taking a pay reduction of 9%, plus some benefits, a concession of $2 billion to their employees.

In 1983, employees of American Airlines agreed to a 32% wage cut — in order to save their jobs.

In June of 1983 the Machinists Union employees of Republic Airlines agreed to a 15% wage cut over the next nine months. That, to save the company $100 million, to keep it afloat — and in order to hold their jobs.

In August 1983, union leaders of Western Airlines agreed to an additional 10% pay cut for which in return they took 25% of the stock of Western Airlines. That watered down the company and there is no guarantee as to the price they will receive for their stock when they sell it. It is a makeshift remedy to keep the company staggering along — in order to save their jobs.

In September 1983, ten thousand non-union workers accepted a 10% cut from Transworld Airlines — to save their jobs.

In September 1983, Delta pilots agreed to work longer hours to help sustain the company.

In September 1983, thirty-five hundred workers at the Ford Rouge Steel Plant agreed to a reduction of $4.15 an hour to keep the plant going.

In November 1983, thirty-two thousand non-union employees of Delta Airlines were told that their wages would be frozen at least through June, 1984.

In December 1983, over twenty-three thousand union employees of Eastern Airlines took reductions ranging from 18% to 22% in exchange for a 25% equity in the company, providing a $290 million relief for Eastern over the next year — to save their jobs.

There is nearly enough evidence now to call this a trend. A trend, once in motion, continues its direction until competing forces make it obsolete.

Now we ask what is causing all this? Why, suddenly in the 1980s, do we run into this trouble that threatens to transform the world? Why didn't it happen before?

Well, there are reasons and we shall come to them but as an early illustration: Those who clung to the bow and arrow when the gun was invented were obliterated; and armies of infantry were annihilated when the cavalry was developed. The cavalry evaporated in front of the thunderous advance of machine guns; as in the glaciated advance over North America, those species that could not adapt to the cold either fled or simply disappeared from the face of the earth.

Nature is one of the few constants, maybe the only constant in this world. It is merciless. It moves inexorably forward according to the realities. The best and the most efficient survive. We've all known that a long time. The question is has the industrialized world reached the stage where its very massiveness has made it obsolete, prey to the new high-tech, lean, efficient and ferocious; and to a frightening degree, foreign?

You may say I'm jumping to conclusions. Ask: Could this really be happening to us? To the U.S.A., the most advanced country in the world? How could this happen so fast?

Electronics is the most advanced technology. It is the newest. It is growing the fastest. At first, calculators spread through the entire world to offices. Clerks were disposed of. Then dictating machines and fast printing machines reduced employment by great numbers, but speeded up the efficiency. And then, finally, computers.

Computers are now marching irresistibly, attacking almost every place of employment in the world. They are eliminating thousands of jobs. They will continue to eliminate them.

It's already a foregone conclusion that the greater part of the steel industry's unemployed will never be hired by the steel industry again. The nature of employment, the training that will be needed for new employees will not let these old workers back. Where are they to find work? As security guards, as railroad engineers, as policemen? Well, maybe.

But this new trend toward slimming the labor force and the modernization of factories will continue to discharge more workers, ever more. The same will apply to the automobile industry, the tire industry. Wherever we have used industry in mindless mass production, it will be supplanted in the computer age.

You must not pay attention to the captains of industry when they evaluate for you their future. About the time the automobile industry took the worst beating it has had in 50 years, their presidents and economists were projecting ever higher numbers of steel monsters. Up and up and up and never an end. But the captains of industry are the last to know. Their noses are too close to the map.

As an example, I want to quote to you an article I wrote in my newsletter of late 1967. Now, remember, back in 1967 none of our conventional economists and certainly no members of the establishment, never in even their gloomiest moments dreamed of possible shrinkage in the automobile's size. A decline in sales was just unthinkable. Across the country the experts were caught flat-footed. Not one of them saw the trouble coming. Yet it was plain to an ordinary man ten years before it happened.

ADAPTION (Nov. 24, 1967)

Adaption to changing conditions is a prerequisite of life. Investors who refuse to recognize a changing climate will meet the fact of extinction.

Every investor should take a course in geology. From the very beginning, life depended upon its ability to adjust. The earliest life, the trilobites, had things pretty much their own way for a long while, but eventually enemies emerged. Trilobites had to see their enemies coming. Those who developed wide peripheral vision survived. Those who did not, perished.

Surviving forms of sea life developed protective shells. Some developed amazing speed. But throughout millions of years, whenever a form of life failed to adapt to meet a changing environment, it disappeared.

Probably the most fascinating geological story is that of the dinosaurs — ponderous mountains of flesh, fighting a losing battle against time in order to eat enough to support tons of living matter. Dinosaurs developed no brain, no defense, as well as brand new enemies — small agile dinosaurs. The carnivores were adaptable. They had vicious teeth, great claws and a ferocious nature. A relatively small carnivorous dinosaur could leap from the ground to grab the throat of a 20-ton monster and bring him down almost in an instant. Naturally, these dinosaurs multiplied and took over the earth while the monsters, ripped and bleeding, fled their feeding grounds and ran, when they could, into the bogs to die.

About three times a year I visit New York and I always go out to Long Island. Every so often I find there is another big freeway. But every time I visit, each of the arteries is more clogged with traffic than it was the time before. I observe that streams of thousands of cars are rolling along like a flowing river, and that nine out of ten of these cars is carrying one, 150-

pound man. Each of these cars weighs from one to two tons, or approximately fifteen times the weight of the cargo.

Men are digging thousands of feet into the earth, all over the globe, to provide the mother substance to push around 3,000 pounds of steel to push around one, 150-pound man. At the same time, this substance throws off its waste in dense clouds of poisonous smoke, polluting the atmosphere, which each of these men then breathes for the rest of the day.

In our dullest moments of discernment we can see clearly the dinosaur was amazingly stupid. I wonder what 21st century man will think of the performance of the automobile. Which brings us now to an important summation.

The trend is for continuing high population growth, increasingly concentrating itself in dense population centers, demanding increasingly more cars per capita. Highway accommodation and parking facilities are falling ever further behind. Now they are talking of building skyscrapers to park these monsters, each taking up 150 square feet for the convenience of the 150-pound man while he works in a few square feet in a nearby office, inhaling the fumes.

Obviously, this whole thing is silly. It will go the way of the dinosaurs.

Today work is progressing feverishly on the development of electric cars, and the development of overhead transportation. These two will replace the automobile as we know it. Automobile companies disparage the electric car. Why wouldn't they? The electric car spells the end of automotive corporate giants.

The complicated assemblies will no longer be needed. Hundreds of smaller corporations will spring up in place of General Motors.

True, the larger automobiles will still be needed for long trips. But 90% of the driving probably consists of not more than 20 to 80 miles per day. General Electric has an electric car with a range of 120 miles, a speed of 35 - 55 mph. You simply plug in the socket at night.

Clearly, the automobile has reached its zenith. The monstrosities must go. That is why in MFE I recommended the SHORT sale of General Motors. For the short term because of the present gloomy market conditions — for the long term because of dinosaurs.

* * * *

(I was the first to draw a geological analogy with any part of our economy. That's because I am a graduate geologist, not

41

economist, and so it was natural for me to make this analogy. Now you see the word "dinosaur" used broadly up and down Wall Street and in nearly all the publications describing this condition or that. Well, it's good that they have caught onto it because this applies not only to automobiles, it now applies to most of the mass production industries of North America.)

The point of this is to show that a layman, without any special knowledge, using ordinary common sense, can make a projection just as accurate and maybe more accurate than the most exalted experts. That's because the layman is objective. His mind has no ax to grind, no wish to fulfill. And that's the kind of judgments you can make.

I want to drive this point home with tremendous force because this ROLLOVER will affect you and your children more than anything else in the next quarter of a century, and it will start affecting you very soon.

IV

AGRICULTURE

Some of our experts are consoling us with the view that high-tech really won't reduce jobs; it will increase jobs — just as the invention of the reaper, and earlier the steam engine, and later the assembly line, increased the social wants so that with each new invention jobs were multiplied.

Well, I have seen high-tech at work. And I will tell you about the results of that.

Along about 1930 tractors were coming into use, replacing horses across the millions of acres of farms in the central United States and western prairies of Canada. It was a revolution. At least its results were revolutionary.

In those days in Western Canada, farms of a thousand acres were thought to be large. There were many farms of half a section. That meant there might be two families on a section. Mostly, you would find about 40 families covering the township. Well, these families would produce about 120 children and, adjusting for the toddlers, perhaps 30 to 50 school children. So there had to be schools to accommodate these children, probably 30 to 40 to a school.

The community life centered around the school, which also served as a church. It was a close-knit society of neighbors. It served as the cultural background, and it produced a lot of independent people, people who thought for themselves. These independent thinkers became the leaders of the world and world business as well as the big farmers.

Along about 1930 came the tractor.

I well remember when our neighbor got his tractor. We

each had about 1,000 acre farms and my friend, who was about my age, was running the tractor.

I would get up at 5 o'clock in the morning, jump on my pony, ride two miles to the pasture, drive the horses into the corral, feed them each in their stalls, both oats and hay, harness them and about 6 o'clock I'd go in for breakfast. At 6:30 I would get up from breakfast, string out the horses (I usually drove eight in two teams of four), hitch them up, two lines in each hand and at 7 o'clock I'd be hollering, "Get up!"

I would work from 7 o'clock till noon on the disk. Covered thick with dust, I'd unhitch, feed, and go in for dinner.

Then back to the barn, bridle them up, string them out, hitch them up, and at 1 o'clock I was saying, "Get up!"

At 6 o'clock I would unhitch, detach the horses, unbridle them, feed them, unharness and go in for supper. In a full day with an eight-horse outfit, I would do about 20 acres.

Along about 9 o'clock in the morning each day I'd see my friend drive up to the tractor. He would get on that thing, quit at noon, rest a couple of hours in the heat of the day, come out and get on the tractor again for a few more hours, – maybe in the cool of the evening – and at the end of the day he had done three times as much as I. I'd start out a quarter section and, when I was about a third finished, he had his quarter finished and was moving on to the next.

It was sure hard to take and I told my dad we'd better get a tractor. And he said we'd have to wait and see how these new tractors worked out. They worked out all right. Inside of a year or two most of the people were getting tractors, including my dad. By that time, I was away from the farm and I never had the joy of doing as much land in a day as my friend, Fred, on the next farm.

Fancy Truck

In the fall we had to haul wheat to town with the horses. We had to go 10 miles and that would take about four hours with a heavy load and, between the two of us, we might haul about 200 bushels. We'd get into town by noon, unload at the elevator, put our horses in the livery stable, feed them and go to the Chinese restaurant for dinner. At 1 o'clock we'd be on our way home. We'd get home about 4 o'clock. But we wouldn't go to the house; we would back up to the granary and with a scoop shovel we would shovel on our loads for the next day. After about an hour of sweating in the granary at the hardest work I've ever known, we would pull our loads to the house, unhitch the horses, put them in the barn, feed them, go in and have supper, go to bed early so we could get up at 5 o'clock the next morning and do the same thing all over again.

I will not forget when our neighbor got a fancy Reo truck. It was harvest season then and he was hauling from the threshing machine. So was I. After about four miles out, or nearly two hours, he would pass me in a cloud of dust. When I'd gone another mile he would pass me coming back. And when I'd gone another couple of miles, he would pass me coming back. And when I'd gone another couple of miles, he would pass me again going into town, and by the time I got into town, he would pass me again. This went on all morning and all afternoon. When I got home, I'd hauled about 80 bushels to town with two horses and he had made seven trips and hauled about 600 bushels. I told my dad we should get a truck, and he said we would wait and see how these new trucks worked out.

No Small Farms

They worked out all right and in another year or two my dad had a truck, too. Tremendous numbers of hours were saved as the combine replaced the binder, and the stookers, and the threshing machine and their wagons and as all loading of grain became automated over the scores of millions of acres in the breadbasket of the United States and Canada. So if millions of hours were saved, people by the hundreds of thousands were no longer needed. And this changed agriculture, but more importantly it changed the culture of the nation. The farms became quickly bigger. The small guys sold out. The young people went to the cities to get jobs. Today you hardly ever see a farm of less than a section and most farms are several sections. The job killers have scourged the land.

Now if you drive around in the country where I lived, you will see the ghost of an era gone — gaping old houses, doors hanging, windows knocked out, roofs leaning, old barns still faintly red and caving in. The laughter of children running in the schoolyard, or the family beings that inhabited that country have passed into history. The huge machines work around the old houses, hardly noticing them.

The descendant children now go to city schools. They get the chance at better education but I doubt if they learn more. When we came home we had work to do, and the city kids miss that; they have nothing to do. In short, the nature and texture of our whole society has changed.

No Country Rubes

There are no country rubes anymore, they are the city smart guys, the motorcycle gangs. To be sure, there are millions of good students, but there are also millions of very poor students and their values are different. They have shaken the dirt from their shoes and they no longer realize they live off the dirt which produces their daily bread.

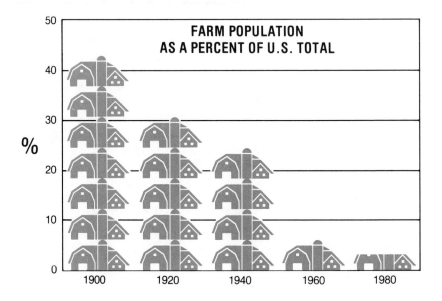

Now this was an evolution, and one of the last ones of the Industrial Revolution. The urban mechanization absorbed the workers fleeing the farms, where now one man with a milking machine could, in half an hour, milk twelve cows, a job which previously would take twelve men half an hour.

The population pattern of the continent was transformed, from predominantly rural to predominantly urban — all in a few decades.

There was a place for the farmers to flee. But where will the industrialized population flee today when their jobs are killed?

I saw these job killers at work. I can drive through there today and observe their handiwork. There's not much life out there today. The people are gone, the horses are gone, the cows are gone, the cats and dogs and chickens are gone. Here and there you will see a cloud of dust trailing a monster machine, blue, red or green, racing along, eating the distance. The revolution is complete.

46

Farmers were lucky because there was a great vacuum to fill, and jobs were created by the millions, but today where is such a vacuum? As these job killers move in to chase the industrial workers from their plants, just as they chased the farmers from the land, where will they now flee?

My point is that the new job killer will not produce new employment as it did in the past. Agriculture is the first obvious victim.

The Vanishing Farm

Nothing could be more indicative of a nation's transformation than when the population moves off the land into the cities. The character of the entire people will change; the character of the economy will change, and the end result will be a **ROLLOVER** of the entire social system. In the year 1900, 40% of the American population was rural, as against only 2.5% today. When most of the people lived on the land the mores, the morals and general character of the population drew from a realism inherently entwined with Mother Nature; unadorned; no sham, no pretense. When the masses move to the cities, their departure from the earthen realities soon results in fundamental changes in how they think, what they think and their attitudes toward the environment and toward one another. Proud, independent people become part of an intricate amorphous banded mass. Serious individualists give way to the rule of consensus. Non-conformists, in time, become quiet conformists, in manner of dress, thought and reactions.

A whole different society soon has developed. The transformation of our old-fashioned agriculture to large corporate business on a grand scale decharacterizes and recharacterizes our country. And this process is moving very fast. So far, we have spoken in terms of general observations. Now an examination of the economic realities leaves little doubt that all of this has, unfortunately, come to pass to a large extent and the family farm will soon be only a ghost in our memories. Here were the realities of the news in 1985.

Naked Economics

The American farmer is facing extinction. Escalating debts, shrinking markets, and falling commodity prices have left him hanging by a thread. When it breaks, the oldest American institution, the family farm, will be obsolete.

U.S. farmers first got into trouble during the 1970s. Huge new export markets, rising land prices, spiraling commodity prices created a euphoria. Certain that these trends would continue, farmers went heavily into debt. Everyone wanted more land and more machines. "Sure," said the bankers, "big profits will pay big debts".

For a time profits surged. From 1976 until 1980, U.S. agriculture exports increased by nearly 64%, from 100 million metric tons to 164 million metric tons. At the same time wheat prices nearly doubled; overall farm income jumped from $15 billion to nearly $20 billion.

Then beginning in 1980 a series of catastrophes occurred.

January, 1980, President Jimmy Carter imposed a grain embargo on the Soviet Union. The intitial cost to the American farmer was the lost sale of 14 million metric tons of wheat and corn. More importantly, the embargo changed the long-term trade relationship with the Soviets, who suddenly looked upon the U.S. as a source of last resort.

The Russians quickly signed long-term grain contracts with Canada, Argentina, and others. The total impact of the action was immense. In 1979 the U.S. accounted for 74% of the Soviets' grain imports; today 17%.

At the same time several big grain importers fell heavily into debt. Unable to meet their loan commitments, they cut back severely on U.S. grain imports.

Also Third World nations, utilizing good land and cheap labor, began to launch major agricultural programs. This not only reduced their need for U.S. grains, but also made them competitors.

"Look at Argentina," said John Urbanchuk, an economist at Wharton Econometric Forecasting Associates: "It has some of the best land in the world, it can produce a lot cheaper than the U.S., and it's just starting to use available technology. This is competition that is going to hurt."

The numbers themselves tell the story. In 1979 Argentina accounted for 5.8% of the world's grain and soybean trade. This year it will account for 11%, and is headed for 15% by 1990.

The Wall Street Journal reported that, "If a contract were signed today, soybeans produced in Argentina or Brazil could be delivered to U.S. Atlantic ports less expensively than U.S. soybeans." In St. Louis, current purchases of Swedish oats are cheaper and of higher quality than those grown in neighboring states.

$$* \qquad * \qquad * \qquad *$$

While the competition was getting tougher, the U.S. farmer faced yet another obstacle; a skyrocketing U.S. dollar. Since 1980 the U.S. dollar has jumped more than 35% against all major currencies. To importers that makes U.S. grain more expensive, and as a result, they have turned to other producers like Canada, whose grain exports climbed nearly 50% in the last five years.

Moreover, the U.S. farmer couldn't have picked a worse time to expand. Interest rates hit 20% in 1980, and have remained at double-digit levels ever since. Also back-to-back recessions cut back demand for several farm products, especially beef and pork.

On top of all this, land values took a severe tumble. Farmbelt land prices have plunged 30% in the past four years. The loss of equity has been widespread. According to U.S. News and World Report, prime vineyard land in California which used to go for $14,000 an acre, now goes for $8,000. Business Week says this is the first farm asset erosion since the 1950s.

Worst of all was the tumble in commodity prices. In 1980 wheat was selling for over $6 a bushel. Today it sells at $3.41. Corn, which was selling at $3.96 a bushel now sells for $2.97.

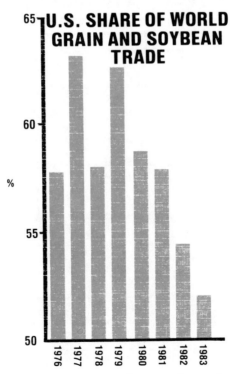

U.S. SHARE OF WORLD GRAIN AND SOYBEAN TRADE

Taken together these factors have hammered U.S. agriculture. In 1979 the U.S. accounted for 63% of the world's grain and soybean trade. Today it accounts for about 50%.

Outlook

The year 1984 gave farmers some hope. For the first time in four years, farm income rose; from less than $10 billion in 1983 to about $14 billion in 1984. During the same period, fuel costs fell 3.4%.

But that recovery may be too late. The major reason: the incredible debt overhang. Farm debt in 1984 totaled more than $215 billion, more than six times the $35 billion owed in 1970.

Farmers also face the threat of losing much needed government support. Congress will introduce a new federal farm policy this year, and President Reagan is pushing to unload some steep farm costs. In 1983 farm support programs cost Americans $19.7 billion (not including the $10 billion Payment in Kind program). That compares to $2.7 billion in farm aid in 1979. In 1985 the U.S. Department of Agriculture has been budgeted $38.4 billion - 10% above 1984's budget.

Now the government **wants out**.

CBT WHEAT PRICE — MAR. 1985

FEB. 1978 - Jan. 1985

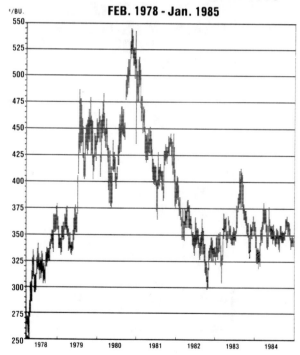

But already a lot of farmers are being **forced out**. One study estimates that a third of Iowa's 110,000 farms may be forced out within this decade.

In the end the banks have been left holding the bag. From mid-1983 to mid-1984, the number of farm banks on the FDIC's problem list jumped 118% to 231. Overall, farm banks represent 34% of all troubled banks. According to Kitty Heller, an analyst at Veribanc Inc., "Fifteen states account for 73% of the banks with problem loans in the first half of 1984, and 11 were states loaded with troubled farm banks."

One such bank is First Chicago, which reported a $72 million third quarter loss, some of it the direct result of sour farm loans.

Some 30% of the $25 billion in Farmer's Home Administration loans are delinquent.

*   *   *   *

Agriculture is America's largest industry accounting for more than $500 million a year in sales and 23 million jobs. Agriculture is one of the last bastions of American economic might. Agriculture was the number one foreign exchange earner in 1984 bringing in $38 billion.

Farm commodities help hold down the huge trade deficit incurred by other industrial imports including cars, clothing, oil and wine.

The recovery of 1984 didn't rub off much on the American farmer, and still the dollar kept rising, commodities kept falling, and the foreign competition kept improving.

In the World Rollover that is underway, we may just lose the American farmer.

Fallout

But the ball does not stop there. The falling mountain climber may take his friends with him. That's what the demise of the American farm will mean.

Farm machinery firms have taken a beating.

In the last four years U.S. farm equipment makers have lost more than $2 billion. Now wallowing in debt, and facing bleak sales for 1985, some big names like International Harvester are packing it in.

Like the farmers, their problems began in the seventies. Assured that big ag profits would continue, farm equipment manufacturers expanded like crazy. Throughout that decade that policy proved correct. Nationwide, farm acreage jumped from 293 million acres in 1970 to 356 million in 1980, and farm equipment profits surged.

Then in 1981 the crunch hit; suddenly the last thing farmers looked to buy was a new tractor. From 1979 to 1984 combine sales fell from 32,000 units to 8,800 units.

Faltering sales meant the loss of thousands of jobs. In 1979 farm equipment factories employed 160,000 people. Today they employ only 90,000.

During the last six weeks of 1984, farm equipment giants shut down most of their plants. On-hand inventory exceeded annual demand. Overall, 1984 sales were 45% of the 1979 rate. "This year will be essentially the same," says Dean McKee, chief economist for Deere and Company.

A.O. Smith Corp. appears convinced. After building storage bins since 1949, the company has decided to sell its unprofitable agricultural business. Ag sales which had totaled 17% of the company's business in 1979, accounted for only 7% in 1983.

International Harvester Co. also wants out. It has planned to sell its money-losing farm equipment division to Tenneco Inc. (subsidiary of J. I. Case). But for Harvester it may be too late. The former giant carries $1.4 billion debt and $900 million in unfunded pension liabilities. Total sale price of the farm division comes to only $430 million. Some analysts now doubt Harvester can survive, can even pay the pensions.

Two giants that will hang on but probably lose more money in 1985 are J. I. Case, and Allis-Chalmers.

The industry is experiencing a violent shake-out.

A New Breed

On the horizon is a new breed of farmer - the professional farm manager. He may work for himself, or he may work for a big corporation overseeing thousands of acres. He will replace the family farm.

"This is the era of the professional farm manager, the traveling farm computer salesman - and soon perhaps the remote controlled tractor. That isn't the era of the old-style family farmer," says the Wall Street Journal.

The process is underway. About 12% of the U.S. farmers account for 63% of the country's sales. The largest farms, those with sales over a quarter of a million dollars a year, have increased in number by 54% from 1978 to 1982. A growing number are run by professional managers, already managing acreage totaling the area of Kansas, says the Wall Street Journal.

The long-term result of this will be cheaper more abundant food, beefing up the export power of the United States.

But that's several years away. Meanwhile, carnage will be immense. Great numbers of American farmers will lose their very way of life. Banks will face billions of dollars in write downs; some will fail. And the U.S. economy will lose one of its most vital generators. All this, as farming, America's oldest cornerstone, is relentlessly rolled over.

V

MINING - AN UNANNOUNCED DISASTER

Ancient kings flogged couriers of bad news from the battlefield. Bearers of bad news from the financial front can expect the same treatment — ridicule at the very least. But the king who successfully squelched the bad battle news took on the risk of losing his neck by failing to realize that his protective armies were in retreat.

Investors will listen to the euphoria out of Washington and Wall Street, bad-mouthing and disbelieving any bad news, taking onto themselves a terrible risk.

The mining industry has usually been a bright spot on the American economic scene and many people still think it is. But in mining we are heading into even a worse future than we can, so far, foresee in agriculture and the smokestack industries. Mining has an added factor working against it — the enormous debt which has to be paid off by Third World mining, as the demand for the products diminishes and the price shrinks.

Meanwhile, Wall Streeters keep whooping it up and are simply unaware, and the bad news out there is effectively stifled before it reaches the bridge.

To use the worst case first, let's start with copper.

In recent years North American producers of copper, lead, zinc, nickel, coal, iron ore and molybdenum have been devastated. In 1980 U.S. mining earned $8.9 billion; by 1983 it earned less than $6 billion. Even during the recent recovery losses have continued to pile up. Today the situation is desperate; some experts contend that unless the federal government subsidizes U.S. mining companies, the U.S. may lose much of its mineral production.

"We are in real danger of losing 75% of our copper industry and 40% to 50% of our iron ore industry," says Robert C. Horton, head of the Bureau of Mines.

That's a long fall for an industry which once dominated world markets. After World War II U.S. mining hit a boom cycle. Throughout the 1950s and 1960s markets continued to expand. At their apex North American companies controlled world markets. In the 1960s Amax Inc. produced 50% of the free world's molybdenum, while Canada's Inco Ltd. produced 90% of the world's nickel.

Then in the seventies, a series of events began to tear at North America's mining industry.

During that decade North American mines were hit by the environmental movement. New legislation to clean up mining practices exacted a heavy price as parts of whole operations were overhauled.

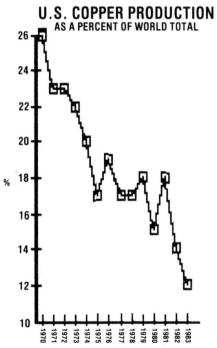

U.S. COPPER PRODUCTION
AS A PERCENT OF WORLD TOTAL

In 1973 the energy crisis hit. Oil prices shot up 1000% in seven years. Mining costs took off. Confident of ever increasing prices, North American companies mistakenly began to borrow heavily.

At the same time Third World countries became major producers. Rich in resources, government borrowed and subsidized, cheap labor produced an immediate impact. Suddenly prices could no longer be set in North American board rooms; now they were set daily on the London Metals Exchange.

Then the 1981-82 recession hit. Two big metal buyers, steel and autos, were rocked. As auto and steel sales crashed metal demand dried up. Big debts began piling up on Third World producers. In desperate need of hard currency they began to push production to its limit, putting further pressure on prices.

Copper, which traded at $1.30 in 1980, fell to 60 cents a pound by 1984, its **lowest real price this century**. From their highs, molybdenum fell 80%; lead 60%; tungsten 50%, and nickel 35%.

North American mining concerns were saddled with big debts, lost markets, and growing debt began to pile up. From 1982 through September 1984, North American mining companies reported total losses of $1.8 billion. Over four years the industry's debt grew from 36% of capitalization to more than 41% — 10% more than the average U.S. industry.

Revere Copper was one of many bankruptcy victims. Many others have been taken over by oil conglomerates, who expected mining economics to reverse. They were wrong. In 1984 Atlantic Richfield Co. wrote off $785 million on Anaconda Minerals Co., a copper producer which it purchased in 1977 for $680 million. Last year Pennzoil Co. was forced to take a $100 million write-off on its Duvual Corp., a copper and molybdenum producer. Standard Oil of Indiana has decided to sell its mining units. More sales are expected.

Today losses stretch across the board.

In copper, Kennecott, Asarco, and Phelps Dodge keep running deeper into debt. During the first nine months of 1984 Phelps Dodge lost $50 million; Kennecott Corp. $41 million, and Asarco Inc. $70 million. Over four years Phelps Dodge has lost $188 million dollars or $8.65 a share. In 1981 its stock sold for over $45 a share; in early 1985, $20 a share. The world's nickel giant suffered worse. Until 1981, it had not posted a loss for 80 years. Over the next four years its sales dropped nearly half ($2.15 billion to $1.3 billion). It posted losses for 13 consecutive quarters. It cut off 7,000 employees, 30% of its work force. In 1980 Inco sold at $33 a share, just above book value.

Lead and zinc are moving in the same direction. During

third quarter 1984 Noranda Inc., a major zinc and lead producer lost $38 million, signaling 1984 as another losing year.

The erosion has been encompassing. **Over the last 30 years America's share of world mineral production has declined 50%.** Mineral imports accounted for 20% of our needs in 1960; by 1985 imports support half of U.S. consumption.

The social costs have been high. **Since 1981 mining employment has fallen from 109,000 to 40,000.** Another 12,000 jobs could be lost by 1987.

In every respect, mining's future is bleak.

The stream of Third World metal imports appears endless. Owing billions of dollars, countries like Chile, Zaire, Zambia and Peru continue to overproduce, while other resource giants like Brazil (iron ore) are just entering the market.

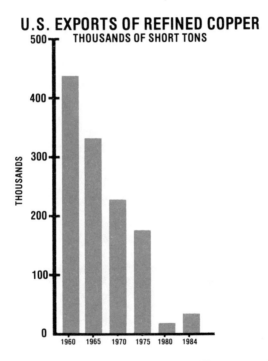

U.S. EXPORTS OF REFINED COPPER
THOUSANDS OF SHORT TONS

U.S. producers are unable to compete. For example Chile, with its rich reserves, can refine copper at a cost of 43 cents a pound, while the best U.S. mines can't sell much below 70 cents a pound. Chile pays its miners a tenth of what U.S. companies pay. Brazil's labor costs are 78% below the U.S.

Finally, the U.S. is running out of cheap reserves. According to BusinessWeek, "Many of the richest domestic base-metal reserves are coming close to depletion, while the low-grade ore that remains is becoming too costly to recover."

Last summer the U.S. mining industry petitioned President Reagan to impose tough trade measures against metal imports - he refused. A key consideration in that choice is the huge debt owed to the U.S. by these exporters. In fact the U.S. government, through agencies like the World Bank and the IMF, has been a major supporter of these countries' mining industries. For example, in 1984 the Inter American Bank lent Chile $268 million to expand its copper production, while the IMF forwarded $600 million to support Zambia's copper production. It is expected that by 1990 Chile, the world's largest copper supplier, will up production 40% above its current 1.1 million ton annual output.

U.S. IMPORTS OF REFINED COPPER
THOUSANDS OF SHORT TONS

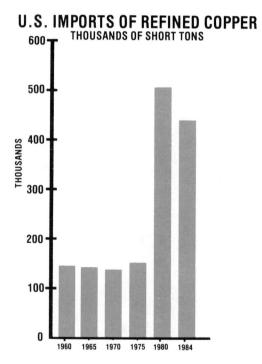

While supplies remain abundant, demand will be shrinking. New synthetic materials are expected to grab an increasing share of the metals market. Firoze E. Katrak, vice-president of Boston commodity firm, Charles River Associates Inc., estimates that in 15 years technological advances will enable manufacturers to use only two-thirds as much copper per unit as they do today. Fibre optics and microwaves have already

58

replaced copper in telecommunications, while lead is being eliminated from gasoline.

Furthermore, says Forbes Magazine, fundamental demand changes have taken place in the economy. "Over the last 30 years U.S. GNP has become increasingly less materials-intensive. Between 1950 and 1981 U.S. real GNP tripled, but steel consumption rose less than 30%, lead not at all and zinc actually declined."

Slack demand and overproduction means weak prices. Katrak predicts that copper will sell for less than 90 cents a pound in constant dollars through the rest of the century while nickel and lead prices will stagnate into the 1990s.

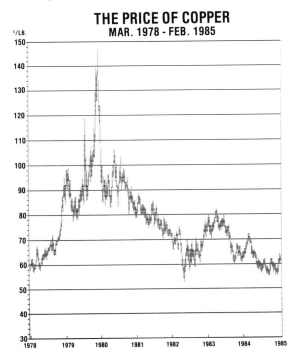

THE PRICE OF COPPER
MAR. 1978 - FEB. 1985

Today these former colossuses tremble. Tomorrow many will be toppled; wasted by debt, overproduction and foreign competition. Like the rest of smokestack America, mining right now is on the ropes, its apex behind it.

* * * *

Reporting bad facts is not pessimism. Failing to report bad facts is bad journalism. The American financial press is guilty of reporting numerous negative stories severally and apart for minimum impact. Reporting separately and unrelatedly justifies us in smearing a black cross over Wall Street, Washington and the press for concealment.

In President Reagan's 1985 euphoric address on the State of the Union, did he even slightly refer to money, agriculture, smokestack industry, this broken banking system, the unpayable debts, the failure of nuclear power? By failing to emphasize the truth, they have all told us an enormous lie.

Meanwhile, the Dow Jones markets proceed in ignorance, and people reporting underlying bad news are called "gloomers and doomers."

*   *   *   *

And all the while a tumultuous **WORLD ROLLOVER** is rumbling just beneath the surface.

VI

CONTRACTION

Basic U.S. industry continues to contract. A fierce foreign assault, when viewed from a 20-year perspective, comes as a shock. The bigger shock comes when you realize that public America is entirely unaware of what is underway.

The growth in the service industries has kept us anesthetized. This growth has built many new jobs and by so doing has covered up the chronic deterioration at the very foundations of industrial America.

A glance at the following graphs on employment, steel production and auto production, will bring you up sharp. Behind these surface manifestations are facts so sobering that the failure to be aware of them could cause you to be led astray to the point where it might even mean economic ruin while listening to all the pabulum being constantly fed out of Washington.

You owe it to yourself to evaluate these next few pages coolly and objectively — then strike down the conclusion if you wish. But, please, first a look at the evidence.

*   *   *   *

In the face of all the talk about the recovery, you should first realize that manufacturing has not made a recovery at all. Says Janet Norwood, commissioner of the Bureau of Labor Statistics: **"Manufacturing has recovered only about 70% of the jobs lost since the recession." And a second contraction may very well be underway.**

Industrial production began falling in late 1984. This was obscured by the fact that unemployment had not risen. But almost all the new jobs that Reagan was able to boast about

61

came from the service industry. Its lusty growth added 170,000 jobs a month during most of 1984.

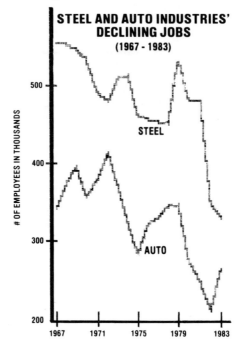

STEEL AND AUTO INDUSTRIES'
DECLINING JOBS
(1967 - 1983)

OF EMPLOYEES IN THOUSANDS

STEEL

AUTO

That may have kept our minds off of the huge trade deficit. But that deficit probably has more meaning for our economic future than any other single factor. It was $12.68 billion in October of 1984 and promised to reach $130 billion for the whole year. That's a new kind of history for the United States. It's never happened before. It has immense implications. But it's easily explained.

Better in quality and lower in price, foreign goods are relentlessly invading the domestic market, leaving U.S. manufacturers floundering and crying for government protection, pleading for restrictions. But the usefulness of restrictions is losing credibility.

In 1980, when free-trader Ronald Reagan came to office, 20.3% of imported goods were under restriction. Today, 40% is not enough. It is clear that the answer lies not in restrictions.

What's killing us now is obsolete factories and wages which allow our competitors to cut us to ribbons. And we have a population which will not accept the wages they must accept if they are to compete against a new breed of lean and efficient industrial nations.

To the steel industry, it must seem as though the recession never ended. After losing more than $6 billion in 1982 and 1983, steel is once again facing gloomy forecasts. Current demand is weak, prices are low, and imports are surging. In November, 1984 the Wall Street Journal commented: *"Over the past six months, steel orders and shipments have plunged, industry operating rates have dropped to a dismal 59% of capacity from 82% last May, and prices are being heavily discounted. Prospects for a pickup in the current quarter or even the 1985 first period are beginning to look bleak."*

Meanwhile, foreigners keep up the relentless pressure. In the first eight months of 1984, imports claimed 26% of the United States market. In a misguided defense, the U.S. is trying now to negotiate "voluntary" import restraint agreements with Japan, Argentina, Spain, Mexico, Brazil and South Korea. The objective is to reduce imports to 18.5% of the market. But even if we succeed − if those countries voluntarily cooperate − imports will still be 80% higher than they were in 1973.

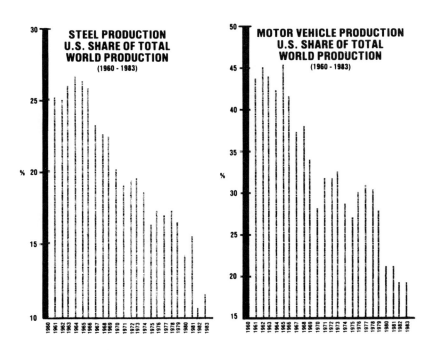

Take the word of Glenn Daniel, a steel credit analyst at Moody's Investors Service: "U.S. steel companies face a race against time."

They must post big gains, he says, before they get hit with the next economic downturn. If not, the steel industry may drown in a sea of debt.

But the question is, how on earth will the steel companies post big gains? Their factories are old, but their sales are too small to justify large debt to build new ones. And even if they could build new ones, the killing wages in the United States would leave their shiny new plants at reduced capacity.

Even autos, the 1984 darling of Wall Street, appear to be skating on thin ice. After posting big sales gains, Detroit seems to be running out of momentum. Domestic car sales for October totaled an annual rate of 6.9 million units, down from 7.9 million in September, and 7.2 million a year ago. That's a long way off the more than 8 million sales pace of spring 1983. The GM strike cannot, by itself, be blamed for the huge difference.

Worse though, the outlook is negative. Import restrictions have kept a lid on Japanese cars, but as of March 1985, they are gone. The result, says one analyst, is that the Japanese will be able **to double their current 21% share of the U.S. car market in just two years.**

The seriousness of the situation is not generally understood. The competitive implications are so great that Detroit is about to throw in the towel on small cars and go back to making medium and large cars. If another recession comes (as it surely will), that could be fatal.

Tentatively, the big three are planning to buy Japanese cars directly, or to buy Japanese components and assemble them here. The estimated savings would be about $1,700 for a subcompact.

Said BusinessWeek: *"Although domestic auto makers will continue to develop and build their own midsize and large cars in the United States, they are turning over manufacture of their smaller cars to an array of joint ventures with foreign competitors, mostly Japanese."*

United Auto Workers president, Owen Bieber, says that will cost his union 500,000 jobs. A badly shaken auto industry will result.

This is hardly a surprise. The auto industry and industrial America in tandem have been weakening for more than a decade.

From 1972 to 1982 the United States posted an annual average growth rate (after inflation) of 2.3%. That put us behind France's 2.5% growth; Italy at 2.6%; India 3.6%; Japan 5.1%; Mexico 6.1%; and South Korea 8.2%.

Commencing back in 1960, the United States produced 29% of the free world's total output. Today that has fallen to 24%.

In 1973 the United States' total share of world exports was 13.4%. Ten years later it was 12.1%.

United States steel is down 45% from the 1973 peak of 151 million tons. U.S. auto production is down 30% from the 9.7 million rate of 1973. In short, the U.S. industrial economy has been outdistanced so far that it may never catch up, particularly under the double burden of new capital requirements and an impossible wage scale.

Year	U.S. Auto Production as % of World Total	U.S. Steel Production as % of World Total
1960	48.3%	26.0%
1961	43.7	25.1
1962	45.0	25.0
1963	44.0	25.9
1964	42.3	26.5
1965	45.4	26.2
1966	41.6	25.8
1967	37.3	23.2
1968	37.9	22.6
1969	34.0	22.4
1970	27.9	20.1
1971	31.7	19.1
1972	31.6	19.4
1973	32.4	19.6
1974	28.7	18.6
1975	27.0	16.4
1976	29.8	17.2
1977	30.9	16.9
1978	30.4	17.3
1979	27.7	16.5
1980	20.9	14.2
1981	21.0	15.5
1982	19.0	10.5
1983	19.2	11.6

In the first place, the United States exported its technology to the Third World, which then improved upon it, while the United States remained static, clinging to the technology of a quarter of a century ago.

As a convincing and irrefutable example: Some 32% of U.S. steel is produced by ultra-modern continuous casting, while 80% of Japanese steel is so produced, and by much cheaper workers. How do you catch up with that?

A Citicorp study revealed that in 1980 U.S. hourly compensation was $11.44 — seventh among 12 industrial

65

nations surveyed; but by 1983 U.S. average compensation had surged to $14.44 an hour, by far the highest.

The cost spread in some industries is out of sight. For example, U.S. automakers earn more than $23 an hour in benefits compared to $12 in Japan, $2.50 in Korea, and $5 in Mexico. In steel, U.S. workers make more than $20 an hour in compensation compared to $12 in Japan, $8 in England, $3 in South Korea.

The answer so far has been to slash employment. In 1969 the U.S. auto industry employed 400,000 workers; in 1983, 265,000 – a **34% decline.** During the same period, steel employment has fallen from 550,000 to 330,000, **a 40% drop.**

The plain truth is that America is no longer the industrial giant of the world.

To survive, smokestack America has but one choice – to move overseas. By making use of cheap foreign labor, U.S. industries will be able to maintain a share of the world market.

But the consequences on America's employment force will be immense. So far, the service sector has been able to take up the slack by providing jobs from soda jerks to heart surgeons. (In the last few years more than two million new jobs have been created by the fast food industry.) But that can only carry us so far. A nation must have the underlying wealth to pay for all these services. Simply put, we can't all run around and sell to each other; somebody has to make the goods.

Investment Implication

In the short run this imbalance places the economic recovery in jeopardy. Unless U.S. manufacturers can begin to sell their goods at home and abroad, their employment ranks will diminish further. Greater unemployment will snowball the problem, eroding personal income and thus diminishing sales. Background to all this will be a growing trade deficit and faltering confidence.

Wall Street is pretty cocksure right now, but that will quickly change as sales stall, earnings fall, and unemployment swells. Smokestack industries appear to be facing possible wholesale liquidations further down the line. This represents basic destruction and deterioration of the underpinnings of the whole Dow Jones.

History has shown us that when a country loses its economic preeminence, its standard of living falls. It happened to Spain in the 16th century, and to England in the early 20th century. It's happening to the United States today, and the ramifications of it are immense because the whole world is involved.

It all forms a part of the pattern of the great **ROLLOVER**.

VII

BIOTECH AND FIBRE OPTICS

Only in 1974 did the first scientists splice genes of a living organism. Ten years later, that technology promises to revolutionize almost every field of industry.

"**Genetic engineering will have more impact than any other technology in the history of man, maybe including fire,**" says Dr. George Rathman, founder of Agmen Corp., and a leading genetic engineer. Rathman and others believe that the manipulation of DNA (coded strands of protein which give order to all life) will be the driving engine for this revolution.

Biotechnology is basically the restructuring or construction (protein engineering) of living organisms. These organisms can perform a huge range of tasks. Says John Naisbitt, author of *Megatrends*: "**Biotechnology will use manipulated genes to alloy, fabricate, and remake living organisms into industrial products.**"

Since the 1975 start, more than $3 billion has been invested in over 100 U.S. biotechnologycompanies. That's expected to reach $50 billion by the year 2000.

Here's what to expect:

Medicine

Biotechnology's benefits to medicine may outweigh all else. Many scientists believe that gene manipulation holds the key for a cancer cure. Hopes are that protein engineering will yield genes which will counteract cancer cells.

Beyond the cancer quest are other vitally important applications. Already, chemicals are being tested which dissolve blood clots, and help regulate the body's immune system. Researchers can already alter animal insulin to treat diabetes.

Work is continuing on bio-reactors – implants which produce and release antibodies into the body.

Writes BusinessWeek: "Diabetics may soon be freed from the tyranny of the needle. Instead of their daily insulin injections, victims of this devastating disease will receive an annual shot of living pancreas cells encapsulated in tiny plastic bubbles."

Agriculture

Biotechnology promises new crop varieties which grow faster, are larger and need less moisture. Genetically manipulated seed industries will become a huge business, says agriculture consultant L. William Tewles, who predicts growth from $8 million next year to $6.8 billion by the year 2000.

Animals won't be left out. Leaner pigs, hardier cows, bigger chickens will soon inhabit the farms as man corrects nature's imperfections. Productivity will increase while costs tumble. Not since the arrival of the tractor will such a transformation have been seen.

(Of course, there may not be many "farms" as such, the technological advance is eliminating farms and transforming "farms" into businesses.)

The U.S. chemical industry sells $50 billion a year in products, most of them oil based. That may change, too. Biotechnology can produce cheaper, more efficient organic-based chemicals. Already, the G.D. Searle & Co. sweetener aspertame (Nutra-sweet) is produced by engineering bacteria enzymes.

Investment opportunities will abound with the **ROLLOVER**. But first, we have to go through the wringer. The bigger question is: "Will we be able to retain the kind of society that will facilitate investments as we know them now?"

Another Buck Rogers frontier is fibre optics.

Fibre optics is the transmission of data via light bursts fired within glass tubes. It began over a hundred years ago when Alexander Graham Bell invented the photophone, a device which used light instead of electricity to transmit sound. Unfortunately, Bell's laboratory device needed a medium; the message traveled only a few feet.

That changed in 1970 when scientists at Corning Glass Works developed optically perfect glass fibers. These thin tubes of glass could carry bursts of infra-red light thousands of miles.

The source of light is a tiny semiconductor laser smaller than a grain of sand. Each device, called an emitter, converts electronic signals into rapid flashes of light. At the end tube lies a detector which turns the light flashes back to electronic signals.

The bottom line is big money. World sales of fibre optics and its components will hit $800 million this year, and a projected $4.5 billion by 1990.

Fibre optics is to copper wire what the car was to the horse. Fibre optics is faster, cheaper, and more efficient than copper wiring. **"The end of conventional copper wire could come as early as the turn of the century,"** is suggested by BusinessWeek.

Fibre optic beams, unhindered by electron drag, can travel 50% faster than copper transmissions, and glass fibers cost less. A long strand of glass is made from a single tablespoon of raw material. American Telephone and Telegraph says that, when completed, its 3,500 mile trans-Atlantic fibre optic link will have five times more capacity than copper cable. That's the **start**.

In 1986, up to 1.3 million miles of optical fiber will be laid in the United States alone. Four years later, almost 5 million more miles a year will be put down. Each line will hold 8 to 48 strands of fiber.

Military Applications

In 1984, the U.S. Navy awarded McDonnell Douglas Corporation $3 million to develop a fibre optic system which will detect and transmit movements of Soviet submarines. Then, at something like 100-mile intervals, a grid of optical fibers will be connected to computers on land.

Ultra fast transmission around the world. That will change man's way of life, says Charles Kao, executive scientist at ITT Corporation.

The technological revolution is only one of the elements that will produce and thrust the **ROLLOVER** worldwide.

VIII

HIGH TECH MIRACLE LOOK AGAIN

It has long been assumed in the halls of Washington and Wall Street that the decline of Industrial America will be offset by the rapid growth of high-tech industries (computer electronics, communications equipment, computer software, robotics, fiber optics, optical instruments, and medical instruments). These new industries, it's been claimed, will launch America into decades of growth and prosperity. Maybe another decade like the sixties, they said. The dream is coming apart. And the key reason the dream is coming apart is unfortunately a generic one.

Fundamental, unavoidable, and built into our economic history is the advantage we've held because we had the technology, and other countries did not. They had to work it out with low wages the hard way, poor slobs. But today the world has the technology or, where it doesn't have the technology, it can import the technology. The generic reason why U.S. industry faces such a terrifying future is that all this ends up as a **function of the living standards** of these competing countries. Our workers are simply unwilling to fall back to a living standard that would accrue from wages of, say, $10 an hour rather than $20 an hour. But around the world, our competitors are willing to produce the goods for that.

Now there's been the mistaken hope that the brains of America can overcome that by becoming the creators of much of this new high tech. And that assumption is true. But what people have not understood is that there are two kinds of high tech; one has the jobs, one has the brains.

Despite reams of new stories, the general public today is in a state of confusion about high tech's potential, mainly because they don't know the difference between high-tech software and high-tech hardware.

The media have had one message to preach and have preached it consistently: The innovations of this new age of electronics will result in many more jobs than it is destroying, just as the industrial revolution did. This is a misconception. It's widespread and it's dangerous.

$$* \quad * \quad * \quad *$$

You can divide the computer industry into two segments: One is the hardware, the other is the software. The hardware is the structure. The software is the brain. The hardware generates the jobs in the new electronics by virtue of manufacturing the keyboards and electrical equipment, for the massive computers coming out and the hundreds of thousands of smaller computers. This is an industry. The hardware, you might say, is the machine.

The software has nothing to do with this. As with a car, the big, dumb car can't do anything without the driver. Software is like the driver in the auto. In a man, it may take the brain a fraction of a second to come up with two or three impulses that command the body to move a cord of wood. The brain can't do anything by itself, but it can tell the big hulk exactly what to do, and the hulk does it. For the amount of energy expended, the brain will use an infinitesimal fraction of the energy expended by the body hulk in moving the cord of wood.

The hardware portion of the computer industry has created and will create a respectable number of jobs. It will not, however, be anything like the number of jobs destroyed by the new machines.

Also, the labor used for the hardware is about as unskilled as any labor can be. That's why it can be done for 50 cents an hour in Third World countries. But that is where the big percentage of the cost is – in the manufacturing of the hardware for the computer industry. So it's not hard to see why this section of the industry is being moved overseas. American jobs are going with it every week and every month. The software is a different matter, but that's not helpful. The software opens up jobs for a tiny number of immensely talented people. It calls on the geniuses in our society.

We have to look only briefly at the reality. There already has developed, in fact, an exodus of the hardware of high tech. To remain competitive, many U.S. companies have begun to pull up stakes. In 1983 Atari, Inc. transferred 1,700 jobs from California to Asia. Many have followed suit.

After losing their dominant positions in computer printers, Diablo Systems, Inc. and Qumen Corp., will move their manufacturing offshore. Seagate Technology — after posting big losses, fired 600 Silicon Valley workers and set up shop in Singapore. TIE/Communications, Inc. has also shipped its telephone product manufacturing overseas.

Even giant General Electric has thrown in the towel. GE has decided to place its new manufacturing plants in the Far East.

Barry Bluestone, professor of economics at Boston College, warns of a disaster.

"The bottom line is that high technology will not be the gleaming white knight that saves industrial jobs of America. Today we are beginning to see the same export of high-technology jobs that we saw with the textile mills, the automobile assembly lines and the manufacturing of television sets; only we are seeing the whole process compressed into a tremendously short time frame."

Many analysts now worry that within a decade Far East countries — who today only assemble parts — will begin producing whole systems, circumventing the U.S. industry and selling directly to the U.S. consumer.

"First you move production to the Far East, then the development of the product will go there," warns C.J. van der Klugt, vice-chairman of Philips, the huge Dutch electronics firm.

Unfortunately, U.S. companies have little choice in the matter. Staying in the U.S. is becoming a severe economic burden.

The Computer Chip Industry

Despite record demand, U.S. chip makers are facing tough times. In 1984 Itel Corp. layed off 900 employees, while Micron Technology, Inc. has cut its 1,250 workforce in half. Even mammoth Texas Instrument has felt the crunch. In 1985 TI was forced to sharply reduce its work schedule, prompting large downward revisions in its earnings forecast.

For confirmation of the trend of high-tech jobs moving out of the United States, we need only take a look at the American superstar:

IBM's PC system screen monitor is made in Korea, the keyboard, the power supply, and graphics printer are made in Japan, and the disk drive system is manufactured in Singapore. The only thing made in the U.S. is the semiconductors. Overall, the U.S. effort accounts for less than 30% of the system's final cost.

Keyboard makers are also facing tough times. In 1985 Idaho based Advanced Input Devices announced that it was forced to lay off 100 employees as a result of IBM's decision to cancel production of its PCjr computer. AID, which manufactured the keyboard for IBM, has been forced to cut its workforce in half overseas.

*   *   *   *

High tech is no bonanza in the United States. It is a job destroyer and it cuts with two edges. In the first place, it greatly cuts back the number of jobs. In the second place, most of the new jobs it creates will move to foreign countries.

From 1980 to 1982 the U.S. manufacturing industry lost two million jobs. At the same time, the high-tech industries provided 500,000 new jobs. This fractional return on lost jobs

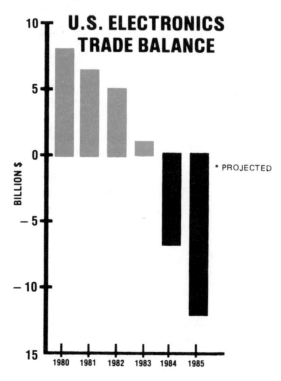

U.S. ELECTRONICS TRADE BALANCE

BILLION $

* PROJECTED

1980 1981 1982 1983 1984 1985

74

will only accelerate. According to U.S. News and World Report, high tech will provide fewer than 10% of the 25 million jobs needed by 1995 to reduce unemployment to 6 percent.

Today, machines are replacing man wholesale. Robots have moved into textiles, automotive, and steel industries just to mention a few. And this trend will accelerate. In 1983 Senator Lloyd Bentsen (Texas) told the Congressional Office of Technology Assessment that millions of jobs, perhaps one-quarter of the nation's factory workforce, could be lost to robots by 1990. General Motors alone will employ 14,000 robots over the next five years, and as machines' exponential development progresses, more and more jobs will be lost.

"By the end of this decade, manufacturing's decline will be nearly complete. The goods will still be needed, but imports and technical change will virtually remove all employment," warns Sir Clive Sinclair, British Industrialist and founder of Sinclair Research.

It may only be the first lap around the track, but Europe already looks to be out of the race. Burdened by old world conservatism, high capital and labor costs, and dwindling investment, Europe appears unable to mount any opposition against Japan and the United States in their quest for high-tech preeminence.

"Europe often looks for safety first. But natural caution may prove suicidal now that the world is in the midst of deep technological and economic change. America and Japan have been racing to meet this challenge. Europe has not," warns *The Economist*.

Unfortunately for Europe, caution is not its only problem. Like the United States, Europe has high capital costs. Nevertheless, America has been able to make do, in large part as a result of the flood of foreign investment. Europe has had no such boom. In 1983 more than $2.8 billion in venture capital was committed to U.S. high-tech industries. In that same year, less than $500 million in venture capital was invested in Europe's high-tech industries.

Europe, like the United States, suffers high labor costs. But Europe, unlike the United States, also suffers from a stagnant and conservative workforce. High tech demands a mobile workforce which will adapt to new jobs and industries overnight. European workers tend to resist such change. In 1981, 30% of all U.S. workers had changed jobs within the previous year; triple Europe's rate.

Europe has also failed to keep R&D (research and development) expenditures in line with the United States and Japan. Together, West Germany, the United Kingdom and France spend only 30% more on R&D than does Japan, alone, and 20% less than the United States.

Finally, Europe has experienced a severe brain drain. On a per-capita basis, Europe has only about half as many scientists and engineers as Japan, and only a third as many as the United States.

All of which spells bad times for Europe. Unable to compete in tomorrow's high-tech world, Europe will be unable to replace its dying smokestack industries. And the net result of that will be less investment, growing unemployment, and an overall decline in the standard of living.

The ongoing Achilles Heel of American industry is the discrepancy in the labor costs between the United States and other countries. Stated more bluntly, our competitors are not specific industries; our competitors are the living standards. How it comes out will narrow down to what kind of compromise can be made toward lowering the U.S. living standard and raising the other standards.

*　　*　　*　　*

In Spokane we have a new Silicon Valley and one of the important North American high-tech companies is I.S.C. Systems. It is building information systems for 1600 financial institutions. It has been a celebrated success. Here is how its vice president, John Lindeblad, assesses the future:

"If U.S. production keeps moving offshore, that is obviously very ominous for the United States. The basic nature of our economic structure will change. Our economy will become even more service based. We will lose our labor intensive industries, and our industry leadership will fall. That presents massive implications for the economic structure of this country. We will have jobs only for the highly skilled and highly trained. Jobs for less skilled and less trained people will simply evaporate."

*　　*　　*　　*

It's not necessarily as bleak as it seems, but it should be obvious to any reader or thinker that we are moving into an imponderable scene. Not one of these things can change without changes in the others. This is the reason we call our concept WORLD ROLLOVER. All of this will have to involve not only our standard of living, but our way of life. And we have to wonder if, indeed, in our new society as it arises, will it be the natural thing for people to have jobs at all. Maybe somewhere down the line having a job will be a mark of honor.

We might, in fact, be drifting toward an ideal world, but I think it cannot come easily. And as we move to this new type of society, we will undergo labor convulsions of this new birth, and many of them.

This raises the point of the type of training you should suggest to your children.

First of all, the basics will always be essential and it is better to learn how to calculate by using your head and the multiplication tables than it is just to do it on a calculator. You'll have plenty of time to use the computer afterwards, but the training of your mind is the essential base from which your facility can be multiplied, accelerated and ballooned by the use of the new technology.

Also language will always be of number one importance in getting along in this world no matter whether they run it with horse-drawn plows or with one tremendous computer in Washington, D.C. Expression of your ideas is the number one development you should aim for. After this preliminary education, you have to consider where the openings will arise as this **ROLLOVER** gets underway.

IX

THE FEMINIST REVOLUTION

The impact of the feminist revolution, the employment of women on a grand scale, from sales persons to chief executive officers, has hardly yet been felt. The reason is the phenomenal expansion of jobs. Even though women were entering the job market in an ever-widening stream, new jobs were coming forward so that the influx of the women created no surplus.

Today it's a different story — a story in reverse.

The trend from an almost unstoppable growth of jobs is now turning around as we enter a trend of almost unstoppable shrinkage of jobs.

Many of the unemployed of today, men generally, including heads of families, would not be unemployed except for their replacement by women.

This is not meant to be critical of women. We are looking for the truth here, and what I have said is a fact. It is a fact that prophesies further conflict between the sexes.

Back in the Great Depression only a small proportion of the working force was made up by women, but wherever a woman was holding down a job — even as low in the scale as school teacher — there was a certain resentment for "taking away" the livelihood of the breadwinner of a family. Of course, this is not surprising considering that women only got the right to vote in 1920 — little more than half a century ago.

Today there is hardly any resentment toward employed women, even as high up the scale as doctors, lawyers, and even corporate executives. But as more husbands get thrown out of work in this trend toward joblessness, due to the new electronics advances, it's very likely that men will be tempted to resentment; first of all maybe toward their wives, and later toward working women in general. It's pretty hard to prophesy such a social development for a fact, but I think it's a good guess that a new animosity between men and women will arise.

If that is so, it is another blow to the structure of the family. And this is a perfect illustration of how a collapse in the world monetary order will strike at the foundations of our social order and change our society.

It's no surprise. It was pretty well recognized all along that men were inferior to women around the house. They couldn't look after it as well; they were more careless, they didn't have the patience with the children. They were content with being inferior to their wives because they were still the breadwinners. So, in that area at least, they commanded importance and prestige from friends and family. Now they will have to face the fact that not only is the wife the superior parent, but also the breadwinner. They become only the inferior parent. It's hard to see this as improving domestic tranquility.

The weakening of the bond between man and wife must inevitably weaken the "family unit" as the building block of the social order. It may well lead to one or more entirely new divisions of business, the foster home for rearing children, simply because elimination of husband and father may become common.

As women have more and more approached equality with men, they have started literally to wear pants. At one time it was only a saying: "his wife wears the pants." Now the wife makes it very clear by **actually** wearing the pants.

What percentage of women would you see in pants on the street 40 years ago, or dressed up in their great finery for the theater, or attending a social function. I would venture it was small; I don't remember any. But now I do believe that women's fashion stores sell more pants than dresses.

This is nothing to be joked at. This is the subconscious reinforcement of women's commanding role. And this is what makes an outlook for depression now differ greatly from the depression of the 1930s. A new condition will be this increasing malcontent among unemployed men. But a greater result will be much higher unemployment overall. During the thirties, unemployed women very seldom got registered as being employed, because most of them had not been employed. Now we will have to add their numbers to the growing ranks of unemployed men.

And that is going to make one whale of a change in our society even if we should be so organized that there were no poverty.

The root of the matter is that men have to work in order to regard themselves as manful. Their power stems from their jobs. When they are denied the recognition of a job, they feel powerless — in other words, impotent.

So the ROLLOVER of the economic order promises the continuation and the acceleration of the sexual revolution. Before it is over, man well may be in as secondary position as the one in which he held his wife prior to women's meteoric advance after getting the vote in 1920. In barely more than half a century after many thousands of years, WOMEN HAVE REACHED A STATION OF NEAR EQUALITY. This has spread from the working place to the general lifestyle and women are now no more criticized for sleeping around than men are. They have asseted themselves with a mighty vehemence that leaves us men flabbergasted.

The reason for their success has been the disappearing advantage of physical strength as induced by the marvelous inventions of the Industrial Revolution, a process now speeding up at a tremendous rate. The product of all this will be the new social order, and a new educational philosophy which must prepare us for a different kind of life — including the productive use of leisure. And that takes us back as far as the Greek philosophers.

*   *   *   *

It was said long ago that "a handful of might is better than a bagful of right." And if we are thinking of justice, we might listen to Plato quoting an angry sophist: "I proclaim that might is right and justice is in the interest of the stronger . . . The different forms of government make laws, democratic, aristocratic, or autocratic, with a view to their respective interests, and these laws so made by them to serve their interests, they deliver to their subjects as 'justice' and punish as unjust anyone who transgresses against them. . ."

So we need not be amazed that women have been subjugated for some scores of thousands of years, since the day of the caveman right up until the 20th century. The laws were made by those with the might.

A caveman was not about to listen to any advice on what was right or not right as far as the treatment of his women were concerned. The greater physical power of men worked to their advantage for these thousands and thousands of years, and it was so engraved in the behavior of both men and women that it was seldom challenged. Women could not challenge them physically, nor even banded together could they challenge them morally, because each one of them would have probably been beaten up when she got home that night. So right has had nothing to do with it. Sheer physical power kept women subjugated.

We have drawn a lot of our customs from the bedrock philosophies of the Greeks, extending through the ages to influence us to this very day.

A part of the bedrock philosophy of Aristotle was his conception of a woman's place:

"Women is to man as is slave to the master, the barbarian to the Greek. Woman is an unfinished man, left standing on a lower step in the scale of development.

"The male is by nature superior, and the female inferior; and one rules and the other is ruled; and this principle extends, of necessity, to all mankind.

"Woman is weak of will, and therefore incapable of independence of character or position; her best position is a quiet home life in which while ruled by the man in her external relations she may be in domestic affairs supreme.

"Woman should not be made more like men, as in Plato's Republic; rather the dissimilarity should be increased; nothing is so attractive as the different. The courage of a man and that of a woman are not, as Socrates supposed, the same; The courage of a man is shown in commanding; that of a women in obeying . . . as the poet says, 'Silence is a woman's glory.'"

* * * *

We may get a good laugh out of it today, but remember, women readily accepted such views 2,400 years ago.

As far back as you can go, the female sex has been subjugated. The Judean beliefs did not challenge the theory of male superiority. In marriage vows, modern Christianity required the woman to swear she would obey her husband. Until about the early part of this century, women were still considered nothing more than helpmates to men and a necessary progenitor of the race.

Long before the Greeks, women had been serfs. Countless societies have killed infant girls if the proportion of the girls in the tribe or the country was becoming too large. That was because the boy children could work and could be used to protect the tribe in war, whereas women were inferior workers because they possessed less strength and, of course, definitely were not qualified for war. It was in those days only a practical matter to keep the male proportion of the population high. Women only meant more mouths to feed.

But it's doubtful if infant female babies were killed solely for the reason of less practical worth. Even the oriental societies kept women subjugated and sometimes did away with girl babies.

After a subjugation dating almost from the beginning, is it surprising that women should have remained subservient? The reason they remained subservient was only because they didn't have the strength to be masters.

I don't mean to suggest that women's march to equal rights was easy. It has, in fact, been a fierce and continuous struggle for 200 years. The beginning of this struggle was marked by the publication in 1792 of *The Vindication of the Rights of Women*, by Mary Wollstonecraft. However, the real advent of women into a man's world came with the breakdown of feudalism, the advent of the capitalistic system and the Industrial Revolution. Women entered the trades in England in the 17th century. Some trades employed three times as many women as men; the woolen trade for example. Under the capitalistic system, men owned their own businesses and when they died the businesses were sometimes carried on by the women. Records back then show women as owners of pawn brokerages, booksellers, contractors.

Young America was the breeding place of many new ideas. Among the most important was the fight for women's rights. This fight marched right along with the Industrial Revolution. The first act culminated in the right to vote in the United States in 1920. As time went by, this right was extended in many countries and finally in Japan in 1980.

The extension of the voting right was a remarkable development in view of the age-old concept that women are the servants of men. In Waikiki I have seen it in great evidence where a Japanese man and woman come into a cafeteria. The man sits down, the woman goes to get their food, makes another trip for the coffee or tea and finally puts it all before her husband. (A meritorious act, but one that is doomed to extinction, **I'm afraid**.)

The marvel is not that it has taken women 200 years to get this far. The marvel is that for 10,000 years it was never attempted.

This supports the point of this whole discussion. As physical strength has become more and more obsolete and used now mainly for sports, the great advantage that men have had over women since man was a mere beast, has been destroyed by the advent of non-muscle industry, new and marvelous machines, and finally the high-tech of today. It is this high-tech that is going to raise woman up to the last rung on this ladder. It will change the proportions of our labor force. It will change man's conception of himself and manhood. That will transform our whole social order further than we can see. And it will all be coming out of, and originating from, the economic explosions that are about to take place all around us.

The feminist revolution has all but succeeded to the realization of its dream — full equality with men. Since women now have the vote, they have every bit as much power as men, and since all they have to do is put an "X" on a ballot in order to throw off their oppressors, they are more likely to vote than men are. I believe we would have to say that the feminist revolution has been a dazzling success in record time.

Now we have reached a stage in the conflict where there are no holds barred. And this is disadvantageous to the men. In this struggle, not a single advantage has been retained by men.

Women are just as bright, just as ambitious, more intuitive and emotionally tougher than men. Men can get out and do great deeds, but usually they are emotionally dependent on a woman somewhere in the background. Take her support away, and the man is a lesser being.

I have often said in jest: "We blew it when we voluntarily gave them the right to vote. Now there are more of them than there are of us and we've had it.

"There's no way we can take the vote away from them; they will always outvote us. In this age of the obsolescence of muscle we may be looking forward to our own subjugation."

And this is no jest. The battle of the sexes is a real one. The ROLLOVER will see it at climax. Already women are moving into high places of power, even as heads of state. When they devise the education curriculum, they will be in the position of the greatest power of all, shaping our youth, and exerting great influence on the future social order, in respect to its morals, perceptions and outlook.

I believe this new social order will grow out of what is happening now; that is, the decay of the monetary system of the world and, as a result of that, the reorientation of our way of life, the reorientation of values will find women dominant just as men had been dominant for scores of milleniums heretofore.

83

If this process develops down through the end of this decade, I believe we will find growing proportions of the jobs in law and education, in medicine, in commerce, even govenment, dominated by women.

As the men find themselves with more leisure time, we may, as a side effect, find that we will run into an age of advancing art, music, and literature.

I hope that, by now, you are prepared to digest some highly unconventional and maybe even unheard-of projections which we ought to take seriously if we believe the feminist movement will continue to advance.

We must know by now that the people with the most votes make the policies of government. That is evident from our system of social handouts and the willingness of candidates to agree to the giveaways as long as they think they will get the votes to put them into office. The increasing strength of the feminist movement means that more and more voters will be voting for more and more women in policy-making jobs. In the end, the result is very simple. Women will rise first to a position of equality in government and an equal voice in government policy. The Equal Rights Amendment is pretty well now a foregone conclusion. It's only a matter of a little more time. This will provide tremendous impetus to the feminist drive to put more women into policy-making jobs, from municipalities right up to the White House.

Those who foresee what is coming and who prepare how to deal with it will be better off than those who are simply overtaken by events. In trying to figure out what changes will occur under feminist equality, or even domination, we need to understand at depth, objectively and with insight, the nature of women.

First of all, is there basically a fundamental difference between women and men in their outlooks and their attitudes, their basic natures? Because remember, the basic nature will always emerge as in Aesop's fable where the cat begs to be changed into a woman. It all went well, she was sedate and poised until a mouse ran by.

A woman will always be a woman; she will always act like a woman. If there is a fundamental difference between men and women, very fundamental changes in our social order are on the way.

We are getting down now to straight opinion. There's not a great deal you can prove about the differences between women and men. But I've been around long enough to observe quite a number of both sexes and I think there is fundamentally a difference in their natures.

First of all, I think women are less aggressive than men. People will tell you that this is because they have always been taught to be less aggressive. But if you watch baby girls and baby boys in your own families and in your relatives' families, you will see it from their early days in the crib. Most mothers will unhesitatingly tell you that the boy was a hellion from the beginning while, generally speaking, the girls are less venturesome, less aggressive, apt to get into fewer fights and generally less mischievous. From the beginning, the male seems to be more prone to assert himself, to show off, to have and to use power over others. The male is, in fact, an exhibitionist.

A society run by women would, I believe, be less likely to make war than a society led by men. They don't need to win a struggle to be fulfilled.

That doesn't mean that women would give in to anything any more than men would. One example is Margaret Thatcher's handling of the Faulkland Island crisis. But I believe they would be better peacemakers than men. I don't believe they would go into a meeting calling adversaries names. Example, Ronald Reagan before starting a meeting on disarmament with the Russians, with a preliminary blast calling them liars and cheats.

I believe that the Russian women, given a chance to agree with American women on the nuclear question, would quickly change their allegiance from the Politburo to the American women.

First off, I believe that the most important and fundamental influence of women would be a reduced tendency toward war. This might not cut much ice at the present time, but if we can keep away from war for another 10 or 20 years, I believe the strong feminist influence will begin to show results.

Oh, I don't say there aren't hellcats in the female sex that would fight at the drop of a hat. But overall, women are kinder, more considerate and more compassionate than men. And you can see it any day of the week among almost any group if you want to look.

Golda Meier was just as tough as Menachem Begin in negotiations, but in warlike decisions she seemed to take less pride out of it than did Begin.

Women may not predominate the scene for several more decades. But it is a question of time until they begin to influence the curriculum, the social laws and, as a result, taxation policy.

In the matter of the latter, I would think that most women would be Democrats. I would be afraid that the social handouts would increase even more. This could only mean a greater distribution of wealth, a general leveling of the classes. It would also mean inevitably less freedom and we are probably heading in that direction anyway, but a dominant feminine hierarchy would speed it up.

Orwell's *1984* may well enough come true as he pictured it with one great change. The bosses will be women.

I don't want you to take this lightly. The very fact that men could keep women suppressed for thousands of years demonstrates that might is right, and that might will work. So why should anyone be surprised if the predominance of female votes changes our social order from one dominated by males to one dominated by females. I can't find that illogical.

For the next suggestion, you are going to kill me. Remember, nature has no emotion; nature has no mercy; nature is relentless, and everything is the servant of truth, and each truth is a natural law. In *The Matter of Justice*, please refer to Page 40, quoting Plato on the making of laws and the definition of justice.

"You must foresee that reality will dictate who our rulers are. This justice will be defined by women."

Now I want to pose a question. If the world population continues to increase and if there is a leveling of the standard of living between countries, and if the dominant feminists encourage and support this leveling process, we will arive at a time when the population is too great.

In the days when muscle was important, the men were needed and they would always have the first priority to life. But in the new society dominated by women, the man's advantage has disappeared. His muscle isn't needed. Under development of the high-tech, the job market will get thinner and thinner and more and more men will be "superfluous." The man's only advantage over women then is his breeding ability. But what sheepbreeder will keep all those unnecessary bucks if the pasture is short — and even if it isn't.

Men got rid of girl babies because they were not useful to the society. Why wouldn't women get rid of male babies and keep only the best of the species for reproduction? It wouldn't be all that tough to do, because in the new society sex of all the offspring would be known well before birth, and male babies could be simply aborted.

It's not as fantastic 50 to 100 years down the line, as some might believe. Think about it.

*   *   *   *

How ever far you want to take it, the feminist movement is going to be one of the biggest factors in shaping the new social order that will follow and be a part of the **rollover** beginning with the breakdown of the monetary system which is now fully foreseeable, although the timing is not.

But from a practical standpoint, the youth of today, especially the male youth, should be taking an early sighting on what employment they propose in the 1990s. We will be able to talk about that when we have developed some more knowledge and better evidence later on and, particularly, toward the end of the book.

X

CRIME ROLLOVER

If you were a second-generation Rip van Winkle, who had gone to sleep in 1934 and wakened in 1984, what would be your greatest shock? It wouldn't be the new kind of houses and apartment buildings. It wouldn't be the affluence of the country. It wouldn't be the debt. It would be the massive crime; the massive, sickening wave of crime. And you would be surprised at the role of women; women as truck drivers, welders, women as policemen, women as heads of corporations, as lawyers, doctors, women as heads of state.

And if you thought about it for a while, you would wonder if the first and the second most shocking waves of change were not related.

Firstly, you would recall how little crime there actually was in 1934. Your mind would posit a great big **WHY**?

You would read of rapes and rapists, of mass murders, and single murders, senseless without the murderer even knowing the victim; murders without motivation, child abuse. What has happened in the 50 years while I slept? Surely, the genes and the chromosomes of the species have not changed. The kids as brought up today must have, in general, the same hereditary characteristics as they had when I went to sleep. Then it must be the environment that's changed.

Criminals are young, mostly under 40 years of age. They were teenagers 25 years ago. From then on, there have been new generations of criminals and now there are thousands of them, from teenagers on up.

How did the environment so change? There is more to eat than there was 50 years ago. The kids have better clothes. Kids have bikes and cars, motorcycles and boats. Surely, they have not been deprived of material things.

Ah — that is it! Not of material things — then it must be of other things. And the deprivation must have been in the home. And what could that be?

And, as I read the newspapers and periodicals, I find that more than half the children come from broken homes. I find that millions of children have been changing parents. Not many enjoy the same two parents while they grow up. The father is replaced by another father. The mother replaced by another mother. I see that the mothers are not at home. Back in 1934, nearly all the mothers were at home. Children came home to their mothers, whom they knew would always be there when they came home.

I think back to my own childhood and I remember there was never a time when I came home from school that my mother was not at home. Most of the people lived in the country, and the fathers were also at home. Even the kids that lived in the cities looked upon home as a haven, a nest of security that would stand no matter what else should fall.

I glance casually at a headline: "Man Shoots Girlfriend and Five Children." I never heard of such a thing.

And I realize that crime has transformed the world. It has changed the social order and the social fabric more than anything else. It seems from newspapers that this crime is a continuing wave and I conclude that it is arising out of a fundamental difference in the environment of children.

Another step takes me to a startling enlightenment: Women are now the equivalent of men. They are in the marketplace with the men, at the factories with the men. Children rarely have full-time mothers and hardly ever constant parents. The criminals are the former children. So the fault has to be in the environment of the former children. And the present children are battering the same environment as the feminist revolution thunders along.

Crime? When could I remember crime? I remember crime; it was at the beginning of the second decade of the century. I was about 10 years old. Although there were no radios, the news of this crime swept the countryside.

This Dorch kid — I only knew him as the Dorch kid — drove into a farmer's yard about 4 o'clock in the morning. Close to the frame house, he honked his horn; the farmer got up, and opened the window. The Dorch kid said he was out of gas; he wanted to borrow some gas. The farmer said he'd be right down.

In his nightgown he came downstairs, lighted a lantern, screwed off the top of a barrel of gas and bent over to get a siphoning hose. As he straightened, the stranger leveled a shotgun and blew his head off.

The Dorch kid was 19 years old. He'd been working for the farmer as a harvest hand. There were underground whispers that the Dorch kid had had something going with the farmer's wife. This was always "hushed" in the presence of us children.

At 10 o'clock that morning, the Dorch kid was playing pool at the town hall. Two Canadian Mounted Police, splendid in their once-famous dress, slapped on the handcuffs and took the Dorch kid away.

We kids at school were breathless for days. We had never heard of a murder. In Southern Alberta there had never been a brutal murder.

In a few weeks the Dorch kid was tried, found guilty and sentenced to death. A very short time after that, he was hanged at the Lethbridge jail a hundred miles from home.

I don't remember anything that left a greater impression on me than the story of this murder and the immutable law which caused the Dorch kid to hang from the neck — this 19-year-old boy — until he was dead. If there was anybody in that whole country, of thousands upon thousands of square miles, who had any idea of killing somebody, he got rid of it pretty fast. I never heard of another murder until 10 years later.

That was in the depression and a vagrant had gotten into a taxicab, killed the cab driver, thrown the body in a ditch, and was swiftly apprehended. The news was inflamed. What a despicable thing! Imagine anyone who would kill an innocent driver.

Could you get a sensation out of it today?

In the United States, the kidnapping of the Lindbergh baby made news all over North America. It was the horror story of a decade. An innocent child plucked from his crib. What a foul and criminal act! Such dogs must die. So great was the public furor sweeping the nation, that the authorities finally ended up hanging an innocent man in order to get the public off their back.

I recall the crime of Leopold and Loeb, who enticed a 14-year-old boy by the name of Frank to a remote place and murdered him for the fun of murdering. The outrage of this horrible deed swept far and wide. How much attention would that crime get today, except a few headlines at the trial. It would be pushed off the front page by updated atrocity after updated atrocity, of murder after murder. Senseless killing upon senseless killing, dope busts, and suicides.

No, it couldn't be that the genes have changed. Surely, inheritance remains the same as it was half a century ago. It has to be the environment. Profound social changes must have already transformed us into a criminal society. And still they keep coming.

So we have traced the cause to the home, and from the home we have traced the cause to parental absence. Kids have been fending for themselves, rarely being punished for doing anything wrong, because most of the while the parents don't have interest to be informed about it. If they are informed, they push it aside. Busy in their own lives, the man's father personality is only half supported by the woman. The woman by day lives in a more exciting and preferable environment. The children become secondary.

The family is disintegrating. The disintegration in 50 years has been swift, dramatic. But in our everyday lives, we hardly notice it.

Worst of all, there's every indication that advancing feminism will advance family disintegration. That means the crime advance will continue until we are overtaken by some huge social **ROLLOVER**.

As a modern Rip van Winkle, I'm appalled. But as a person who was a boy 60 years ago, I understand what's happening. I do not forget the great fear that overtook me when my parents quarreled seriously. But I didn't leave home; I just went out to the barn until it was over. The kid today might leave home. Or his mother might leave home. Or his father might leave home. The disintegration of that rock of security shatters the kid. He seeks a substitute, solace; he seeks drugs or sex, any palliative.

My mother never left home because there was probably no place for her to go. She didn't have a job on equal standing with men, or perhaps a job superior to my father's job. My father didn't leave home. It was the only home he had. Home was a fortress, indestructible. I knew they'd never leave, and I knew it would all blow over.

The breakdown of marriage is the breakdown of the home, and the breakdown of the home pressures and maybe cracks the moral fiber of the child.

This is not critical of the feminists, but it does say that this social world of ours is in the first revolutions of a complete **ROLLOVER**. The way of life is changing. Common sense tells you this can't keep on growing without destroying the whole society. It is changing in tandem with dozens of major transformations in our economy, our workplace, our mode of making a living, our sources of power and heat, our trembling economic and monetary structure. All of these things are in the midst of profound changes. And the process has already begun and is underway.

The crime wave is only one of all these forces that will be brought into focus.

It will not happen like clockwork, and at once. There will be deterrents here and there. For example, if Rip van Winkle woke up in Japan in 1984, crime would not stand out as the most shocking change in the last half century. There, he would be most impressed by the tremendous changes in the standard of living, the better way of life, radios, motorcycles, transistors, cars, televisions, even housing. The home customs may have changed, but the structure still stands. The crime wave never developed there.

Likewise in Western Europe. Except in the United States, women have stayed more with their traditional roles. Only in America are the militant feminists out waving the flag.

This is not a doctrine of criticism. It is a doctrine of insight. It is a search for reasons. No one any longer doubts that women can fill most of the roles filled by men. But one thing comes out very clearly. They cannot fill the role of men and, at the same time, the role of the traditional mother.

Can any working mother honestly claim that she has the capacity, coming home dead tired from the office, to make the relaxing dinner for the family, to read the children bedtime stories, or just to engage in motherly talk? Can the children come home to the smell of cookies, or just the smile of the home's guardian? Can any woman claim she can give herself twice? If she has given herself to her career, she cannot give it again to her children at night. Her husband can't give himself twice. He believes that his main thrust should be out in the world, as it was since earliest society. Who gets left holding the bag?

The crime figures give you the answer.

Feminism is on the march. It's likely to increase. And crime is likely to increase. And this condition will continue to progress until women can either find a substitute for themselves in their children's lives, or make a clear-cut decision to have a career or to have children. Emotional neglect is the mother of insecurity, and insecurity is the mother of crime.

*　　*　　*　　*

This has meaning for the economic front. Positive results often arise out of the worst disasters.

The meaning is that crime will undoubtedly increase. That means there will be an increasing emphasis on security devices. Securing and protecting oneself will become a part of the curriculum. All kinds of locks, alarm systems, defense systems have been in a period of growth. This growth will continue. There's room for new, bright ideas, room to capitalize and exploit the new needs of the social order.

If that's not for you, at least be mindful your home will be needing attention and constantly more foresight. All of this is one of the birth pains we must suffer in the **ROLLOVER**.

Great revolutions and evolutions never happen without pain. You can see the pain quite plainly as it has commenced to happen, is indeed well advanced, on our economic and monetary scene.

XI

EXPLODING THE MYTH

If a stone is thrown in the air, it will come to a complete stop before it starts coming down again. This stop at turning points of civilization becomes a long plateau. The result is that people who are living during the plateau are not quite sure if the trend is merely stopping for a rest or if it is really the signal that the whole trend is soon going to reverse.

If we take the long-term view of the Industrial Revolution, we will see that the social order and the standard of living has been rising for over 200 years. We will see that the markets have always been going up. Sometimes they stop going up for a year or two or even more, but never before in the history of markets have we traversed a plateau of the duration of the present one. And if you listen to Wall Street analysts, the federal government and economists in general, you will think that the Dow Jones Industrial Average has just performed miracles since the war. In 1945 the Dow Jones Average was slightly over 150. Today if you read the newspapers, you will find that the Dow Jones Average is 1,250.

If you use constant dollars, however, that is to say dollars adjusted for inflation, and you take a measurement of the history of the Dow Jones since 1945, you will be flabbergasted. At that time, the Dow Jones stood at about 150 as calculated in 1940 dollars *(we use 1940 because that was the last time money was really stable)*. If you look at December's end, 1983, you will find that the Dow Jones Average of 1,250 converts to 172 as measured in 1940 dollars. Imagine, 150 to 170 in 38 years. That's fast?

The Dow Jones first hit a 1,000 all-time high in 1966. But the 1983 DJ at 1,250, when converted to 1966 dollars, was at 420. In 17 years, not only has the stock market failed to gain a dime – it has actually LOST two-thirds of its value.

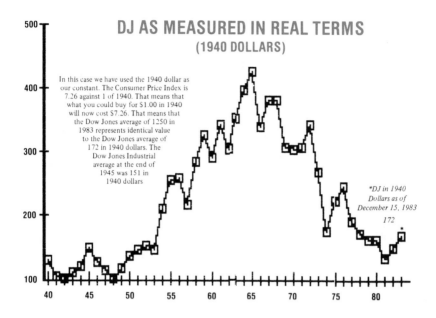

DJ AS MEASURED IN REAL TERMS
(1940 DOLLARS)

In this case we have used the 1940 dollar as our constant. The Consumer Price Index is 7.26 against 1 of 1940. That means that what you could buy for $1.00 in 1940 will now cost $7.26. That means that the Dow Jones average of 1250 in 1983 represents identical value to the Dow Jones average of 172 in 1940 dollars. The Dow Jones Industrial average at the end of 1945 was 151 in 1940 dollars

*DJ in 1940 Dollars as of December 15, 1983
172

People have great difficulty in believing that the fall in the Dow Jones Average since 1966 translates into actual loss in their bank accounts. The real truth, of course, is obscured by the numbers, but the value of stocks owned in 1966 has tumbled disastrously.

To make sure that you comprehend how terrible our losses have been in the period from 1967 to 1983, I prepared a table covering the stock market quotations of the stocks which are used to make up the Industrial Average, as of January 1, 1966, and as of January 1, 1984.

You understand that 30 of the leading industrial stocks of the U.S. are picked to indicate what is happening to the economy. During the years, some stocks become less representative and others more representative.

Of the stocks that comprised the Dow Jones Averages of January 1, 1966, seven have been dropped and seven new ones have been added. To keep our eye on the ball, I have limited this

DOW INDUSTRIALS

Company Name	Symbol	'66 Price	'84 Price	Splits Since 66	Real '84 Price	Gain or Loss	
Allied Chemical	ALD	$49 1/8	$55 3/4	0	$17 3/4	$31 3/8	−64%
Aluminum Co. Am.	AA	76 5/8	45	3/2 '73 2/1 '81	43	33 5/8	−44%
American Can	AC	55 5/8	46 3/4	0	14 7/8	40 3/4	−73%
AT&T	T	60 3/4	61 1/8	0	19 1/2	41 1/4	−68%
Bethlehem Steel	BS	40 3/8	27 7/8	0	8 7/8	31 1/2	−78%
DuPont	DD	239 1/4	52 5/8	3/1 '79	50 1/4	189	−79%
Eastman Kodak	EK	117 3/8	76 1/4	2/1 '68	48 1/2	68 7/8	−59%
General Electric	GE	118	58 3/8	2/1 '71 2/1 '83	74 3/8	43 5/8	−37%
General Foods	GF	82 1/2	51 3/8	2/1 '71	32 3/4	49 3/4	−60%
General Motors	GM	103 1/2	74 3/8	0	23 5/8	79 7/8	−77%
Goodyear	GT	47 1/2	30 1/8	2/1 '69	19 1/8	28 3/8	−60%
Internat'l Harvester	HR	45 7/8	11 3/4	0	3 3/4	42 1/8	−92%
Internat'l Paper	IP	30 3/4	59	0	18 3/4	12	−39%
Johns Manville	MAN	55 3/8	11 1/8	2/1 '69	7 ,	48 3/8	−87%
Owens-Illinois	OL	63	37 3/4	2/1 '77	24	39	−62%
Proctor & Gamble	PG	69 3/8	57 3/8	2/1 '70 2/1 '83	73	+ 3 5/8	+ 5%
Sears Roebuck	S	66	37 3/8	2/1 '77	23 3/4	42 1/4	−64%
Standard Oil Calif.	SD	79 7/8	34 1/4	2/1 '73 2/1 '81	43 5/8	36 1/4	−45%
Texaco	TX	80 3/8	36 1/4	2/1 '69	23	57 3/4	−72%
Union Carbide	UK	68 1/2	62 3/4	0	20	48 1/2	−71%
U. S. Steel	X	52 1/4	30 7/8	3/2 '76	14 3/4	37 1/2	−72%
Westinghouse Elect.	WX	62 1/4	55 1/4	2/1 '71	35 1/4	27	−43%
Woolworth	Z	31 5/8	35 1/4	0	11 1/4	20 3/8	−64%
*IBM	IBM	499	123 1/8	50% '66 2/1 '68 25% '73 4/1 '79	588 1/8	+89 1/8	+18%

*Not in 1966 composite

96

record to the 23 stocks of 1966 that still remain in the Dow Jones Averages.

Pay attention to the quoted price of January 1, 1966, January 1, 1984, the 1984 price conversion to 1966 dollars by means of applying the Consumer Price Index (inflation of 3.14). The sixth column gives you the purchasing power of the quoted stock price January 1, 1984, in 1966 dollars. (*No comparisons are worth beans unless you use constant dollars.*)

Notice that, out of the 23 stocks, only one has made any increase at all. Proctor & Gamble rose 5% in 17 years in real purchasing power.

Proctor & Gamble quoted at 69 3/8 in 1966, split two for one in 1970 and two for one in 1983. The result is a stockholder who had one share and now has four shares. The price on the market as of January 1, 1984, was **57 3/8**, so the four shares are worth $229. Divide that by 3.14 for 1966 value and you get $73 as against the quoted price of 69 3/8 in 1966. The stock's value has **appreciated 3 5/8** or a rise of **5%** in the course of 17 years.

The other Dow Jones stocks are down.

Aluminum Company of America was quoted at 76 5/8 January 1, 1966. There was a stock split of three for two in 1973. That means that the man with a share of Aluminum Company of America turned it in and got a share and a half in 1973. Then, in 1981, there was a stock split of two for one. The man turned in 1 1/2 shares and received three shares. The price quotation of Aluminum Company of America on January 1, 1984, was 45, so if he sold his three shares he got $135. The inflation factor since 1933 is two-thirds. Specifically, it takes 3.14 1983 dollars to buy what could be bought with one 1966 dollar. So the value of his three shares of Aluminum Company of America as of January 1, 1984, is $135, divided by 3.14, or 43 1966 dollars. So the owner has a depreciation in 1966 dollars of $31, which is a real decrease of 44%.

International Harvester is down 92%; Johns Manville is down 87%; DuPont is down 79%; General Motors is down 77%; American Can is down 73%; Texaco is down 72%; U.S. Steel is down 72%; Union Carbide is down 71%; Woolworth is down 64%; Allied Chemical is down 64%; Sears & Roebuck is down 64%; Owens Illinois is down 62%; Goodyear is down 60%; General Foods is down 60%; AT&T is down 60%; Eastman Kodak is down 59%; Standard Oil of California is down 46%; Aluminum Company of America is down 44%; Westinghouse is down 43%; International Paper is down 40%; General Electric is down 37%; and Bethlehem Steel is down 31%.

*   *   *   *

IBM was not in the composite averages for 1966. But since it is the star performer of all major corporations and people have it in their minds that it has appreciated some thousands of percent, I think we ought to know its real performance just for our own mental balance.

On January 1, 1966, IBM was $499 per share. It was bonused by half a share so that, at the end of 1966, the shareholder had 1 1/2 shares of IBM. In 1968, on a two-for-one split, the total shares became three. A 25% share bonus in 1973 gave him 3.75 shares. In 1979, in a split of four for one, his IBM shares totaled 15. The quoted price on IBM January 1, 1984, was 123 1/8. Fifteen shares, therefore, have a quoted value of $1,847. Divide this by the Consumer Price Index of 3.14 and we find that IBM has a value of $588. Therefore, the share that was worth $499 January 1, 1966, is worth $588 today, an appreciation of $89 which amounts to 18%.

Here we have 200 million Americans and hundreds of millions of Europeans and Japanese who are under the general impression that IBM has multiplied in value by some thousands of percent since 1966 and we find it has increased only 18%. Now don't let someone talk you out of the truth of this statement. It is a fact, a known fact, an established fact that the $500 value in IBM in 1966 bought three times as much as $500 buys in 1983. This is a literal and statistical **REALITY. AND IT IS AN ESTABLISHED AND UNALTERABLE AND UNCONTESTABLE FACT THAT IN REAL TERMS – IN REAL PURCHASING POWER – IBM HAS RISEN 18% OVER THE LAST 17 YEARS.**

*   *   *   *

We are looking at industrial America. Surely no one of an objective frame of mind could view the above wreckage of the stock market and doubt that it's a forewarning of some grave and monolithic change. The stock market is merely the rumble of thunder.

When will it happen?

*   *   *   *

Before a system breaks down, various warning signs occur. The fractures in the foundation. Tiny cracks in the horizontal walls. Unlevel floors. Many, many signs multiply until finally the strength of the structure is cracked in its main supports, and the building tumbles.

We have many signs today that our present system is undergoing tremendous stress. One of the signs is that the

98

growth of this system has practically stopped. The second sign is that we are subjected to an **ILLUSION** that the growth is continuing, "It's seven bells and all is well!"

Since our system absolutely depends on and demands growth, any reversal of growth endangers its existence. We have to have growth for many reasons.

Firstly, the population is continually increasing and so the gross national product — the definition of the total product of the country — must always expand at least to the extent of the population increase. But more importantly, the system carries a debt load of some trillions of dollars. The servicing of this debt (interest) at current interest rates consumes much more than a trillion dollars. If our gross national product doesn't grow as much as our outflow for interest and other reasons, then it follows — in common sense — that we are falling backwards.

If you look at the figures published by the authorities and the figures accepted by the economists everywhere, you will find out that we are doing just great. The following graph shows you how "great" the gross national product is doing.

The 1983 gross national product is not a lie, as such; it's a distortion and an illusion because it is denominated in dollars changing year by year, the value shrinking year by year. So the

99

only way we can find out what the gross national product has really been doing is to apply constant dollars. That is, the purchasing power of a dollar. If it took $5 to buy a pair of shoes in 1940 and it took $10 to buy them in 1950, the cost in 1950 is five 1940 dollars. If the value of the dollar fell by half again by 1960, then the cost of the pair of shoes would be published as $20, but in constant money – in 1940 dollars – the right figure is $5. The only thing that had changed was the number on the bill. It now took four printed dollars to buy as much in 1960 as one printed dollar would buy in 1940.

In arriving at the gross national product of the United States, I have done something a little different than we usually see. Usually, the 1966 dollar is taken and, using the Consumer Price Index which is published by the government and which gives the comparative purchasing power of the dollar of various years, they use 1966 dollars as a base for all calculations. So in 1983 the Consumer Price Index is about three times the 1966 figure. That means a dollar in 1983 was only worth one-third as much as a 1966 dollar. And there's nothing wrong with that figuring except that 1966 is not basic. The money had been inflating before 1966. So what I have done here is go back to where I knew money was good and stable, which was 1940, shortly before the United States entered the war.

In those days, no one ever heard the word "inflation." I doubt that it was in the vocabulary of 10% of the people. Money was good and stable. If you had $1,000 in 1940, it would buy you $1,000 worth of goods tomorrow, or 10 years from tomorrow, or presumably 20 years from tomorrow.

So I went back and looked at the gross national product in the year 1973 and calculated it in terms of 1940 dollars using the government's own formula for the change in purchasing power of a dollar. I found that in terms of 1940 dollars, the gross national product in 1973 was $418 billion. By 1983, it was barely more, about 9%, a little over $458 billion. Meanwhile, the population of the United States had increased 10% from 210,000,000 to 234,000,000. Thus, the gross national product incease just about matched the population increase. **In other words, the gross national product on a per-capita basis had not grown at all between 1973 and 1983** —even while the government drums were beating about the financial prosperity and the tremendous outlook for our future. They were promoting the great illusion **WITH DRUMS!**

The following graph heightens and emphasizes the great ILLUSION to which we had been exposed over a couple of

100

decades. Personal income did rise somewhat in real terms between 1967 and 1983, but notice this increase only came to the end of 1980; that it stopped in 1980. The year 1983, in spite of all the praise of the great recovery, did not show a rise in personal income to REAL TERMS. The personal income increase as reported by government just about equals the inflation of 1983. What is most startling about this graph is its confirmation about the great illusion.

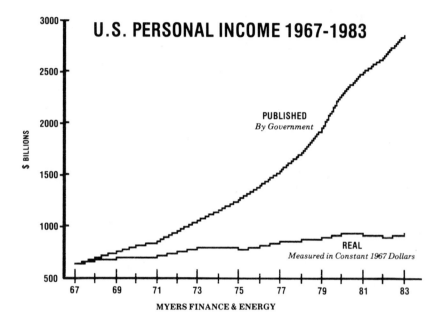

U.S. PERSONAL INCOME 1967-1983

PUBLISHED
By Government

REAL
Measured in Constant 1967 Dollars

MYERS FINANCE & ENERGY

Various influences are pulled together here to show that the years of inflation have reached a plateau; disinflation set in about two years ago. The plateau now seems to be turning down. Actual shortage of money, falling prices and falling wages, will be the biggest single factor in producing the **ROLLOVER**.

When future historians look back at the beginning of the **ROLLOVER** they will be able to nail down its advent by (a) the performance of the stock market, (b) the nearly flat projectory of the gross national product, (c) slow growth of personal income. And surely they will wonder why economists, government experts, and forecasters in general wouldn't have spotted the fact that we were moving into historic new territories. By hindsight, it will look as though this huge and imminent transformation was practically announcing itself. But everyone had been seduced by the ILLUSION of the numbers that arose out of inflation.

We must realize here that we are dealing with a major turning point in human history. These turning points take a long time. Normally, they may not be visible very much short of a generation. But today our whole machine has accelerated to dizzying speeds, and changes that might have taken a generation, may now be accomplished in only a few years.

However, it's not so fast that if you read this book in June you can expect the **ROLLOVER** by January. The events will seem very gradual and very slow to us. Only when looked at in the perspective of history will they seem extremely fast. Projections made here are not to be nailed down to a particular month or even year.

But it is now apparent and will become increasingly apparent that these changes are underway. These same changes talked about in **The Coming Deflation**, of 1976, are considerably further advanced. The process will speed up now, leading to a precipitation of events which will convince everybody that a **ROLLOVER** has indeed arrived.

XII

ROLLOVER IN GROWTH

Our whole economy is predicated on perpetual growth. Even if we come to a point where we have everything we want, we must keep on buying or our factories will slow down, profits will shrink or disappear, unemployment will spread. In short, we will be plunged into a depression.

We dare not stop growing. This was made all too clear by the policy of waste which reached its peak in the 1960s and early 1970s. Planned obsolescence became the cardinal policy with industry. If the products couldn't be made to wear out soon enough, the obsolescence could be established by changes in fashion. The textile industry could be kept growing by constantly changing styles. One year women's coats would be long; a couple of years later they would be short, then long again. The stamp of style had to be put on everything so people could see how dated they were and thus the status of the wearer or user could be impugned. Auto makers made sure that each year's model would carry enough cosmetic changes to emphatically date it. Most of the population had enough goods already to enable them to afford to trade in their cars to ensure that everyone knew they could keep up, and maybe pass, the Joneses.

Unless car owners could be encouraged either by mechanical obsolescence or by fashion, what would happen to the auto companies? The answers added up to colossal waste.

And that's still the way our society is structured. We must continue to get rid of the old in order to buy the new. At any price, the GOD OF GROWTH. Continual sacrifices of good and perfectly usable products must everlastingly be laid at its feet.

And WASTE was the key to GROWTH.

Now, I think that sensible people — lacking any education at all — who know that the earth is finite and that its resources are finite, always becoming scarcer, will judge these practices unintelligent, in fact stupid, and moreover that this deliberate and uninhibited waste is a sin against mankind and creation. And down deep, we know that such a philosophy will have to undergo drastic change, maybe even reversal; that, since enforced growth is the key to economic prosperity, we've got to change our philosophy. This is but one more factor forecasting a flipflop in our social order.

In the 1970s, I attended the annual meetings of the International Monetary Fund. Here is a world organization of tremendous influence. The meeting was attended by most central bankers of the world, finance ministers and deputy ministers of most countries, top-ranking economists and government advisers. Probably no group with greater power over the masses ever assembled in one place. Out of the three thousand or so attendees, about 200 among them controlled the finances of the world to the extent that it is controllable by man. I was impelled to write a piece called:

Cups of Copenhagen

These people controlling the finance ministries, and the Central Banks of the western world, are moulding policy — whether they realize it or not — which will set the pattern of the lives of hundreds of millions. They control the machinery that sets the limits within whcih millions will shape the pattern of their existence. The enormity of this concept, when it struck me quite by chance, was shocking.

What was the objective of these men?

Clearly, it was this: To maintain the status quo, to maintain the affluence; to prevent recession; to keep things moving; to project into the future what we have; **more of the same**.

At the Bella Centre there was a free coffee bar. I used it a lot. Every time I got a cup of coffee, they took out a new, sparkling clean plastic cup. Every time I turned it back, they threw it into the garbage. They threw away thousands and thousands of these cups. They gathered them up and presumably took them to some dump to burn.

And I thought: This is the affluent society — this is what we are striving to preserve. PLANNED WASTE. Surely, this wanton dissipation of the fruits of our earth must be a sin.

Think of the search for these raw materials, the production, the manufacture, the design, the machines involved, the packaging, the journey to market. The cup is used for a single fill and the resources of our earth are tossed away. But we are not satisfied with that. No, we now must set these resources to the torch, using them to destroy the environment which supports us.

Those cups were good cups. Believe me. During the depression, I know my family would have been mighty glad of those cups. I believe Asia would be glad of those cups. The peasants of China and India. But there is no profit in that. The manufacturers wish to keep on making the cups. Producers of plastic wish to keep on producing the plastic, so that there can be jobs and profits. And so that always the cups can be destroyed, so that they can make new cups.

It's a tiny example. Projected, a nylon stocking is worn five minutes and catches a run. The pair goes up in smoke. Think of the work. The fine material. Millions of pairs of nylon stockings every day — into smoke. It is not enough to have one car. Our affluence demands two or three cars. These, too, are planned for waste. The tin and the steel, the generators, the rubber, the enormous effort — the treasure of the good earth — they are all soon relegated to the junk heap, so that auto companies can make more autos, because we'd better not have a recession.

You get a little wear on the corner of your rug, and you throw it away. You don't cut it down to make it do for another room. You throw it away and the smoke circles into the blue sky. We must not have a recession. We must make more rugs.

The bankers had better not let anything happen, because the politicians would lose their jobs if people couldn't throw their plastic cups away, and burn their stockings.

Tell me, where is the joy in this? **This mad rush to consume as fast as possible all the fruits of our planet and destroy them in order to poison the air we breathe?** Indeed, has not the whole world become infected with a strange insanity?

The United States is fighting might and main to avoid any hint of recession. The Federal Reserve dare not allow the credit to be tightened. Otherwise, people could not burn stockings every day, could not toss used mixmasters into the dump; and would be stuck with the wonderful products until they have served their owners well.

More steel and rubber for the dumps, more unmended socks into the ashcan, while the wife drinks gin or watches

105

television. The chemicals that produce these products lay spoil to our sparkling rivers. The rivers reach out into our oceans until they lay waste to the habitat of the fish of our earth.

Now clothing manufacturers press hard on us to junk hundreds of **millions** of mini-skirts so they can make hundreds of millions of midis, also later to go up in smoke for something new.

And a thousand bankers who shape the economic lives of the millions struggle in Copenhagen to assure that this "prosperity" will go on.

Apparently, only a deep worldwide depression can bring us to our senses.

*　　*　　*　　*

Those cups in Copenhagen told a very big story, but the world money barons didn't tumble to it. Over the four-day conference, I doubt if the word "waste" was once uttered. Listening to money managers of the world, I came to realize there was no great wisdom there. Impressions of wisdom arose out of complicated jargon which a layman couldn't understand. But I know that where there is wisdom, it can always be stated in simple terms. These people were too entangled in the complicated mental threads they had spun. I felt they had bypassed reality long ago.

Today, people are confused by the jargon of the economists to the point they begin to think economics is an intellectually impenetrable jungle — and they throw up their hands content to let the experts run it. If they knew the pitiful limitation of the experts, they might not be so ready to let them run it.

I speak to you as a layman because I consider myself a layman. I am not an economist. I'm glad I'm not an economist. If I were shouldered with such a rotten record of forecasting, I don't think I'd have the nerve to pop my head up in public any more.

I speak to you as a layman, but I've been writing *Myers Finance & Energy* for 18 years. During that time, I've picked up quite a lot of knowledge, and to this knowledge I try to apply ordinary horse sense. That brings me out at a point in the future which discredits the trained economists.

As a layman, I know the economists have consistently made the "wrong calls." Gold was only an example of one megablunder by the economists. Hardly an economist foresaw the greatest commodity price increase in history. And they had all their tools, and they had all their graphs, and they had all

106

their experts, and they had long handles from the most prominent universities. With all this, the economists scoffed at the thought of gold ever hitting $100, much less $800. They ridiculed those who thought so. And none, as far as I have heard, has even had the courtesy to openly admit the extent of that blunder. They have chosen to ignore that it ever happened. Alan Greenspan, for instance; have you heard an apology from him? How about Walter Heller or Milton Friedman?

As a layman, I know that is only one example of the non-brilliance of the economists. So when I hear them prophesying long-term recovery, higher interest rates, lower interest rates, a stronger dollar, a weaker dollar, I don't put two cents of stock in it. But as a layman I have some very basic questions that I would like answered. I find that economists, politicians and government never deal with long-term questions; never want to look beyond the day after tomorrow. Never like to spread an uncomfortable truth. For example, did you ever hear one of them get up and say, "The Dow Jones has been absolutely slaughtered in the last 17 years, and people who put their money in it have now lost about half of their substance – even as they think they have gained."

No, expediency is their specialty and "**all is well**" is their motto.

As a layman, yes, I would like to have some questions answered. Question number one is how do they figure this out: A continuing and never-ending growth rate? The government aims at 4%. Well now, I'm a layman so I didn't figure this out, but I read somewhere that if you had a 4% per year growth rate, you would increase our standard of living by 30 times in 100 years. Can you imagine a standard of living 30 times as high as what we have? And in 200 years – if these bright people ever took time to think about it – our standard of living would be about 1,000 times as great as it is now. How could this be? I would think that the whole population would be eating nightingale tongues as their main course. As a man of common sense, I would have to believe that this whole thing will blow up if this growth keeps accumulating year on year. Uninterrupted growth, even if possible, is a formula for self-destruction.

Growth just in prices, in stock market quotations is meaningless. Double the price of everything including wages and what result do you have? Just a change in numbers. For real growth, you have to have more productivity by workers either through ambition or, more likely, advanced technology. But I know that the advanced technology will produce more good with less work — so I see unemployment — and I wonder with growing unemployment how you can have healthy growth at all. I think it's myopia, even nonsense, to formulate our policies — stake our future — on the impossible premise that economic growth can go on and on. I mean, the growth could go on, but what would you do with all the stuff?

Yet it seems to be true if we don't have growth, the monetary system is going to collapse. In the first place, we must have about $2 to $3 trillion foreign debt in this world, and with interest rates as they are, that will cost $200 to $300 billion each year. But where is that to come from? If it's merely produced by the printing presses — it will be worse than meaningless — because it will renew inflation — which will kill us. I mean that **literally**.

Where would we get all the energy for this growth? And what would we do with all this growth? Give computers to illiterate kids in Nigeria?

I think the politicians ought to figure out some way that we can tread a steady course without always having to have growth.

It seems to me this is like a snake swallowing its own tail. Ever imagine that? What happens when a snake has swallowed its tail? Is he a thick ball — or has he exploded?

The next question I have to ask as a layman is, how are we going to produce growth in even the near term of 1985 and 1986 as economic ruination now becomes evident in the Third World countries and facing the $700 billion debt there? Well, the obvious answer is more and bigger loans. But who's going to do that? Well, I know from my experience as a farmer that if I borrowed $100,000 two years ago to buy machinery and special feed, and maybe some dairy cattle, and after two or three years are up I go to the bank and I say I'm sorry but I can't pay my interest, they're going to ask what results I got out of the loan. If I tell them I bought a Cadillac, and I bought an airplane, and remodeled my house, I don't think they're going to be very happy about lending me some more money. And, in my layman's view, that is what the poor countries have done. They have borrowed all this money and have spent it unproductively; some of them have bought gold-plated Cadillacs, great mansions, concubines, not to mention tanks and guns.

But the big question is how can the banker lend these countries the money again? The chances of success are less now because the poor countries will have to use half of any new loan in paying the old interest and a large part of the remainder in paying the new interest.

As a layman, I can't see any way these foreign debts are going to be paid and so I have to wonder about how the banks are going to live with it and if they will have any money left to lend business at home — and so are we going to have any growth when the federal debt alone (let alone foreign debt) is $1.6 trillion, and when you consider that consumer and business debts are nearly $5 trillion, can you believe in the long-term survival of our money system even domestically?

Can you blame a layman for doubting if the country can get back on its feet when he knows that the federal government is (for its deficits) borrowing just about all the money that is saved by all the people? So how can we get capital to bring on a great new period of building and boom? And what is going to keep the stock market up there, sound and strong — as we float on this growing sea of debt? And I say, out of common sense, the rosy forecasts are pure rubbish — I don't believe it! This debt-ridden system is breeding a hoard of parasites (interest rates) that will soon be big enough to destroy their host — that is, the economy.

And I have to wonder are we going to let the Third World shrink into starvation, disease and debt — or whether we are to share our dwindling wealth with all of them.

When we say "ALL," we have said a mouthful. Sub-Sahara Africa is reported to have almost doubled its population in a dozen years to 400,000,000. If that happened again, by 1992 and again in 2004, we would see 1.6 billion starving human beings, near death, their petitioning hands stretched out to the West.

But will this happen? Won't something even worse happen long before it gets this far? Won't nature step in somehow, as she does with other species, and strike down a cancerous population growth? No more can this continue than can perpetual economic growth continue. So it stands to reason, something will stop it. Isn't all this just another element of a global **ROLLOVER**, the outcome of which no man can foresee?

Africa is only a sample of what we face by the year 2000. The world's four billion people will probably double in the next quarter century. That's not very long. How far back does 1959 seem to you?

One might say this whole thing is already upon us. At least it is clearly in sight for anyone who wants to see.

Making the African situation more hopeless is the corruption in its governments, smelling worse than the rotting carcasses of cattle on the desert sands. Simple laughing people who were willing to tolerate colonialism and imperialism now cringe under the heel of heartless dictators, tyrants, murderers, executioners like Idi Amin of Uganda. You can roll off the names of the leaders of most of the countries and put them in a similar class. Even those under colonial government were better off than the millions of roaming refugees, sick, helpless and hopeless, an ever-expanding horde.

These are the rumblings of the small earthquakes that may very well be the first signs of a tremor building at the global core, a tremor which will cause the earth to shudder, shaking the human race. And it may begin as close as Mexico and as soon as 1987-88.

Where we are heading now is a confrontation with nature, itself. The winner will be nature.

Nature is eternal, and it sits in the sky and watches its handiwork. If you were one of nature's gods satelliting the earth and you saw a limited forest in the midst of a desert, populated with a species of, let us say, vigorous antelope which had no peer in this forest, and if you saw them multiplying to the extent where hordes became swarms, and swarms devoured each year more vegetation, you would say quite matter-of-factly, and without sympathy, they will perish; or perhaps a few of the stronger ones will survive the starvation when enough have died to let the forest grow again.

See how ridiculous the projections of the present economists are? The growth now envisaged, at the rate of the population increase, will be doubling the requirements of the people of this earth every dozen years, drawing twice as much petroleum, twice as much of all ores, twice as much timber, etc.

The doubling of industrial growth would tend to double the pollution in 10 years, and again in another 10 years to where the atmosphere and the seas would be damaged to the extent of no return — which would not make much difference to nature.

But the earth is only one of nature's planets, and nature did not provide the resources for such kind of consumption. There are good reasons to believe, and not a few, that the human race has already approached the limit of industrialization without passing the barrier of permanent damage to the environment.

So we know that this cannot go on.

Knowing it can't go on, we must conclude that it is going to at least slow down. That's because we are up against nature which is unflinching and unyielding. But under our present system of debt money, any time we slow down beyond the critical point, we face a certain collapse.

A wide-angle lens would be very deficient if it didn't spread a little wider to include the population problem.

We know there are four billion people in the world; a billion live in the advanced countries, including Russia, Europe and Japan and North America. They get enough to eat. Half of the other three billion are suffering malnutrition and retardation. One-fifth of these are starving or on the borderline of starvation. Having failed with four billion, how can we handle eight?

The one billion people of the advanced and adequately fed countries, having stabilized their population growth, will add about 50% to their current one billion. For example, the United States under just a replacement program − but including those coming up − will grow from 220 million to 330 million people. That, in itself, will result in a large increase in food requirements.

But you have seen nothing yet:

The underdeveloped countries with now a population of three billion, approximately half of which are underfed, is doubling about every 25 to 30 years. So, under current conditions, look for six billion people there − all of the additional of which cannot be fed − and one billion more in the developed countries − seven or eight billion in 25 years!

It's comforting to say that birth control will help solve the problem. But the awful truth is that if the populations of those countries were stabilized by the year 2000, we would still have 10 billion people on earth by the year 2050. And, of course, there is no hope, whatsoever, for the stabilization of those populations.

It ought to be clear that we don't have to dig around with a shovel anymore to come to the conclusion that the current trends have run slam-bang against the immovable wall of nature.

Fair conclusions are:

(1) There is very little more potential food than we are producing now − or if there is more potential, the underdeveloped countries are in no position to take advantage of it. Moreover, they wouldn't even have the mechanisms to distribute it if they had it.

111

(2) The diminishing natural resources of the earth are being tempted to their capacity, except at a very high production price, which would mean a large reduction in the standard of living everywhere.

(3) The margin of safety of the environment cannot be tempted much further, the clock is running down.

So the overall conclusion is that we have about reached the confrontation with the limits of nature.

XIII

RELIGION IN A VISE

All of this brings us unavoidably to the subject of religion, for what is embodied in the hearts of men eventually becomes embodied in their laws. Therefore, if man's environment is subjected to far-reaching changes, that will send repercussions backward into the religious beliefs.

If the population of a species, for instance, exceeds the ability of the environment to support its growth, man will have to come up with beliefs that make it **"right"** to limit the species' growth.

Then the religion will have to yield to the new environmental realities and undergo these fundamental readjustments, or fall from grace.

Man will always invent beliefs that will suit him in his environment. Age-old history tells us this.

From the very first, man feared the elements and so he began inventing gods to save him. He invented sun gods, rain gods, sea gods, wind gods, gods of thunder. He enlarged these imaginations to include gods of fertility, gods of love, and gods covering almost all of his fears and desires.

One by one, these gods fell when after millions of years, it was found that the gods did not live. The gods did not respond. The gods were non-gods. The Jews saw that the Egyptian gods were non-gods, and the Babylonian gods were non-gods, and that all the gods were a lie. The Jews came up with Jehovah as one god above any and all other gods, and all of these past lies crumbled. For a lie cannot live even if it is a religious lie.

The test comes through a confrontation with nature.

113

When we discuss religion, we too frequently refer just to Christianity, only about 2,000 years old. Actually, Christianity only represents the last few moments of the history of Homo sapiens.

Christianity represented a **ROLLOVER** in religion that spread to meet the developing needs of civilized man. But it preserved the ancient common thread running through all religion. The most fundamental teachings are geared to the basic needs of the society. It's a fascinating history.

The first enduring God was Jehovah. It seems fair to ask a question or two about Jehovah.

If Jehovah was there all the time, why did He allow dozens of previous civilizations to remain ignorant of His being? Why did He allow them to stumble along in worship of fake gods? Why did He not reveal Himself to those people?

If Jehovah only wanted to make Himself known to the Jews, what were the reasons for His preference for the Jews? Indeed, was it quite fair that God should withhold Himself from all of the other peoples over the millions of years preceding, and not even allow them to know of His existence?

The realistic explanation seems to be that the Jews were a cut smarter than other people. They saw that these gods of worship were constantly being knocked around. When one nation would conquer another nation, it would either smash its god or haul it away somewhere else. The victorious nation thereby gained certain allegiance of the defeated because the victors held and possessed **the god worshipped by the defeated**.

As long as the gods that man invented were physical in nature; as long as they could be pictured, created and sculpted, they were subject to destruction, thereby devastating the spirit of the peoples who worshipped them as immortal.

But if a god existed only in the mind, then no conquering nation could destroy him or take him away. The religions of those peoples whose god existed in their minds would be eternal and they could go on praying to God through all their adversities forever. Their spirits were less easily broken. Even though the enemies had enslaved them the enemies could not touch their god. God was immune to the enemies and would probably later rescue them. They could go on praying to god, their spirits could not be broken.

The invention of a faceless, imageless god was the greatest forward step in the history of religion.

Others caught the idea and Allah was also a faceless, non-materialistic god. In the long run then, it became quite easy for

114

people who worshipped Jehovah to suspect that the Allah of the Mohammedans was merely another name for Jehovah. Immunity to man's powers became a very important part of these religions, and one of the most important planks of the religion of Jehovah is the admonishment not to picture his face or any physical image

Thus we see one of the strong examples of how religion is tailored to serve the purpose of the society. The Jews got knocked around just too much to be able to withstand such repeated destruction of gods. But their indestructible God took the edge off the worst and was one of the mainstays in the perseverance of the Jews throughout history.

Nearly all aspects of religion can be shown to have served a very vital need of the social order. But when an order is revolutionized, you have to expect a **ROLLOVER** in religion as we first had 2,000 years ago with the advent of Christianity.

New social orders can put strains on old religions. The social order always comes to rest on the concept of the religion. The two must go in tandem.

There are, of course, religious principles that remain eternally unchangeable. Every religion has a capital tantamount to "**THOU SHALT NOT KILL.**" Had this commandment not become a deep belief in the minds of the people (that it was wrong to kill), then anyone could kill anyone else. And society would soon be reduced to the bands of the followers of tyrants who each then tried to kill one another.

The commandment, "Thou shalt not steal," is likewise essential to any orderly society. If men believed stealing was permissible, it would be impossible to have a surviving society, no matter what laws were made.

It took a great deal of time, of course, but somehow the religion of today is falling behind new realities that have developed because of science and the drastic effects of the Industrial Revolution — now already itself beginning to change.

At one time it was highly desirable to raise as many offspring as possible. If you refer to the graph on Page 18, you will see that the world's population barely grew at all for the first six hundred years A.D. and did not reach any dramatic proportions until 1700 but that, in the last 50 years, the curve is practically exponential. Earlier, humanity had all it could do just to hang on to the population it had. Therefore, it was necessary to start as many new babies as possible and to raise as many as could survive. So fertility became a very important plank in many religions. Except for a reverence of fertility man might have disappeared from the planet. And so, man was admonished by God to: "**multiply.**"

In some societies where manual work and soldiering were vitally important for the survival of the tribe or nation, the boy babies were naturally valued far above the girl babies. So it was quite proper according to those religions to kill girl babies. In other words, religion will preach what seems to be the most practical.

Thus, right and wrong came to be defined as to whether certain acts were good or bad for the propagation and prosperity of the society.

For example, polygamy may be a good practice for a society whose male population has been decimated by war. Large surpluses of the female productive apparatus are unemployed at a time when the need for more offspring is urgent. In order for the rules of the society to be carried out, it is important that they be profoundly respected (believed) by members of the society.

The laws of countries are based on their religions and the laws are much more easily and competently applied if they are an inherent part of the religious belief of the subjects.

*   *   *   *

These observations may seem random and obvious, but taken together they loudly pronounce a truth that is universal, timeless, and crystal clear: **The religion of a society will always be tailored to the best interests of the society.** If the condition fundamentally and permanently changes, the religion will be altered by one means or another over the course of time to coincide with the needs of the society.

*   *   *   *

This brings us to the religious **ROLLOVER**, the **biggest ROLLOVER** to take place in the 20th century. For ages in the past, there has been plenty of fertile land in the world to feed the people. The religions of the past have not had to deal with massive populations overrunning and destroying the environment which supports various sections of humanity on the earth. Whereas, before it was becoming that the religions should preach fertility, favoring large families to keep the race going, the conditions today suggest that this teaching is out of date, even counter-productive.

The pictures we see today of the starvation in Africa are only the beginning of a long period ahead when this starvation, now evident in Ethiopia and the Sudan and earlier in Nigeria, will spread to most of the continent of Africa. And this foretells

116

a world catastrophe, largely as the result of too many people on that continent. The teeming population of Central and South America may be on the verge of producing similar problems in the future. This has already happened in China and the Chinese government has taken the realistic view that failure to stop procreation of the race will result in nationwide starvation. The hard-headed attitude is entering the law and gradually it will work its way into the religion.

WORLD ROLLOVER in religion may come as a result of the failure of the Catholic Church to realize and recognize that the projection of current population trends in Africa, South America and Asia presents a problem that will grow like a whirlwind and which the affluent world will not be able to escape. Along the way, the church – promoting maximum births – will find itself wrong, and therefore outmoded.

Blocking birth control and early abortion must, even now, if it is applied in Africa, lead to sickening starvation of innocent children unwisely brought into the world which cannot feed them.

Unless the pope will see the writing on the wall and gradually relax the inflexibility of the Catholic Church on reproduction, then the Catholic Church has already begun a descent which will weaken it, if not eliminate it, as the major Christian religion in the world. It is questionable whether these doctrines can be altered early enough to escape the collapse of much of the rest of the accepted dogma of the church.

Already the church has lost credibility through its violent opposition to birth control. Now it is splitting apart some societies on the highly emotional issue of abortion. Somehow the propaganda has gotten around to calling fetuses babies. Years ago I never heard that idea expressed. Its introduction has caused the controversy to burst into flames.

They claim fetuses are babies. Well, are they?

To get to the truth, you have to move a step away. Let's not consider the human fetus. Let's consider the principle. An egg is an egg. A fertilized egg is a fetus. When does the fetus become the mammal, the animal, the chicken?

I was raised on a farm, so I know that most of the eggs we ate were fertilized. When the fertilizations got to the size you could see them as red spots, they were often discarded. Was that fertilized egg a chicken? Did we kill a young chicken?

When the egg under a hen for three weeks was broken, out came a half-formed chicken. As a boy, when I broke the egg did

117

I kill a chicken? I never thought so. It never seemed to me like much of a chicken.

It seemed like a chicken when you could hear the pecking inside the shell. But still, if you broke the egg at an earlier stage, you did not have a chicken. It was not a moving chicken. I must tell you in fact, in reality and in the name of common sense, I never thought of a broken egg as a chicken until the chicken had come out. That was when the chicken breathed the air, squeaked, took unsteady steps, and had consciousness.

Once in butchering a cow, with a broken leg, we came upon a partially developed fetus. Did we ever consider it to be a calf? Did my dad say to me, "We have just killed a calf?" No, the fetus was treated just like any other part of the cow's innards. As far as I could see, it had no life. It did not make a sound. It did not breathe. It did not move its eyelids, and I presume it did not hear. Certainly it did not see – it was no calf. Now you might be able to get your university friends to say this was a calf. The readers of books may say it was a calf. But I was there. I was a 10-year-old boy and I know it was no calf, and you would know it, too, if you had been there.

I don't believe there can be life without a conscious state and I believe that consciousness can only come with experience.

The fetus, whether it be a chicken, or a calf can have no background because it has no recognition. How can you recognize something where you have not yet been? It could only recognize a smell if it has already smelled. It could only recognize a sight if it had already seen. But having not yet heard, hungered or felt, there can be no consciousness! It does not smell. It does not see.

Now, coming back to humans, we have to consider the same principles. I will concede that in the later part of pregnancy we may be dealing with something different – a time when artificial help might save a life. But in the first three months, do we have a baby? Be fair – the first second after the sperm has entered the ovary – is that honest-to-goodness human life – ten seconds later? Is it within one hour a human life? Ten hours later? Two days later is this fertilized egg a baby? Certainly, it is a fetus. Twenty days?

The "right-to-lifers" make their arguments on viable interpretations. Preachers get up and pound the pulpit in front of millions, claiming that fetuses are living beings. If they want to know, on the basis of the Bible, when life begins, why don't they go and look at the Bible? The Good Book tells them when life begins (Genesis 2:7): **"The Lord God breathed into his**

118

nostrils the breath of life and man became a living soul."

It must be clear that this was an emerging infant. Until then, it had depended upon the natural processes of its mother's body to keep the development process going. We have here an infant with nostrils and when this infant took its first breath, it became a living soul. I don't want to get into the argument, but why don't the Bible quoters just go and look at the Bible?

I am not pursuing an argument here. I am dealing with a physical point of religion which is falling behind world realities, failing to see the projection of ever-increasing births, ever-increasing longevity, ever-dwindling resources and a resulting population explosion that could inundate civilization. I am trying to point out that religion was right in its earlier stand when we needed population. The pressing populations require that the religious take cognizance of the growing limitations facing the ever-growing demands. It is a point that urgently needs to be recognized by world leaders now.

One would look for some common sense from the president of an enlightened nation. But now the president is calling fetuses babies. It's not Reagan's first brush with scientific knowledge. Before his 1980 election, he allowed as how people weren't so sure about evolution anymore, inferring that evolution might be nothing more than a theory. Apparently his aides got to him quickly about that one, maybe by showing him some ordinary rocks and fossils. It's dangerous for a president to think so erroneously.

Remember, when the pope preaches and the president proclaims all the world listens, including the starving nations. And Mexico is listening. Some future president will have to deal with an almost unsurmountable wave moving in from the south.

The pope says, "Keep on breeding in accordance with nature."

China has taken issue with the pope and has foreseen that if its population growth is as projected, there will be massive starvation throughout the nation of a billion people, and it has been forced to come to very strict laws to limit the population, first of all by birth control and when that doesn't work by abortion. They've decided to be warned by an everlasting truth: **Whether the species be deer, antelope or wildcats — or humans, Jehovah's law is written in granite. It says: "If you overproduce, you must starve!"** This is not subject to appeal.

(That certainly is not to be taken literally. Of course, it is not written in granite, but nature writes it in bleaching skeletons across the land.)

It's to be hoped that the church and the political leadership will recognize this primordial wave that is now advancing upon us.

If it is not recognized, we will be consumed in a world population firestorm.

Whereas once the purpose of a realistic religion was to populate the earth, now the purpose is to limit it.

XIV

ROLLOVER IN
THE THIRD WORLD

It is human nature to survive and to fight to survive. It will be a manifestation of human nature that those who are starving will claw and fight to get enough food to survive. If the underdeveloped countries get atomic weapons, they will be tempted to use them for blackmail, and then the larger powers will have to decide whether to give up continually increasing quantities of food – or to wipe out the underdeveloped countries with nuclear weapons.

Even if there is no nuclear contest, the best that could be hoped for would be widespread starvation. It will not be a part of human nature for American citizens to voluntarily say, we are now eating 500 pounds of grain and 100 pounds of meat per year. Because our brothers are starving, we will cut our consumption to 250 pounds of grain and 20 pounds of meat. Human nature, being a part of nature, can be counted upon not to do that.

It follows that, beginning now, it will be a mistake to provide food to encourage the expansion of the doomed populations. Intellectually – dealing strictly out of reason – one has to say, better to let a half billion starve now than three billion starve 20 years from now.

Obviously, we are coming to a point of decision – fateful for the whole human race – and within these next 10 years. We don't have to know what the decision will be to be sure that we are faced with unfamiliar and unprecedented troubles.

And this is all beginning to happen as the **ROLLOVER** starts, beginning barely to move. That means we have started the advance toward the unavoidable confrontation between humanity and nature.

I know that people claim we are going to solve all these problems, the do-gooders, the eternal optimists. But anyone who claims that, really hasn't even seen the problem. I doubt if most of the leaders in Congress have tumbled remotely to the problem. And if they had tumbled to it, would they be apt to get up and talk about it from a platform? That's what makes one wonder whether the country is run by dreamers, hypocrites, or just empty-headed, unthinking, run-of-the-mill politicians who believe that the safest and surest way to prominence is to always "follow the crowd." **Don't dare to look ahead! And if you do — keep your mouth shut.**

When I look at all this and see a very expensive American dollar causing foreigners to avoid American-made goods, thus putting a damper on U.S. factories, thus causing unemployment to grow — when I see all this, I come to the conclusion that our planners ought to know for certain that present policies are leading us into the epicenter of a hurricane — worldwide. It would be more accurate to say that present policies are "**blundering**" into a hurricane. There is no leadership.

You come to the conclusion after awhile that no intelligent being is at the helm of the ship. It is drifting aimlessly in the area of the maelstrom. (If you haven't read that story by Edgar Allan Poe, do so. It is a very apt analogy.) For once having entered the rim of the maelstrom, the ship will be relentlessly sucked in deeper and deeper.

*   *   *   *

As folks of common sense, you will know right away that this monetary system, this economy, hooked as it is on a mandatory growth rate, must sooner or later get locked into an exponential curve. That is, the curve gets steeper and steeper and the steepness of the curve continues to accelerate, until the curve becomes, to all intents and purposes, perpendicular, at which point it can't get any steeper. You can't get more vertical than vertical. But our system mandates that the rate of growth must continue because:

(1) The population is continually increasing so the economy must grow in order to accommodate the increased population.

(2) More and more money is borrowed, more and more interest is due, and more and more is compounded on more and more, until the money system finally explodes into suicidal inflation or catastrophic deflation.

Both the bicycle and the airplane have critical speeds. If the man on the bicycle stops making the bicycle move forward, it will fall over. If an airplane drops below its critical speed, it will fall out of the sky. If the economy loses the necessary momentum to keep it going, it will collapse.

It's absolutely necessary that people must buy and, over the course of the years, they must always buy more and then still more. But finally you come to the point, as in the Great Depression, where they can't buy more because they don't have more dollars, as a result of bankruptcies — the crashing of the curve of growth.

Then they have less money. Then comes growing unemployment, bank failures, a whole host of troubles that can be grouped together to be called **DEFLATION**.

They have been making use of a method to get around this. That is, the manufacture of more money. When we were on the gold standard with gold at a fixed price, the treasury of a country could not manufacture more money than its gold pile would allow. If the country had to have more money, it had to raise the price of gold (devalue its currency) and then it could increase the printed money supply. That was devaluation. Other countries didn't like devaluation because that made the money cheaper, and it gave the devalued currency an advantage in selling to their markets and it put them at a disadvantage in selling to their own market. All that is still true. Nevertheless, since we no longer work under any such restrictions as called for by the gold standard, the treasury of a country can simply devalue against the U.S. dollar. But with the dollar being the standard (not gold) the United States has nothing to devalue **against**; it can only devalue by inflation. That is, by making more dollars available, issuing more credit.

I shouldn't have used the word "simply," because it's not quite that simple. It's done this way: The banker may have lent out his depositors' money and have nothing more than a line of credit with the Federal Reserve. You go into the bank and borrow $1,000. The banker issues you a credit for $1,000. You have now added $1,000 to the money supply of the country. Multiply that a few thousand times in big figures and you can see how the money supply of a country can expand enormously through debt.

Now you write checks on your $1,000 and that money goes into someone else's account, and that goes into the deposit of some other bank, and the other bank then can lend out that money. Then it goes to another bank. All in all — including the

123

mandatory amount the bank has to keep on deposit, your $1,000 becomes $6,000. By borrowing that $1,000, you have increased the money supply by $6,000.

Now that is one of the main cylinders of the engine of growth. Continually borrowing, continually increasing the money supply, starting new businesses, etc. And that coincides with the whole picure of the never-ending growth.

But there are two bad things about this. One is that when the Federal Reserve backs the banks with great reserves of credit, the money supply is increased far and beyond the amount of goods on the markeplace. In simple terms, if you were to double the money supply of a country, and if all of the money before was worth all of the goods, you would now have twice as much money for the same amount of goods. The prices would double, reflecting the amount of added money. And there would be INFLATION.

A second and more horrible result is that all the loaned money demands interest. For instance, the U.S. government debt of over $1.4 trillion in 1984 demands interest of approximately $140 billion. Well, one fifth of the budget is going to be paying the interest. Now, as the debt continues to grow, the interest continues to compound, so the interest is always higher year by year. That requires always more money, without having added one iota to the gross national product — just more money.

The private debt of the United States is over three times as much as the public debt. As this debt grows — and it always seems to be growing — the amount of interest continues to grow. So there you will have $300 to $400 billion more cash needed next year than was needed this year.

If this extra money is created, it adds to the total money supply — UNLESS the money can be put to work productively — in other words, to grow more crops, produce more goods and services. If that happens that will restrain the inflation by adding to the goods and services available.

But if the money is given away as social handouts, it will simply be spent for consumption and it will be inflationary money implanted into the money supply.

Now this may give a clue as to why the leadership of this country has been so hellbent on increased spending — as illustrated on Page 22 in the satire on President Johnson. People simply have to keep buying more to keep the factories busy. Also, people mustn't pay off too many of their debts.

When people go bankrupt, that erases the debt and that reduces the money supply by many fold. When people pay debts, the same thing happens.

The result is that we are on a course in this economy where the debt always has to increase. So the interest always has to increase. So there always has to be more money and more money as a perpetual growth factor. So there always has to be more and more consumption. And whenever that stops, you have the bust.

So it is absolutely inherent in our system that we must have the growth. But if the growth falls in on itself — as I have pictured above — then we don't have a system. And, in a nutshell, that is what this book is about. **The system itself is on a collision course with the necessity of growth.**

*   *   *   *

Now that is what you had in 1929. You had the bust and it got worse and worse. We never really did recover from the bust until the war came along and huge amounts of money were siphoned into the economy for the war effort. The real, hard-earned savings of the American people went into it. But that did stimulate the beast. Nevertheless, the Great Depression is still not understood by economists and they still don't know how they would have gotten out of it had it not been for the war.

But what I am talking about in this book is no mere depression like we had in the 1930s. It's like comparing a battle to a war. To the conditions of 1929, we must now add the illiquidity of the whole Third World, which is into us for hundreds of billions of dollars. We must add the fact that all of the western nations have been in a recession — bordering on a depression — and the United States is the only one to have staged a recovery.

No nation today can live in prosperity and continue to enjoy good times while the other nations of the world flounder. Today, the world is one big integrated and confused mass of interaction. You'd have as much chance of tracing all this out as you would have understanding the inside of a modern computer.

The point is that, in addition to the monetary problems which broke the system in 1929, we now have overpopulation in the poor countries of the world to where many of them are facing starvation, as they wallow in a sea of debt. We are laboring under the highest real interest rates in history, even as we enter these tempestuous seas. We are coming face to face with high-tech which will reduce our jobs drastically from now on, so that the army of the unemployed will continue to grow.

125

We are dealing with the Feminist Revolution which will produce unprecedented strains on our social order that reach right down to the bottom of the family. All of these things are in addition to the comparatively small crisis of 1929 and the resulting 1930s.

That is why I call this book **ROLLOVER**. We are coming to a point where the whole society, not only its money system, not only its debts, not only its jobs, but the very roots of human existence and the concept of the purpose of life itself are coming into question. And it looks like it's all coming up at once.

Of course, talking about a movement like this "all at once" doesn't mean all in one year, or all in four years. But it does mean the whole thing comes into question in a relatively small number of years, certainly faster than we can digest it.

Therefore, it means a crisis, a crisis for banks, a crisis in savings, a crisis in jobs, in money itself.

And on top of that, we now have a danger of a war that could never have even been imagined in 1929.

It is all so overwhelming that I am inclined to believe it will bring common sense to the world leaderships and that war, the worst of all dangers, may be avoided.

Meanwhile, we will not be finished with the dangers of nuclear disaster. For as all of this comes unstuck and gets glued together, we have to face war by terrorism, the only way our poor and starving countries can deal with big neighbors relying on clumsy armies.

For the most part, all of this happened so gradually that you hardly realized anything new was taking place. The big **ROLLOVER** is comprised of countless trends and countertrends, forces and counter-forces, even new forces and counter-forces that will arise within the drama, not yet foreseeable. Each of these in itself will be some kind of a crisis. The **ROLLOVER** is only the sum of all of these conflicts, stresses, and climaxes. For instance, a weekend crisis in world banking, although it should shake the world, would be only one of the many elements that will enter into the sum of the **ROLLOVER**. Each will make its contribution so in the end, the **ROLLOVER** will not be one event at all. It will be the RESULT of all of them put together. And this result will eventually be the new way of life for the human race upon this planet. And all of it will take years, but at the rate things move today, it might not be many years.

For example, if terrorism becomes a way of fighting wars between big nations and little nations, rich nations and poor nations, this will be a process causing perpetual havoc and unremitting strain.

Under conditions as they are in 1985, can anyone doubt the trend toward the escalation of terrorism? Can you rule out a suicidal raid into a nuclear plant, leading to a melt-down, atomic fusions, radioactive clouds and the near destruction of the population of certain centers? Such an event would terrorize the entire populations living around other nuclear plants. As embattled smaller countries become embittered, this war by terrorism would tend to accelerate. And the truth is we don't know how to deal with terrorism. Just as a relatively small number of guerrilla warriors could inflict damage all out of proportion to their strength in Vietnam, so the terrorists have the advantage of small numbers and small organizations and big damage.

And why does it happen? It happens because our civilization has not developed the wisdom nor the means to deal with the relationship between the extremely poor and the affluent. The structure of our social order, mandating perpetual growth, is itself a death sentence to the social order which has been built upon that philosophy. The Industrial Revolution showed us how to produce more, but not how to distribute it.

I wish to emphasize that the mere fact you don't pick up the paper six months from now and read about foreseen and projected events, doesn't mean you forget about them. The forces that will bring them on are working all day and all night every day as time passes.

But the **ROLLOVER** in growth — the shrinkage of growth — is likely to be one of the earlier of the major elements of the big picture that will produce a new way of life for the human species on this planet.

XV

ROLLOVER IN DEBT

Having progressed thus far in an understanding of some of the naked but **hidden** truths of the economic conditions, as we approach the end of this massive industrial era, you must now prepare for haymaker punch that will knock you right off your feet. And when you get up, your brain will clear and you will know, without any doubt, that the day of the **ROLLOVER** is upon us.

As a layman with common sense, start off with this. The total debt of the world is well over $8 trillion. The interest is over $800 billion a year. If not paid, the interest is simply added to the debt and the compounding process continues.

In order to believe that we can live with this, we have to come around to a philosophic line that contends "debt doesn't matter." If we go along with this idea of President Reagan that a $200 billion deficit doesn't matter, I suppose a $500 billion deficit doesn't matter? And take that to the end of the logic and a deficit, no matter what size, wouldn't matter. To look at the way the United States has been going into debt, glance at the graph on Page 143, and if you think debt does matter, then you have to go along with me and say there's going to be one enormous bang one of these days.

Now I have a law. I stated it some years ago. I have never seen it stated before by anyone and I believe I have every right to call it *MYERS' LAW*. It is as immutable as Newton's Law of Gravity, as simple as nature, as inescapable: **A DEBT WILL ALWAYS BE PAID — either by the one who borrowed, or by the one who lent.**

*   *   *   *

128

If I can convince you that every loan in the world will be paid either by the debtor or the lender himself, who unwittingly made the bad loan, I will not have very much trouble in convincing you of all of the rest of the conclusions in this book.

This becomes the most important fundamental which you must absolutely accept as true beyond doubt. Then you will know that one of these days credit will explode with unimaginable force. This is the handwriting on the wall, and there is no escape from it.

First of all, don't be fooled by the propaganda which states "countries don't default." Answer them by quoting the following dispatch from Rio de Janeiro:

"Official announcements, that a partial moratorium had been obtained on foreign debt payments, was made today by the Brazilian Government publicity bureau. The government, it was stated, has decided to suspend temporarily foreign debt payments with the exception of two funding loans and the Coffee Loan." – London Financial Times, August 30, 1930.

That was just a year and five days after the world had been assured by Thomas W. Lamont, senior director, J.P. Morgan and Co., as follows:

"Mr. Lamont in his capacity as chairman of the International Committee of Bankers of Mexico, felt nothing but pride and satisfaction as he ushered Sr. Luis Montes Fioca, the Mexican Finance Minister, into the Morgan Bank's opulent boardroom on Wall Street."

The two were said to have successfully concluded the biggest renegotiation and settlement of a defaulting country's foreign debt. Here was rosy new hope for the financial world, after a year of continuous disasters. But that hope had lived just six months. It turned out to be only the beginning of a long string of default. The big restructuring celebration triumphantly held on July 25, 1929, was knocked in the head by the Bolivian moratorium six months later on January 1, 1930. Then in March, the Peruvian finance minister wired Mr. Mitchell, chairman of City Bank:

"I am addressing you with respect to the interest due, April the first next, on the Peruvian National Loan. This government took office on March the eleventh last, after a period of political disturbance extending over six months. It finds the treasury bare of funds, both as a result of these political disturbances and of the economic depression which has obtained for more than a year. As a result of these conditions, for which the present government is not responsible, it has not

the capacity at this time to pay in full the service charges on the Republic's entire debt."

Mr. Mitchell, chairman of City Bank, had barely had time to digest the bad news of March when the hail started coming thick and fast. A similar letter was received from the government of Chile. Then came the bolt from Brazil, followed in quick order by similar cables from Ecuador, Colombia and Central America. Within a year, only three major Latin American countries — Argentina, Venezuela, and the Dominican Republic — were meeting their obligations in full. Then came defaults from Hungary, Yugoslavia, Rumania, Poland, Bulgaria and finally Germany under the new Chancellor Adolf Hitler.

This information, drawn from the Financial Times, paints a picture which may well be a dead ringer for upcoming events in 1985-86.

The pity of it is that the American people have been exposed to so much untruth that they fully believe these foreign debts can be kept under the rug indefinitely. They think these debts can be dealt with as fantasies are dealt with. Nothing has happened yet over these tremendous debts, so nothing will.

But if I have convinced you that a debt will always be paid, then you **KNOW** that this matter will come into the open sooner or later, and perhaps sooner. The difference between the debts today and the debts that were largely responsible for the last depression is the fact that today's debts are giants compared with the debts of 1930.

That doesn't necessarily mean that the precipitation of today's debts will come faster than it did in 1930, but the history of the early 1930s tends to indicate that we can become accustomed to any facts in fairly fast order. The Financial Times said:

"No nation in Latin America explicitly repudiated its debts, but by 1933 there was no longer any thought of loyally complying 'with external obligations,'" as expressed by the Peruvian minister in 1931. Indeed, when the Mexican president asserted publicly in September, 1933, that the present and future financial policy of the government "does not permit any idea of renewing service on the foreign debt," his statement did not even rate a report in the financial press.

"The bond market even picked up slightly when Brazil converted its 'temporary' moratorium into a permanent default by stating that it would issue newly printed bonds for twenty and forty years in lieu of cash interest payments."

130

As for the dire threats of what will happen to any country that defaults, that too is mostly fantasy. Back in the 1930s, absolutely nothing happened to those who defaulted. No trade was cut off, and Mexico had defaulted for 30 years, from 1914 to 1943, and then even after the confiscation of American oil interests in Mexico, the country was back at the lending desk again and, specifically in 1981, asking for a $50 million loan on behalf of Pemex, the lucky recipient of the U.S. oil companies.

* * * *

Here is what happened half a century ago as a consequence of default by countries. The following was the assessment of President Herbert Hoover:

"The Great Depression of 1932 resulted not from the market crash of 1929, but rather originated with the heritage of war which led to a financial collapse in Europe, and its subsequent default on billions of dollars in loans to the U.S. government."

Before the war's conclusion, the U.S. government lent its Allies $10 billion to become the largest creditor in history — lending $4.3 billion to Britain, $3 billion to France, $1.6 billion to Italy and over $1 billion to a host of other nations. In return, the treasury held obligations in the form of certificates of indebtedness, which were payable in gold, bore interest ranging from 3% to 5%, and originally had early maturity dates.

However, repayment really depended on creditors receiving reparation payments from defeated Germany — which after the treaties of Versailles and Saint Germain, had been assessed $33 billion worth of guilt. But war-torn Germany was in no position to meet its obligations and in 1923 the system seemed ready to collapse.

However, the United States government came to the rescue with the Dawes Plan — a large guarantee loan to Germany enabling it to make reparation payments, thus enabling the allies to repay the United States. This plan not only averted a major financial crisis, but also induced private U.S. investors to make further German loans. The system looked secure — then along came 1929, when the boom induced capitalists to draw funds from Europe to the United States to invest in the New York Stock Exchange. By 1929, Europe was hanging by a thread. Then came the crash in New York, and the panic withdrawal of funds from Europe. That resulted in the collapse of the largest bank in Austria, owing $76 million abroad, most of it to Great Britain and the United States.

131

According to noted historian, Broadus Mitchell: "Failure of the Kreditanstalt meant the failure of Central Europe; the financial strain was communicated everywhere because important banks must bring home other foreign assets to compensate for funds tied up in Austria."

President Hoover, facing what he believed to be a complete international banking collapse, called for a one-year moratorium on all intergovernmental payments in the summer of 1931. But by then, it was too late.

In December, 1932, France, Belgium and four other governments defaulted on debt installments due the U.S. government. By June, 1933, Great Britain was only able to make a token payment — including silver calculated at twice its market price. Newly elected President Roosevelt went on record saying that he did not consider these debtors to be in default. By December, 1933, France had failed on its third payment, calling its action a postponement.

But American holders of German, British and French bonds found our the "postponement" would last forever.

But that was the final pretense. The world was now mired in its deepest recession and Adolf Hitler was on the verge of seizing control in Europe.

Then we had the same kind of fiddle-faddle we have now. The United States agreed to spread out British payments over 62 years with interest at 3% for the first 10 years and 3 1/2% thereafter. Similar "restructurings" were made with France, Italy and Yugoslavia with interest rates averaging 1.6% in the first 10 years and 0.4% thereafter. Today, these agreements are worthless pieces of paper in the files of history. In this case, the lender (U.S. taxpayers) paid the debt.

So much for the precedents of default. Who will pay now?

Well, in the past as you can recognize, a very great deal of this debt was paid by the lender. In today's world, it won't be any different; the lenders will be stuck. That means the huge western banks, and especially the massive banks of New York. But some people say the government will never allow the banks to go broke. If you believe that, and if that is true, then the taxpayers will pay for the loans that were made to these foreign countries. Let's see what that might amount to.

There are approximately 200 million people in the United States. Look at one country alone: Brazil. The acknowledged debt at the end of 1982 was $90 billion. It has to be more than $100 billion in 1985.

If you believe that the loan will be paid either by (a) Brazil, (b) the banks, (c) the taxpayers, then let's see what your bill, in the last instance, would be. At $10 per person, 200 million people could pay $2,000 million — in other words, $2 billion. At $100 per person, it would be $20 billion. If every person — man, woman and child — chipped in $500 ($2,000 per family of four), they could pay off Brazil's debt.

But the total debt of Latin America is about $300 billion. If every man, woman and child paid $1,500 ($6,000 for every family of four), we could pay off the debt of Central and South America. But if we wanted to include the other shaky loans in communist countries and so on, we would have to pay about $750 billion in all. Every man, woman and child would have to pay $4,500 ($18,000 for a family of four). Now the interest at 10% adds nearly $500 a year, so if you don't pay it, next year you'll owe $5,000 instead of $4,500. And in about seven years more, you will owe a total of about $10,000. If you are a family of four, you will owe $40,000. (We haven't even started to talk about your own debt yet, nor the debt of the United States.) The U.S. government is in debt for more than $1.5 trillion. That is, $80,000 for a family of four. Every single working man or woman owes $20,000.

If you believe that **a debt will always be paid by (a), (b), or (c) as listed above,** then you can readily see that most of this debt in the world is going to be paid by the people who lent it.

And that will produce the **ROLLOVER** of our civilization. Not only will debtors be bankrupt, but lenders, too. What you are projecting right now is a social order that has gone bankrupt.

Don't think it's maybe. Sooner or later this thing will burst. When it does, it will be like a giant firecracker, filling the monetary sky as far as your eye can see in any direction.

The banking situation seems always to be clouded in the newspapers. People get nervous about the banks, but they don't exactly know why. Sometimes I think the banking facts are purposely kept complicated and incomplete. Actually, the banking structure is quite simple. Very large questions are nearly always simple. Their answers may not be simple, but the questions are simple. How do these big banks work? Just like any little bank.

Suppose you and I and a couple of other fellows put a million dollars into a bank. Now we are ready to set up business and to loan money. We are also ready to receive deposits from customers.

133

For simplification, let's say by the time we have received $100,000 in deposits we find what we think is a good loan prospect and we loan our original million dollars plus most of our $100,000 deposited with us.

Now, let's say that although we don't know this loan is bad when we make it, we find out later that it is. The debtor defaults. The sum of $1,100,000 has been lent out. That means that the money you and I and others put up is completely lost. We have lost our million dollars. Beyond that, though, the $100,000 comes out of the hide of our depositors. That is why the bank inspectors have to keep watching these banks. The Federal Insurance Depository Corp. is very interested because they guarantee that extra $100,000 on any deposit not exceeding $100,000. So it's the job of the bank watchdog agencies to keep examining these banks to monitor how much the FDIC might lose if the bank had to close. Now, if you look at banks like Continental Illinois and Citicorp, for instance, you see that each has lent out a lot more than the total equity of all the shareholders and anything in excess of that would be the depositors' money – if there were a default – exceeding the shareholders' owners equity. So for the FDIC not to get caught with too big a problem on its hands, it watches this and it is the duty of these watchdog agencies to force the bank to close if they think that default would exceed the total value of all the shareholders in the bank stock.

People unaccustomed to bank jargon may get confused over the two words: "assets" and "equity." We are used to thinking that our assets are what we have. And that's all to the good. It doesn't work quite that way on the bank balance sheet.

If you go to the bank and borrow $10,000, that is marked up against you and immediately placed in the asset column of the bank. Your loan is their asset. If International Harvester comes along and borrows $100 million, that goes into the asset column, too.

If Brazil borrows $2 billion from the bank, it is also a bank asset. Notice these are all assets and will be assets IF they get paid. If they're not paid, they're supposed to be called into default and the property is to be seized.

However, in the case of Brazil (as we have seen), there isn't much to be seized. But interest is due – let's say in the amount of $200 million. If that interest isn't paid, the bank is forced to call the loan into default.

Well, how could Brazil get $200 million that it doesn't have? It could **borrow** it from the bank. So the bank lends Brazil $200 million to pay its interest and that, as a new loan, becomes a bank asset. The assets of the bank are miraculously now improved by $200 million. The debt is just as good, and not one bit better, than Brazil's ability and willingness to pay it.

The equity is quite a different matter. The equity is what all shareholders of the bank own.

If the shareholders of one of the big banks have an equity of $2 billion, and if it has deposits of $3 billion, and if it has bad loans of $6 billion, then of course the bad loans of $6 billion will have to come out of the equity. Well, there's only $2 billion of equity, so immediately that is all gobbled up and every shareholder of the bank has lost his shirt and the bank must close. Additionally, the bank has been using the $3 billion of its depositors, and of course it cannot now pay its depositors because it has lent their money to Brazil — and Brazil can't pay. So the FDIC theoretically is required to pay all the depositors of this defunct bank. (It's not required to pay any deposits over $100,000.)

All of this goes along quite smoothly until something happens to upset the applecart. So far, in 1982, 1983 and 1984, the Fed and the FDIC have been arranging for other banks to take over banks that are about to close. The FDIC, in many cases, made up the difference so that all the depositors could be paid. They absolutely have to do this because if it ever happened that the depositors didn't get paid, it would send a scare througout the whole country and there would be runs on banks all over the country — and then they would go broke. So they have to keep the subject quiet and copacetic. Now they are able to do this to a limited extent, although the FDIC funds of $15.4 billion insures $1.3 trillion in deposits (1.19%). But let this happen to a megabank. It would likely nearly break the entire Federal Depository Insurance Corporation. If that became known, there would be a run on banks all over the country.

At any cost — no matter what the cost — if it is at all possible, the authorities will block, by fair means or foul, the bankruptcy of any megabank.

But the question remains. What happens if Brazil defaults? There is no banker in the world with an answer to this. They just HOPE it won't happen. And I guess you and I had better hope it won't happen, too.

Brazil, approaching a debt of $100 billion, is unable to pay any of its creditors either the installments or the interest due on these loans. Its reserves are almost nil. There is, of course, no hope that the country can meet its commitment in this next year. The question is can the tiger be kept in the cage for a year after that? And, if so, for a year after that?

Of one thing you can be certain. The big banks will not call the country into default. Try to imagine a board meeting at Citicorp discussing this extremely sensitive situation behind closed doors:

FIRST DIRECTOR: If we had followed good banking practice, we wouldn't be in up to our necks in Brazil.

SECOND DIRECTOR: Let's call them to default right now. This is not going to get any better.

THIRD DIRECTOR: I agree with that, but what are we going to seize to get some of our money back?

CHAIRMAN: Well, there may be a few ships here and there in some of our ports that we could seize.

SECOND DIRECTOR: That would mean maybe a few scores of millions of dollars — not much help against a debt of $4,350 million Brazil, alone, owes us.

CHAIRMAN: That's true — we wouldn't get anything.

FIRST DIRECTOR: And that would mean we'd have to write off the $4,360 million?

CHAIRMAN: Yes.

FIRST DIRECTOR: But this loan is on our books as an asset of the bank of $4,360 million. When we write this loan down, we write it down as a total loss. But we can't lose more than we've got and be in business, and we've only got $4,833 million counting down to the last pencil. So we'll only have $473 million left. My God, Mexico alone owes us $3,300 million. If they cop out on even $500 million, we are worth less than zero.

CHAIRMAN: That's correct. No share of Citicorp would be worth a dime. We will go under into bankruptcy, still owing hundreds of millions of dollars,

	ourselves. We would be wiped out. And maybe we'll take the FDIC with us.
SECOND DIRECTOR:	Isn't there some way around it?
CHAIRMAN:	Yes, there is a way around it. We can see if we can get Brazil to promise to make payments next year and we can call that PUBLICLY rescheduling of the loan. I wouldn't give you fifteen cents for such an agreement, but it will mean that we don't have to write off the loan. That will mean we don't have to declare bankruptcy ourselves.
ALL DIRECTORS:	Well then, there's no choice. We will have to make — if necessary — a bogus agreement with Brazil for them to pay into the future. Even if they don't pay, we could reschedule it again later on and in the meantime we could stay in business.
CHAIRMAN:	Yes, but some day the problem will have to be met. Meanwhile, we will have to keep lending them more in order to keep the agreement on the books. Interest is $450 million for this next year. Well, if they can't pay the interest then you know we have to LEND them the money so that they can pay the interest. That way, the loan looks okay on the books.
FIRST DIRECTOR:	Yes, and that helps us some too, because when they pay us back that $50 million we lent them, we show that as earnings. So it makes our profit picture look better. And if we lend this money to all those illiquid debtors around the world, these earnings look very, very good. Of course, if the countries don't pay, those earnings are all really losses. And so, of course, is the entire loan.
CHAIRMAN:	Well, that's right. And meanwhile we don't have to close our doors. We can go on acting and performing like one

of the richest banks in the world. We also keep our jobs. We also avoid a domino bankruptcy throughout the United States which would be sure to spread to England and most of Europe and around the world. Gentlemen, you know as well as I that would be a world catastrophe. AND IT CAN'T HAPPEN.

FIRST DIRECTOR: I agree and I think we all agree, there is nothing to be gained by calling them into default. We must go on lending them more money for the simple reason that we dare not stop.

CHAIRMAN: That is, I think, what we have to do. But that doesn't get us out of the woods entirely. It's possible there might be a revolution in Brazil and BRAZIL ITSELF might simply announce a default on the loan. In that case, we have no choice but to write it off.

SECOND DIRECTOR: Not really!

CHAIRMAN: WELL, WE CAN HANG ON AND HOPE.

*   *   *   *

Here is the table of three of the world's worst debtors. An examination of the debt of only three countries will serve our purpose here: Mexico, Brazil, and Venezuela.

Bank	Mexico ($ Mill)	Brazil ($ Mill)	Venezuela ($ Mill)	Others ($ Mill)	Total ($ Mill)	Net Worth ($ Mill)	% of Net Worth
Man. Hanover	1,730	2,014	1,100	1,967	6,811	2,780	245%
Chase Manhattan	1,687	2,362	1,012	1,012	6,073	2,760	220%
Citicorp	3,270	4,360	1,090	1,090	9,810	4,833	203%
Chemical	1,500	1,300	-0-	741	3,541	1,946	185%
Morgan Guaranty	1,082	1,688	543	759	4,072	2,715	150%
BankAmerica	2,500	2,300	2,000	-0-	6,800	4,595	148%
Bankers Trust	875	875	475	-0-	2,225	1,560	143%
Continental Illinois	695	490	463	381	2,029	1,705	119%
Security Pacific	525	490	-0-	175	1,190	1,488	80%
First Interstate	680	474	-0-	-0-	1,154	1,803	64%
TOTAL	14,544	16,353	6,683	6,125	43,705	26,185	169%

Column five is the total debt involvement of the banks and column six is what those banks are worth. Notice in the case of the first, Manufacturers Hanover Trust, they have loaned $1,700 million to Mexico, $2,000 million ($2 billion) to Brazil, and $1,100 million to Venezuela, plus nearly $2 billion to other countries. Thus, their total outstanding, nonperforming, shaky loans amount to over $6 billion. But the net worth of all the buildings and all the assets of Manufacturers Hanover Trust, everywhere in the world, is only $2,780 million ($2.78 billion). So their questionable loans are two and one-half times as much as their total equity. Notice in the case of Chase Manhattan that it has lent over $2,360 million to Brazil alone, and its total net worth including all of its shareholders and assets is only $2,760 million. So if Brazil alone defaulted, the Chase Manhattan Bank would only have $400 million left. And if the others among them defaulted a total of no more than $400 million – Chase Manhattan would be without assets – and it would close. Any one of these banks that closed its doors would shake every other bank to its very foundations and probably close some of them. Then this would bring on the closure of other banks. I believe we can take it for granted that if any one of the giants goes down as a result of a default (declared by either side), the result would be a world **ROLLOVER** of the debt structure. Businesses that relied on these banks would also close. People would lose their jobs right and left. You go on with the chaotic results in your own mind. But I tell you, these debts will be paid!

None of this is fiction, none is alarmist. There is no fantasy in it.

Still, the system persists. It persists because there is every effort by the combined authorities in the world to glue it together, patch it together. But it is only a delaying action. A debt will always be paid. Certain events could precipitate this brew without warning. The banks don't know any more than you or I whether there will be a revolution, for example, in Brazil, Argentina or Mexico. Maybe no, maybe yes.

We do know that these countries are politically unstable and that their economies are in a deplorable state, and that they have virtually no net reserves to pay out. We also know that you can't take blood from a stone. And we know that millions live at the level of starvation.

A Salomon Brothers analyst was quoted as saying: "There's a day coming when a number of these big banks will have to sell equity capital at punitive prices." Analyze what that means in plain English. That means BROKE!

139

To destroy this fear, the banks are saying that the likelihood of all of these countries going broke is practically zero.

Well, of course! But even if one of them goes broke, we would have a banking crisis that might well paralyze the world.

* * * *

A very detailed study of 14,000 U.S. banks has led a specialist group, Veribanc (P. O. Box 2963, Woburn, Mass. 10888, phone (617)-245-8370) to draw the following conclusions:

"The figures indicate a problem of considerably larger scope and magnitude than has yet been made public.

"Actions such as defaults on the part of the debtor countries, payment moratoriums or formation of a debtors' cartel would cause U.S. banking chaos which could well be beyond even the Federal Reserve Board's ability to control."

Veribanc makes the flat statement:

"Foreign loan commitments and holdings of U.S. banks are considerably higher than have been reported by the banks and government authorities to date."

The figure of $98.6 billion foreign exposure, reported by the Federal Reserve Board, and publicized as the total amount outstanding to non-oil-producing countries is far short of the Veribanc mark.

Records of 14,000 U.S. banks show that the total long-term and short-term debt owed by overseas borrowers to U.S. banks is not $98.6 billion, but $235.7 billion. And that's only to the end of the third quarter 1982, and it's based on computer-aided examination of the most recent Federal Reserve Board report.

The unthinkable thought is that if there should be a rash of foreign defaults or moratoriums, the FDIC could pay only a small fraction of the amount required to pay depositors, even after the banks' total net worth had been absorbed. Depositors of over $100,000 would lose everything above $100,000.

Equity means the net worth of the bank. Bad loans have to be written off from equity. If the bad loans exceed the equity, the bank must close. It will still have depositors' money and it still may have large so-called "assets." But if the bad loan total exceeds the equity, that comes out of the depositors' hides.

For example, busted Seafirst still has $9 billion in assets. But those assets are, in reality, large debts due the bank. When it comes to the crunch, losses can only be charged off against the

140

net worth — that is, the equity of the bank, including shareholders and properties.

We are expected to take the following for granted: If a foreign loan of a bank is defaulted, and if that default exceeds the equity of the bank, then even though the bank must close, the Federal Deposit Insurance Corporation will pay off all the depositors. No danger!

That can only hold true, however, if the tidal wave of bankruptcies does not exceed the amount of funds set aside by the FDIC to pay the depositors.

The Veribanc study shows that the 90 leading banks which account for the bulk of the assets of the industry (over $1 trillion) have a foreign loan exposure of $221 billion which exceeds their combined equity by $185 billion. They would be $185 billion short of paying their depositors. So that would be up to the FDIC. But the FDIC has only less than a twelfth of that amount, a total of $15.4 billion on reserve.

Another group of 59 banks has foreign loan exposure of over $100 billion and this exceeds its total combined net worth by $64.5 billion — over four times FDIC reserves.

The report goes on to state that while the bulk of foreign loans are held by the large U.S. banks in the money centers, there are surprising numbers of medium-sized banks throughout the country which are in over their net worth, i.e. equity.

That doesn't mean we are going to have a banking crisis tomorrow morning. It does mean that the foundation under the banks is woefully inadequate.

It doesn't matter that the Fed is expected to control it all. The Fed is not omnipotent, not an invincible monetary force. Also, the word "control" can have quite a wide range of meaning.

Control might involve placing limitations on deposit withdrawals. For instance, I could easily imagine a release something like this: All depositors are safe. However, during the present emergency, withdrawals will be limited briefly to 25% of any bank deposit or in any single amount exceeding $20,000. Larger withdrawals will require a special permit.

Of course, those figures are just picked out of the air. It's meant only as an example of a type of restriction that could be used. In an emergency, almost any numbers can be used.

The guts of this story is that it is possible that substantial foreign defaults could jeopardize, indeed, overwhelm the Fed's ability to pay off more than $1 trillion of depositor money.

It's natural that the banks should "pooh-pooh" any such idea in order to sustain at all costs "confidence." Without confidence, the banks, because of overwhelming non-performing loans, are finished right now. No one knows this better than the banks.

*   *   *   *

The news is bad even if there is never a default. It means the immobilization of $700 billion in the world. The interest and payments due on this huge sum of money simply don't come in. Therefore, they simply can't be lent out again. This tightens the money all around the world and its effects have been felt and will continue to be increasingly deflationary as each year the debt grows by 10% through interest. If we were ever to classify these loans as lost, the monetary supply would come down like a deflated balloon.

Now, what chance is there that this money will be repaid? Most perceptive observers expect there is very little chance. One of the reasons is the capital flight from these countries.

In the case of Brazil, they already sold their gold. The treasury is bare. They have no dollars with which to buy any foreign products. Oil has to be paid for in dollars. The only way they can earn these dollars is through their exports. But the world in 1985 still remains in recession. How can these countries get back on their feet? No one has the answer for that. The experts just advise them to tighten their belts. How far can you tighten your belt? The impossibility of payment closely parallels the inability of Germany to pay the war reparations. Yet world brokers kept the debts on the books as assets for more than ten years. Then the floodgates broke.

If you believe a debt will always be paid, then get ready to see one of two things: Either to pay it out of your own pocket as a taxpayer, or the closing of many of the world's biggest banks.

Domestic Debt Rollover

So much for the debt of foreign governments. What about the debt of our own government, now standing at $1.4 trillion.

The United States itself has been a repudiator. Just prior to the depression in 1837, several U.S. states defaulted on English credit just as now a number of South American countries couldn't pay the interest on their debt, let alone principal. The answer was the repudiation of debt by Pennsylvania, Maryland, Michigan, Indiana and Mississippi.

Defaults led to the almost 10-year depression of the 1930s. These were triggered by liquidity crises and the failure of

142

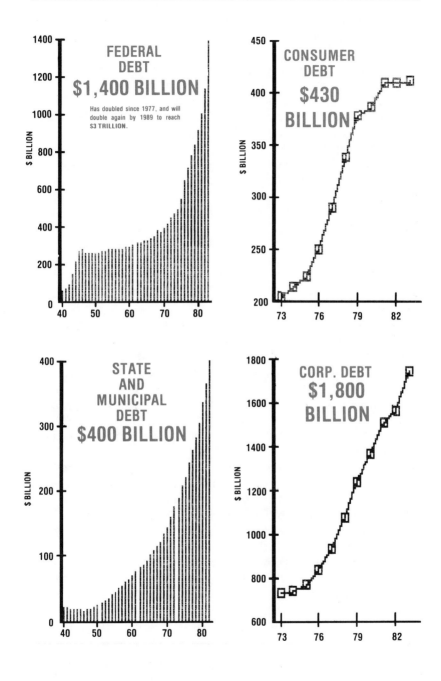

FEDERAL
DEBT
$1,400 BILLION

Has doubled since 1977, and will
double again by 1989 to reach
$3 TRILLION.

CONSUMER
DEBT
**$430
BILLION**

STATE
AND
MUNICIPAL
DEBT
$400 BILLION

CORP. DEBT
**$1,800
BILLION**

financial institutions. As now, nobody foresaw these. They took an unbelieving world by shock and surprise.

The graph on Page 143 shows you how the U.S. government debt has increased over the last 35 years. You can see here the rationale behind the concept of a complete **ROLLOVER** in the system of debt around the world. Then consider the following which was arrived at by calculations of newsletter writer Jim McKeever. He makes these assumptions:

That the annual deficit between now and the year 2000 will be 10% of the total federal debt, currently at $1.4 trillion. This year's budget deficit is more than 10% of the federal debt, so his assumption is conservative. You come out with a federal debt in the year 2000 of $38 trillion. And the interest on that debt, assuming constant interest rates (and they may be much higher) would be more than $4 trillion. Our budget would have to pay $4 trillion interest a year, which is seven times the total budget at this time.

Even a simpleton will see he has to conclude that the projection of the present debt practices would capsize the world's trade and every semblance of monetary order in the world. I will say flatly that such astronomical heights of debt will never be reached. That means a total collapse before the year 2000, or immediate remedial measures raising taxes substantially and cutting social payments substantially. Since neither of these two matters, particularly the second one, is likely to take place any time soon, we must expect the "crisis scenario" – that is, the breakdown of the world monetary system.

What we talk about here is only one of the elements contained in my concept of **ROLLOVER**. You see it coming from every direction and there is a very good chance that the debt structure will be one of the earliest rollovers, but all of the contributing factors will dovetail into one huge restructuring of the social order of the world.

The Ballooning Cancer of Debt

They talk about mortgage debt, and they talk about consumer debt. And all these statistics and many more are available through the Wall Street Journal or a hundred other publications. It's like describing a patient with cancer and one report tells you how deeply it has penetrated the liver, another the heart, another the spleen, another the lung. Each one of these reports, bad enough in itself, fails to give the doctor any idea of the terminal condition of the patient. To judge that, you must have them all. I have tried to put together on these pages

144

the major debt positions of the U.S. economy. They are produced here in graphic form payable in 1984 dollars.

The total debt comes to $5.8 trillion. Earlier on I stated that your indebtedness to satisfy the debt of Brazil, alone, would be $2,000 per family of four. But the U.S. federal debt is 15 times as great as the debt of Brazil, so what do you do to satisfy the U.S. federal debt of $1.5 trillion? If you are a single person, you owe a little over $7,000.

Many writers today say the U.S. federal debt can never be paid. But I have to disagree with them if the U.S. government will keep its fingers out of satisfying any other debts. Spelled out over 30 years, and assuming some repayment along the line, a single U.S. citizen multiplied by the total could pay off the federal debt in 20 to 25 years. We have lots of houses mortgaged for that period of time. Parts of two generations would be paying this debt. If we had a healthy, free-rolling economy, it's not at all impossible that the United States could pay off the federal debt, but what they have to do first is stop its growth. And being realistic and understanding that politicians buy votes by promising entitlements to the majority of the people, you have to give debt repayment a pretty slim chance.

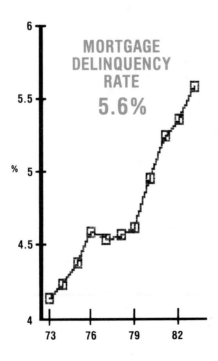

The graphs on Page 143 show a frightening pattern throughout. For instance, the graph on the state and municipal debt is almost a parallel in trend with the graph on the federal debt. Even so, the roads and public services of the cities and municipalities have been allowed to deteriorate and municipality budgets would have to be increased if we are not going into a state of serious disrepair.

The corporate debt of $1.8 trillion will probably soon stop, as it will have to stop under conditions of the upcoming shrinkage. Likewise with the mortgage debt.

Nevertheless, the total debt per capita in the United States, including these five, is over $26,000. This is a burden so immense that no reasonable man can think the domestic debts of the United States can possibly be paid.

Moreover, the total net worth of the United States, including every brick and toothbrush, is estimated to be between $7 trillion and $8 trillion. Collectively, we owe for almost everything that exists in this country. What we have done is to build the future on the present — maybe the future that ought not to have arrived for half a century.

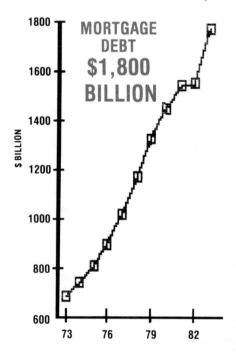

But a debt is always paid and that means that the lenders behind these sums totaled up on the graphs have already paid when they lent the money; they will not get it back, so the bankruptcy epidemic, once it starts, will be completely beyond the realm of our experience. We will have nothing in the past with which to compare it.

And that is what I mean by **ROLLOVER**.

I believe if you will study this chapter intensely, you will not be able to come away without the conclusion that such a ROLLOVER cannot be avoided.

When you have digested the meaning of this monolithic condition that grips the world, you will understand that no president could ever solve it, no congress, no groups of bankers, no mortal man or men. This has built up over a period of a great many years. It can't be canceled out. **A DEBT WILL ALWAYS BE PAID.**

XVI

STOCK MARKET ROLLOVER

The human race has drifted so far from the basics that it has lost its ability to discriminate between reality and illusion. Hollywood trained us to accept illusion. The Hollywood set brings us illusions by the score — more believable than the real thing. We have come to prefer illusions. The greatest illusion ever is the published record of the stock market over the last half century.

In 1934, deep in the depression, the Dow Jones Averages were 184. In early 1984 the averages were nearly 1,300. So how much has the value of the stock multiplied in this half century — between 6 and 7 times? Wrong. The value is exact level of the Dow Jones Industrials, as measured in constant 1929 dollars, is at exactly the level it was in 1934 — 184.

How come such an illusion?

Illusion was created by inflation, insidiously, slowly, inexorably advancing. As the inflation reduced the value of the dollar; that is, as it reduced the purchasing power of the dollar, the measurement values increased. If you kept shortening the inch on your tape measure, the same amount of cloth could always be shown as more.

The government keeps tabs on the purchasing power of the dollar. It's called the "Consumer Price Index." You can find out fairly simply how many dollars you have to earn in 1984 to be the equivalent in purchasing power of 1980 or 1960 or 1929 or any year whatsoever. And so we have applied the purchasing power values of the American dollar to the values of the Dow Jones Industrials as quoted every day on the New York Stock Exchange. The results of this are shown on the following pages.

148

AFTER HALF A CENTURY BACK TO SQUARE ONE

The graph below tells you what has happened to the stock market in the last half century. In order to bring this **ENORMOUS TRUTH** home to you dramatically, I have started off with a dollar of 1929. I have traced the stock market, plotting month-end readings from the high of August 1929 to the present time. And I have converted the figures allowing for inflation or deflation along the way to show the exact Dow Jones reading adjusted to 1929 dollars, right up to March 1984.

The first thing that becomes immediately clear in the graph is that during 11 years, from 1954 to 1965, the Dow Jones had risen from a reading of 166 to its peak of 524 in early 1966. For the next 18 years the Dow Jones has been in a steady fall (in real terms) until, as of March 1984, we were back to a reading of 1,154 which is equal to the Dow Jones reading of 186 (1929 dollars) where we stood in 1930.

In 1954 the stock market began a rise that would last for 22 years. All of the highs were higher than the previous highs until we reached early 1966. **Since 1966, all of the lows are lower than the previous lows.** Since 1967 we have been in a down channel, inexorably losing ground. All of the lows are lower than the previous lows. And all of the highs are lower than the previous highs. In essence, the picture is this:

A QUARTER CENTURY OF A BULL MARKET AND
A QUARTER CENTURY OF A BEAR MARKET

It would appear to me that we would have another three or four years of bear market ahead of us. It also appears to me that there will be a dramatic downside climax. And that could lead us back to the reading of less than 100 on the constant Dow Jones or a **reading of 600 on the quoted Dow Jones on the New York Stock Exchange.**

If that view of a half century of economic history proves true, it will place us again at the level of the Great Depression.

For that to come true, you will see one of these days disaster in the marketplace and you will see some volumes of up to 200 million shares and falls of maybe 70 or 80 points in a single day.

For that to come true, there will be a very dramatic and devastating event. We do not know what this event will be. But I personally believe that it will center on the world debt situation. It would mean the fall of giant financial institutions and the resulting havoc.

Let's try to be optimistic. What do you see in historical evidence that would lead you to believe the Dow Jones at these

low readings would turn around and pass its old high? Can you
say with respect to any of the fundamentals, that we are now in
a position to reverse the trend of 25 years? You cannot say it.
The domestic debt situation has never been worse. The
international debt situation is trembling on the brink as now
even whole countries are vulnerable to default. Even if it is
called some other name.

Where is the great rebuilding going to take place? Of
course there are new industries that will germinate and flourish,
but these new industries are industries of low employment.

When we began the quarter century rise from 1954 to
1966, we were on the edge of huge new demands and
employment for the smokestack industries. This was their
zenith. This was their growth. This was the apex of the
Industrial Revolution and of every industry on a massive scale.
So we had a great potential there to bring men to work and sell
the products which had been in short supply during the war. We
had an immensely rich United States not greatly troubled by
debt, a gold hoard bigger than ever, and the bulk of the gold
belonged to the United States. Inflation was a word you rarely
saw in the newspapers.

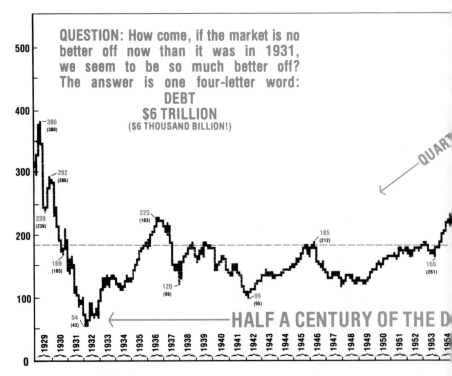

In short, we were starting out from a period of deflation and with low interest rates, and nowhere to go but up. This time we are starting out crippled by the worst inflation in the history of the United States with high interest rates. Can it be said that we now have no place to go but up?

The debt structure amounts to hundreds of billions of dollars of **fluff**. The most effective riddance of this fluff would arise out of a worldwide deflation.

(The graph is based on month-end Dow Jones ratings as they are published in the daily newspapers.)

Here is the comparative value of your dollars. You can calculate the worth of a 1984 dollar against any dollar back to 1929 by dividing your present dollars by the Consumer Price Index. Or you can rate the purchasing power of the dollars of any year to any other year. I have started with the 1967 dollar at $1 because this is the year generally used as a base by economists and publications.

This table will allow you to make your own comparisons, based on the 1967 dollar. Notice that in 1929, one 1967 dollar was equal to 51.2 cents in January 1929; also notice that one 1967 dollar was worth $2.92 at year end, 1982.

The green dotted line marks the level of the Dow Jones 1929 to March, 1984.

It shows that the current DJ 1159 matches the 1931 level DJ 186 in constant dollars.

So here's what it means: If you have about $300,000 now you are only as wealthy as you would have been in 1967 if you had $100,000 then. And if your father had $51,000 in 1929, he was as rich as you were with $100,000 in 1967, and nearly $300,000 today.

By use of this table you can compare the worth of your present take-home pay with what you made in 1958, 1967 or 1973, or anytime.

If your grandfather left you a share of GM stock in 1934 with a value of $36.50, his share is quoted on the New York Stock Exchange today at $66.

CONSUMER PRICE INDEX
1929–1984 (Year end close)
(1967 = 1.00)

1929	51.4	1957	85.2
1930	48.3	1958	86.7
1931	43.7	1959	88.0
1932	39.2	1960	89.3
1933	39.4	1961	89.9
1934	40.2	1962	91.0
1935	41.4	1963	92.5
1936	41.9	1964	93.6
1937	43.2	1965	95.4
1938	42.0	1966	98.6
1939	41.8	1967	101.6
1940	42.2	1968	106.4
1941	46.3	1969	112.9
1942	50.6	1970	119.1
1943	52.2	1971	123.1
1944	53.3	1972	127.3
1945	54.5	1973	138.5
1946	64.4	1974	155.4
1947	70.2	1975	166.3
1948	72.1	1976	174.3
1949	70.8	1977	186.1
1950	74.9	1978	202.9
1951	79.3	1979	229.9
1952	80.0	1980	258.4
1953	80.5	1981	281.5
1954	80.1	1982	292.4
1955	80.4	1983	305.0
1956	82.7	1984	316.7

What you see in the first quarter century of the graph is the apex of the Industrial Revolution and the zenith of the smokestack industries. Some of them didn't hit their high points until 1978, but generally speaking, 1966 was the turning point. And it turns out that because of the advances made up until 1966, your investment in the leading industrial, which is General Motors, would have been quite satisfactory. A share of GM in 1934 was quoted at $36.50 on the New York Stock Exchange. The stock was split two for one in 1950 and three for one in 1955. So in May of 1966 you had six shares to sell at $90 per share for a total of $286 in 1929 terms. So you had a gain of

684% in this leader at the zenith of the Industrial Revolution – plus the dividends you had received in the interval.

Unfortunately, after 1966, it went the other way and, as of May 1984, GM was quoted at $66. You may realize $396 for your 1934 share, but the inflation factor since 1934 has been 7.7, so to get back to 1934 you would divide $396 by 7.7 and you arrive at $51.75 per share. While your investment had appreciated 684% from 1934 to 1966, the net appreciation has been only 40% by 1984. But in GM, we have picked the outstanding performer of the last days of the smokestack industries.

The overall picture of the Dow Jones shows that the level of 200 in May, 1939, is just about equal to the market reading of approximately 200 in 1984.

It is unrealistic to expect that the smokestack industries, having gone through infancy, youth and maturity, and having commenced their deterioration, will ever see a growth period to match that of 1954-1966.

That is one of the big reasons why this book has been entitled ROLLOVER. The biggies of the old era have seen their day. As of yet, we do not know the biggies of the new era.

We have been feasting on this enormous illusion of greatly increased wealth.

We have been able to maintain the illusion by virtue of two other illusions. The one is that we are always progressing. Would it not be impossible that we could not have progressed in real goods after all this time? The other illusion is the numbers themselves. People will say numbers don't lie. Nearly all of us believe numbers don't lie. But you can make from numbers the greatest lie on earth.

The first illusion – that we are always progressing – has been kept alive by the fact that we do have a lot more material goods than our grandfathers had; we have a lot more advantages; a lot more pleasures. Then how come the values are down where they were?

The answer to that is a four-letter word – DEBT.

The value of America today figured down to the last toothbrush and up to the highest skyscraper and throughout the irrigation dams is reckoned to be $7 trillion to $8 trillion. The debt today is $5.8 trillion.

You went over to your friend's place and you talked glibly about your house. What do you mean your house? That's not your house, that's the mortgage company's house. You have let it from the mortgage company and someday, if you live long

153

enough, it will be your house. If you do not make the payments the mortgage company will sell it. And that alone proves it is not your house.

You talk about "my car." That's not your car, that belongs to the acceptance company. You talk about our vacation — I guess it's your vacation, since you already have taken it, but since you haven't yet paid for it, it will come off your wages next year. Your son is already college educated, but that's not paid for yet.

The government has been handing over millions of dollars to our elderly people, but that isn't paid for yet.

We have mortgaged ourselves into the future. We have mortgaged our children's and the government's future. We may have mortgaged our grandchildren's futures. And all of these debts are piled up to one huge debt of $5.8 trillion. It's all in the inventory.

We have been content with this because the stock market has been telling us about our fantastic progress. We have enjoyed the illusion of numbers and don't we have the Dow Jones Averages to prove it? Wasn't it nearly 1,300 in 1983 and only 297 in 1930? No one had told us that 297 in 1930 was the equivalent of 1,300 in 1983.

In the history of stocks it also happened that a vigorous, forceful, sustained and seemingly unending advance has turned around imperceptibly somewhere back there and has gone all the way back to where it was in 1934.

You recall when the United States Treasury lost control of the silver price in 1967 and silver jumped in a single day from $1.29 to $1.65. Do you recall that it went up to $2.35 some months later. And more IMPORTANTLY, do you recall that in the following months it went back down to $1.29 again?

This is not truly unusual. It has often happened in the past. Look what happened to real estate values in the time of the Mississippi bubble. It happened in the 1930s where the real estate values of the early 1920s multiplied hundreds of percent and then fell back to less than they were when they were bought. It's now happening in some instances in real estate.

And with the Dow Jones Averages computed in constant dollars, as I've said, although quoted at 1,300 are really equal to $297 in 1934, I believe they may retreat to 54, that low of 1930, that is to say 600 in the modern Dow Jones.

By looking at the graphs on pages 150 and 151 you see how many years it took the Dow Jones to recover. In 1928 and

1929 the stock market was on everyone's mind. The newspapers and the radios wouldn't think of passing up a broadcast without voicing the principal prices. Every average working Joe had some stock or had a relative who was buying and selling stock. But in the years following the bust nobody at all talked about stocks. The financial press, of course, published prices but very few stories about investments made the front pages of the papers.

This speculation in the market is a game that gets played every half century or so. In a broad way, it goes up for a quarter of a century, down for a quarter of a century, and then up for a quarter of a century.

The reason for great fluctuations of prices is not usually fluctuation of values. The reason is based in people's imaginations. They buy and sell stocks on what they THINK the price will be later on. They don't buy and sell stocks because of the value today and a reckoned increase because of solid growth.

It is neither natural nor productive that people shall make fortunes by simply uttering orders to buy and sell. If it were that easy, why would anyone work? And then no stocks would be worth anything.

Most of the people who play the stock market lose. And if they don't lose, obviously by the figures quoted on the board, in the long run they lose by a gradual depreciation of the dollar.

I heard it said that in the long run nothing is made in the market. And I am inclined to believe that is true if you take the full mass of all the people dealing on the stock market. Of course, certain people make money and certain people lose money. In the intervals over the long haul, though, the increased values are usually symbols, and as they are shown on the graph on pages 150 and 151 — just illusions.

Of course, you can carry a line of reasoning too far on anything. For example, let's say you and I are prospectors and we have found very rich signs of gold, very extensive signs, and we envisage a huge gold mine. But we know that to get at this gold may cost hundreds of thousands and maybe millions of dollars. So we organize a company and we get people to share this risk and they buy shares in this company. And it turns out we were right. We have an enormous gold mine. People who bought shares for 25 cents are able to sell them for $25.

Yes, that is an illustration of a legitimate investment.

A company comes along with a new invention of great potential worth. We buy this stock and end up with a profit.

In the long run, however, the stock usually goes too high, far above any potential value, and people are still buying, and

155

those people found in the long run the stock was going backward. A lot of the money we made as investors on a sound basis is being lost by speculators and gamblers who only expect to issue orders to buy, and then sell to some other person even more foolish. Suddenly the new fools stop coming and we have a stock market bust.

We will always have these rollovers. They come in small editions in certain stocks or families of stocks or they come in larger sweeps within the great, great waves of bear and bull markets. The graph on pages 150 and 151 are a dramatic presentation of the truth over half a century.

*   *   *   *

The stock market rollover, however, is different from the others we are discussing. Fundamentally, the stock market never changes.

In the days of the herdsman, even prior to agricultural populations, trading was done among them, sheep for salt, hides for beans; the trading was never-ending. Standard prices emerged and each sale was judged on how it stood up to the standards in quality and in relation to other current sales. The market could tell you the worth of the time.

But if a tale of that bad winter hit the broad geographical area and most of the lambs were lost, the price of wool skin for the next fall would be much higher. That was the start of the commodities futures market.

As civilization became more centralized, as roaming herdsmen became stationary agriculturists, as towns grew to cities, trading intensified and finally began to be carried out in recognized centers. The prices eventually evolved in these centers, and they became guide prices for trading in the hinterlands.

Today you have the New York Stock Exchange, the greatest trading center in the world. As communications have speeded up, we are aware of instant changes in values, in instant changes in the volume of demand, Paris, London, Hong Kong, anywhere. As long as people inherit the earth and as long as their natural instinct to acquire can be sustained, there will be markets of the same type as we have today. In dealing on these markets the age-old principles of trading will still apply. I have put together a series of principles which I think are eternal in the markets. They would have been true a hundred years ago; they will still be true a hundred years from now or indeed a thousand years from now if the human race persists.

XVII

PHILOSOPHY WON'T ROLL OVER

Market Philosophy
Greed

In participating or observing the market for more than a third of a century, I have come to some broad conclusions and philosophies which I would like to share with you. Among them are:

(a) The greatest hazard - *Greed.*

(b) The greatest foundation for profit - *Well-based confidence.*

(c) The time to buy - *After a movement is already in swing.*

(d) The time to sell - *After the bull movement has lost momentum and has declined.*

(e) The time to rest - *When you can't seem to do anything right.*

Probably the most important of these is THE GREATEST HAZARD — GREED. That's because greed caused some people to actually go broke. It's not so bad to fail to make money as it is to lose what you've got.

In watching people in the market for nearly four decades, I have seen the devastation resulting from greed many times. And yet I don't like to define the characteristic I am talking about as simply greed. It is something more. It is an emotionalism, a semi-euphoria, a departure from reality, generated by the volatility of rising prices. It's best illustrated by making a case:

About 35 years ago they discovered the Leduc field in Canada. I was oil editor for the Calgary Herald at the time. The discovery of Devonian oil caused great circles of excitement throughout the petroleum world. The Devonian was a formation which underlay all of Western Canada. And some people thought that if oil was found in this formation in one place, it would be found in this formation all over Western Canada. Some even dreamed there was an ocean of oil under the millions upon millions of square miles in Western Canada. Of course this was total nonsense to a geologist. People who savvied oil production knew that fields occurred in pimples on formations. That is, in certain upward bulges, there the oil had been trapped as it strove to rise, in its mixture with water, to the surface — just like it would in any container. And so they knew that the oil would be in these pimples or bulges. No one knew how many pimples or bulges there would be. No one could tell, in drilling the high pimples and pinnacles, if they would prove to be full of oil or not. No one could tell the shape of them exactly until they have been drilled.

In any case Imperial Oil discovered this Devonian field near Edmonton. They drilled another well two or three miles to the northeast and it was also a producer. And it was a producer in a second deeper zone than the first well. Then some independents got busy and leased the land around there and one independent called *Leduc Consolidated* bought two quarter sections of lease and started three wells on those quarter sections.

Now it looked very good because the land adjoined Imperial No. 3. It was a new stock; it came out at 25 cents a share. I had very little money but I put in $250 for a thousand shares, and later I was able to buy more. Finally I was able to obtain 5,000 shares. Partially this was done by margin because my broker told me that when it got to $1 a share I could margin at 50% and therefore have twice the stock.

Now I tell you this to demonstrate how absolutely certain we were about these two quarter sections. Because of this great optimism, *Leduc Consolidated* went to $1 and then even up to $1.25. Meanwhile, the wells were drilling, and meanwhile, another well called Central Leduc was getting deeper — but it was hitting all the formations higher! Now we had learned in Turner Valley that when formations came in higher that was good news. The higher you hit oil the more certain you were to be free of water. That's always so. And so a feeling of euphoria swept the western independent operators. *Leduc Consolidated*

158

began to move very fast, past $1.65 a share, as Central Leduc went down nearby. Another well nearby called Okalta No. 1, also was getting pretty deep as we expected news momentarily of another strike. Then I stopped getting reports. The industry stopped getting reports. Then the well stopped drilling, ostensibly for some reason of repair. I became suspicious. I had researched enough to know that the Leduc field was a coral reef. Also that corals built reefs in peculiar fashions and sometimes you might climb gently up one side of a reef to find the other side was a precipice. Being too high might indicate you were just over the precipice. I went to my broker one morning and I said, "You know, it's possible that *Leduc Consolidated* will have three dry holes." He threw up his hands and said, "It can't be possible. If it does have three dry holes a lot of guys around here are going to be bankrupt." "Well," I said, "I think it's possible and I think it may be that Okalta is a dry hole, and possibly Central Leduc as well." The idea was unacceptable and unthinkable. Nevertheless, I showed my broker on paper why I thought it could be a dry hole. The stock was selling at about $1.85 a share.

Meanwhile the promoter of *Leduc Consolidated*, who owned 500,000 shares — and was, therefore, worth nearly a million dollars — determined that all three wells would be oil wells and that $5 a share would be a cheap price for *Leduc Consolidated*, and he was buying more on margin. I knew of this and, of course, his courage caused other people to buy still more. But I said to my broker, "You know I don't have anything beyond what I have in this stock. It was next to nothing to start with and now I have enough to buy a house." (You could buy a nice house then for $10,000 and easily with 50% down). "I know I have a house in my hands now; I didn't have one two months ago. If I hang onto the stock and if they get dry holes, I won't have a house. So it seems to me I'm betting my house that these are going to be oil wells. And I want you to sell all my stock today."

He did. I bought the house the next day. The promoter — whom I won't name, although he must be dead by now — continued to buy on margin, and then we found out that Okalta was a dry hole! *Leduc Consolidated* plummeted but of course the die-hard euphorics wouldn't give up yet. Then it turned out the Central Leduc was a dry hole also. The *Leduc Consolidated* wells were still drilling, and the die-hards held on, although the stock declined to about $1.25. Then the first one came in with salt water. In a matter of days the second well got down and it was a dry hole, and the stock fell to 50 cents. And then in about another week or so the third well was a dry hole. And the stock, in a month or so, went to 15 cents. Today it does not exist. The promoter who had one million dollars gambled the whole million and lost the whole million. The last I heard of him, he was operating a service station in a small town in Alberta.

That taught me a very powerful lesson. There are several lessons in it:

(1) There is no such thing as unthinkable.

(2) Nothing is more uncertain than a lead pipe cinch.

Always figure out how much you are betting and what you are betting on – and if you weren't already betting it, would you place the bet right now? Never get carried away by "moddism"; that is, by the infectious but unfounded enthusiasm of a crowd. Be as greedy as you like as long as you don't risk your neck.

I concluded then, and it has remained always a conclusion of mine: The greatest hazard in the stock market is to forget what you are betting and to fail to be aware of the consequences if your gamble was wrong. Bull-headedness, if you stay with it, sooner or later will kill you.

Market Philosophy
Profit

I just commented on the greatest stock market HAZARD. Now I would like to comment on what I believe to be the best posture for PROFIT.

Over the course of four decades I have observed probably three types of stock market investors. On the one extreme there are the blue chip purists; at the other extreme the gamblers. In between you find the speculators.

The purists make very little money but also they lose very little. In the long run (except for this period of horrendous inflation) the purists have usually made money. Gamblers usually end up broke.

In between are the moneymakers, the careful speculators.

The purists are so afraid of losses, they will not take a big enough risk ever to give them a handsome profit – except by luck. The gambler is so eager for a fast buck that he will not invest in anything except with a view to large and fast profits – forgetting that along with the prospects of those profits goes

160

commensurate risk. The trick of the stock market is to pick a speculative risk with great care, and having picked it to pursue it with great patience.

Avoid speculations dependent on a single throw of the dice. The converse is to choose a speculation involving a whole SITUATION.

Bernard Baruch, one of the great wizards of the stock market, always specialized in situations. And he never went into a situation without having examined every aspect, every cross-current, every tributary. Once having zeroed in on that situation, and having made the initial investment, he was hard to jar loose unless he found something occurring now which would have undermined the original evaluation, had he known of it.

Another important aspect of "situation" investing is the courage of a conviction, even in the face of a market decline. You can't be jarred loose every time the market goes against you. That is not to say that one should FIGHT the market. It just means that the investor, once having drawn what he considers a completely founded conclusion, must not abandon that conclusion because of surface turbulence, or merely because events have not moved as fast as he thought they should. I can best make the point by illustration.

After I sold out of OilWeek magazine, in 1963, I had to make choices on the disposition of the proceeds. I reserved a large part for the stock market. Early on in my search for an investment I noticed a stock called United Oils, which had recently begun to move. For more than a year it had languished between $1.20 and $1.30. I noticed it selling at $1.35 and most importantly on considerably larger volume. I suspected something might be up.

This United Oil controlled Home Oil, which was the biggest independent oil company in Canada. R.A. Brown was the president and driving force in Home Oil. He had a big stake in both Home and United, but to control Home he needed to control United.

From a study of the stock it appeared to me that no one other than the Browns had a real chance of getting controlling interest of United. I came to the conclusion that they had set out on a program to control Home Oil through United. With this in mind, I made a first tentative purchase at $1.38. It was not too long thereafter that the stock sold at $1.45, which was a notable new high and at that time I made further commitments.

161

All along the line I followed a policy of buying more of the stock as my most recent purchases had been confirmed good. Every once in a while I would test the market by the sale of a few thousand shares, just to make sure that the demand was not artificial. My stock was snapped up every time. I continued to buy United through $1.85 and through $2. By this time huge volumes of the stock had moved on the market and it was a hot item. I stopped my purchases then and sure enough, not long after, we received the announcement of a meeting of United shareholders to draw up resolutions which would result in the objectives I had envisioned.

As always, the stock had gone too high. It went up to over $2.25 and started to recede. I found that I was selling the first of my stock at a price almost equal to my latest purchases, but I continued to sell. I got out about four or five months after I first started to buy and at a very tidy profit. I had used about one-third margin.

This was the case of picking a situation. I didn't buy United because of any oil wells it had, which might come in or might not. It was a broad, well-based, and likely situation. It confirmed the validity of the investment all along the way.

Later on I became interested in Texas Gulf Sulphur, after they had made a huge discovery of copper and nickel in Ontario. I bought the first shares at $35. We were able to tell from the releases the size of the reserves that had accrued to Texas Gulf Sulphur as the result of this discovery. We were able to figure, in a rough way, what the stock ought to be worth. I decided that this was a situation which had to win in the long run. I followed the same policies as I had with United. In this case it required a lot more patience and once or twice the price tumbled frighteningly. However, I could not see where my original reasons had been undermined. I stayed with it. It took almost a year and a half for the situation to mature. Texas Gulf went to $125, later fell quickly to $115, and when it was selling at $111 to $112, I sold out the works. That didn't turn out to be too bright because the stock immediately recovered and went on up to $140. I'd held 8,000 shares of Texas Gulf Sulphur.

Picking a situation was also the case with MFE in 1967. At that time I saw – as anyone could see – that the U.S. Treasury was fast running out of silver. A trend had developed. The trend was enormously increasing volume week by week. Simple arithmetic showed that if this continued very long the Treasury

162

would lose control of the silver price because they wouldn't have the stocks to sell. I concluded that the Treasury would have to abandon its policy of buying or selling unlimited silver. I bought a lot of silver in February 1967 and advised the clients of MFE to buy heavily at the price of $1.32 predicting that the Treasury would lose control in 100 days. The price shot up 35 cents in one day. The price of silver rose to $2.35 an ounce in a relatively short time. Once again the SITUATION game had paid off.

By 1971, various aspects of the monetary situation throughout the world convinced me that it was only a matter of time until the United States lost control of the gold price, just as they had lost control of the silver price. Sure enough, in August of 1971, President Nixon backed away from the dollar's convertibility into gold.

Here was a place where many investors would go wrong because immediately when Nixon announced abandonment of the gold standard, the price of gold fell sharply on all the world exchanges. It continued to fall for some time. But we had zeroed in on the SITUATION which Nixon's action really confirmed and we couldn't logically change. As it turned out, the market itself was wrong.

Through the 30-odd years that I have been watching the market, I have never seen a fortune made by fast traders. I have seen them make good and handsome profits. Often I have envied them. But none that I knew got rich. Quite a lot of people that I know got rich by latching onto a total SITUATION and staying with it.

Market Philosophy
When to Buy

The most important step you will take when you enter the market is the very first one. That's to buy. It's not the most difficult step. The most difficult is the last one — to sell.

Nevertheless, buying right is difficult enough. And it's vital. It's a step that should be taken very carefully, but boldly and with confidence, once the decision is made.

When to buy can be answered somewhat more easily, I think, if we first attack it from the standpoint of WHEN NOT TO BUY. I'll list a few of these and then deal with them:

(1) Never buy on news.
(2) Never buy an unlisted stock.

(3) Never buy a thin trader.

(4) Never buy on a tip.

(5) Never buy because your friend is vice president and he's very excited about it — avoid insiders.

Now for every don't there's not only one exception, there are several. The first rule in the stock market is that THERE IS NO RULE. Nowhere else is the rule so unreliable as in the marketplace. Still it is well to be guided by a sound policy, and if you operate under sound policy, chances are in the long run you'll do much better than operating without a policy. If you depart from your policy at least the reason will have to be very compelling.

NEVER BUY ON NEWS. I'll tell you why by an example.

In the late 1940s, when I was oil editor for the Calgary Herald, huge volumes of gas had been discovered in Northwestern Canada. It wasn't long before an application came before the Alberta government for a permit to export this gas to the United States. The hearings lasted for several months. I attended most of them. I knew the reserves were there and I knew that the company, *West Coast Transmission*, was able to get the financing to build this pipeline. Still I wouldn't buy the stock until I was quite sure that the permit for export would be given.

As the Alberta government considered the recommendations of its board, the price of several of the stocks surrounding *West Coast Transmission*, including *Atlantic Oils* and *Pacific Petroleums* were moving strongly. One night at 6 o'clock the phone rang. *West Coast Transmission* was on the line. The Alberta cabinet had approved the export of the gas only 10 minutes before. I was asked to come down to the office. There I found a state of euphoria. Frank McMahon, probably the most colorful promoter in the history of the Canadian oil industry, could hardly contain himself. This was the crowning victory for him; an international artery of world importance. I knew all the people there and naturally we discussed which stock would be the best to buy in the morning — *Atlantic Oils* was the consensus, considering the holdings that it had in *West Coast Transmission* and the gas reserves it had.

Sure enough, in the morning I entered the market with market orders. I put all the money I had, something like $40,000 to $50,000, in *Atlantic* and then I margined about a third besides.

The day before, *Atlantic* had been trading at about $7.85 a share; my average purchase price was around $8.50 per share. Actually I was surprised I didn't have to pay more. I wasn't sure that I liked it, and by the end of the day I didn't like it.

The stock, after being up to about $8.75, sold about 15 cents below my buy point. *Atlantic* fooled around there for quite a while and gradually sank to $8. I used to call the McMahons frequently and always I was told everything was fine. I really believe they thought everything was fine. They knew they had to go through the U.S. application. They knew they had to go through the American hearings. I believe they were confident there would be no trouble.

However, the hearings kept being put off. The stock continued to slide. After about two months, and a bad case of nerves, I decided the process had gone far enough. The stock was down to $6.60 — considering the margin I was on, I lost almost 50% of my capital at that price. I had to decide whether to stay with it or let go. I was sure that gas export to the United States would take place. But I didn't know when, and the market was telling me that nobody was very enthusiastic about early success. If it had looked good in the United States, I reasoned, certainly officials, bureaucrats, friends of bureaucrats and connections in Canada would be buying the stock. The lack of strength convinced me that I had made a bad mistake. I sold all my stock in one or two days at between $6 and $6.25. It was pretty bitter medicine. But I was glad that I had swallowed it, because in a few more months, *Atlantic* was down around $3 a share and, had I stayed, I would have been called for margin and lost every cent I had.

Much later it became a very high-priced stock when American approval was finally obtained.

This also illustrates rule No. 5. Here is a case of knowing the insiders. The trouble with insiders is that they are so enthusiastic they cannot be objective. It takes these kinds of people to make a success of things. If Frank McMahon had been the type of person to doubt that the United States would quickly accept his proposition to sell gas, he would never have found the gas in the first place, or brought it so close to fruition. He had to be a great optimist. I knew those men would not deceive me and that was why I went in so heavily. But I had not yet learned that the insiders of the company have to be prejudiced if they are good company men. Be very careful about

165

investing on the strength of insider information. (There are always exceptions to the rule.)

Never buy an unlisted stock. The trouble is you can't tell what's happening. You don't know how much stock is trading half the time. The regulations are less stringent and there is room for behind-the-scenes manipulation. As a general policy, don't touch it.

Never buy a thin trader. Oh, it's all right to buy a few hundred shares. But if you buy several thousand shares of a stock that is a thin trader and if you decide you want to get out, you may find yourself locked in. Every time you go to sell, the market bid seems to disappear. There are no bidders out there in the woods; it's a thin trader. (Only rare exceptions to this rule exist.)

Never buy on a tip. Unless your tip comes highly authenticated, the source is probably questionable. Tips often originate with promoters who get it whispered around that something is going to happen. They tell their friends very confidentially. A friend tells a friend; and especially in the case of a thin trading stock or an unlisted stock, it may start to rise with some excitement. This produces more excitement even to the extent when some of the tipsters begin to believe that the trading is imparting knowledge of great value.

An old wildcatter went to heaven. It got so boring up there he thought he'd have some excitement and he told somebody not to mention it, but they had discovered oil in hell. Very shortly, the ranks in heaven began to thin. And the old wildcatter, after a week or so, wondered what was happening. By now the crowd was leaving in great numbers. He asked a passerby, "Where is everybody going?" The man replied, "Haven't you head – they've discovered oil in hell."

"Just a minute while I get my hat," said the wildcatter. "I'm coming, too."

That's the kind of stuff most tips are made of and they're usually unreliable. The most use that can be made of a tip is to alert you to a possibility. You check it out – and if you're tempted to buy – check it out once more. (There often are exceptions to this rule.)

Market Philosophy
When to Sell

The most fundamental law I know for investment success

is: Let profits run, cut short the losses. Thus you are doomed never to get the top price.

Let's use gold as an example. It began to show some action in 1972. A lot of people had bought gold at $35 an ounce. When gold rose to $65 an ounce, it was a great temptation to sell it. Those who did were highly reluctant to buy gold again at $80 an ounce. For the most part, they were out of the market. Again, when gold reached $85 an ounce, there was a great temptation to sell it, and again at $100 an ounce, and at $125 an ounce. Many people sold gold and South African gold stocks. MFE subscribers did not. The reason I did not recommend the sale of gold was that I did not know how high the price would go. In fact, I was astonished when it passed $100 an ounce. But gold was in a very strong upward move. Your chartists might give you objectives where it might go but I could never believe much in that. I believe that nobody ever can judge the ultimate price until the ultimate price has passed them. In other words, until the commodity has started to come down.

Even then you cannot safely sell because this more than likely is an adjustment still in the upward movement. What you have to wait for then is a sign that you are not experiencing a simple reaction but that the price has actually turned around. After gold passed $200 an ounce, it came down — I believe to about $185 — and then went up. It was not logical to sell it there because it might still be in the strong upward movement. But it failed to pass the old high and indeed it went down again to about $165. And then it recovered but it did not recover to $185. It fooled around in that area between $165 and $175, as I remember, and it was at this point that I advised the subscribers of MFE to sell. I felt the tide had turned. Then gold dipped to $105.

But he who follows this policy is doomed never, never to get the top price. Those who got what they thought was the top price on the way up, actually sold at a great sacrifice. There was no more logic in holding gold and selling it at $200 than there was in selling it at $100. But there was strong logic in selling it at $165 to $175.

Still, such action is by no means certain. Sometimes the signs of reversal are false and you can find yourself out of a market that is still going up. But in my experience, this is quite rare.

We had a repetition of this scenario late in 1980. We had bought back into gold at $135 in 1977. And it took off on the most phenomenal bull market I have ever seen. Once again there was no way to tell where to sell on the way up. Even the $850 mark had no support in logic as a sale point. But that spike in gold did not last long and we did not give it a great deal of credence. The average price for gold at the high – where a lot of volume traded – was around $700. Again, there was no way we could expect to get the high because we simply did not know whether gold might revive and go up to $1,000. But after making new lows and failing to pass old highs, I felt we were supported by reasonable logic to sell at $665. As gold continued to fall, I was convinced that we were in a very strong down movement on gold – a tidal movement, not a correction.

So I think that here we uncover a very worthwhile rule. The successful speculator will never hit the top price and he knows that. Also, he will never buy at the bottom price and he knows that. In order to choose the right time to enter the market, it must already have been advancing and have given evidence that it has changed direction. So while gold bottomed at $103, we did not get into the 1977 market until $135 to $140 an ounce.

I believe it was J.P. Morgan who said, "I always miss the first 20% of the market move, and I always miss the last 20%, but I'm satisfied with the 60% in between. I'm happy to leave the 40% to others."

But now what happens when you've bought a stock or commodity after a very thorough study and with all the conviction in the world and then the stock, for no reason, starts going down? Yet you have no reason to believe that your original judgment was wrong? You check everything out again. Well, then it is quite possible you are in it too soon. Maybe circumstances have arisen that have delayed the fruition of your investment. You have two choices. You can stay with it and some substantial time later, if it seems to have bottomed you can increase your holdings. Normally, I don't like this but in some cases it is the best policy.

The other way to handle it is to sell and take your loss, watching the market for signals that your stock will not drop any further. You will have to let it go up a way. You will have to let it prove itself. At that time you may go back again. This is always a personal decision and it depends on one's temperament. The majority of the people that I know would rather stay with the purchase that they have made, even if it goes down, as long as they remain convinced that the value is there.

Professionals, by and large, would be inclined to cut the losses and watch for a better day.

A brief example: In April 1981, Pittston Coal traded in enormous volume day after day, sometimes half a million shares. This was at the time of the Conoco takeover. I could not see such volume without believing that some movement in the background was causing a huge and vast accumulation of Pittston Coal. Without bothering to study the fundamentals, I bought 50 calls of Pittston Coal at $7. But, lo and behold, a few days later the market started to dry up, and soon the price began to slide. This was a bad sign. It hinted to discredit my basic theory. I let it go on a little longer, and when Pittston options were $4.75, I sold the lot taking a loss of about $13,000 on a $35,000 investment. Later that loss looked good.

Maybe the second most dangerous thing in the market is the refusal to take the loss in the face of an obvious misinvestment. Second only to greed is bullheadedness. Related to that is constant manufacture of excuses for the equity you own. Even when it's going down, you pardon it repeatedly, as if a wayward child. You must be cold-blooded. You must be the executioner. You must cut it loose without heart.

If I were confined to two policy sentences on the subject of selling, they would be: "Cut losses short, let the profits run."

My second sentence: "Selling is a very personal decision. You make it in the night and you make it alone. (When you become emotional about your investments, it is time to leave the market.)"

Market Philosophy
When to Stop

It's easier to start an investment than to stop one. It's easier to pick a buy point than to pick a sell point.

When you pick a buy point, you are very conscious that every dollar that goes into it is yours. It's very dangerous to drop this attitude when it comes to selling a stock on which you have made a large profit. Too many people say, "Well, it's really not mine." But on the day you consider selling the stock, the money is yours if you want to take it. To say to yourself that it's profit and you are not losing anything is wrong. The adjudged value of the equity has deteriorated. Some people will quibble over buying a stock for a quarter of a point — and then maybe even miss getting it. But when it comes to selling the stock, they don't worry themselves if it goes down $5, or maybe

169

even loses a third or more. If you are going to think about it that way, you ought to think to yourself: I bought this stock at $30 and now it's $65. If I didn't own any of it, would I be buying it today? Is it a good buy at $65? If not, stop the investment. You've had your gravy. Nothing goes on forever.

A standard piece of advice is that if you have bought two stocks and one of them has gone down and the other has gone up, then sell the one that has gone down and keep the one that has gone up — just the opposite practice from what most people do. And I'm in agreement with that. Because when a stock is in an uptrend, chances are very heavy that it will continue that uptrend for some time. But you cannot be complacent in the view that it will keep going up forever. You have to pick a point when you think it is no longer a bargain for people to buy. And that is the most difficult part of investing. And that's why it is so much easier to start an investment than to stop one.

A second important maxim is this: If you have been into a situation and you have come out of it with a very large profit — stay out! So many people enter into the picture again, only to lose their shirts the second time. If the stock has gone up, they feel they have sold too soon. So they buy in. If the stock has gone down, they feel it's a bargain, so they buy in. Never do that. Once you have had a fine and profitable association and you've said goodbye, wave a fond farewell and try to forget the stock.

You may enter the situation again at a later date if it's an altogether different ballgame. That is to say, if new reasons have entered the picture to cause the stock to become a bargain a second time. But there must be brand new factors, that were not in consideration at all at the time you owned the stock on the previous turn.

If you played a situation and made huge profits, it's a good idea to stop investment altogether for awhile. If you immediately plunge those funds into some other situation, you begin to lose track of the fact that you are dealing with actual dollars. With actual hard cash. You have never seen it. To you it is a fictitious entity. And once you do that, you don't pay enough care to either the dangers or the opportunities.

I read this advice from Jessie L. Livermore many, many years ago and it has always helped me. When Livermore came off with a great coup, he would often not only put the money in the bank, but take large gobs of it out in cash. Sometimes he would take a quarter or a half million dollars in cash and put it in the safety deposit box just to make sure that he was dealing in the real thing. Then when he went to reinvest that money, he took the proper care. It also provided him with the proper attitude about the money that he had in the bank that was not in the form of cash. But as long as one sale is always represented by immediately another purchase, without ever getting the money in the bank, your perspective is in danger. And the most important thing you need in the stock market is a down-to-earth perspective.

When nothing works right — stop! You may buy Stock A and it promptly goes down and in a few weeks it has lost maybe 10%. You decide the stock is not living up to the expectations that you had for it. Your judgment is not being proved out. So you buy Stock B. The same thing happens to Stock B. Maybe you switch to a commodity or maybe from an electronic stock to a mining stock. The same thing happens. You are accumulating a number of small losses. STOP!

Take those losses and lick your wounds and retire from the picture. The chances are that in subsequent months you may be able to look back on this as a bear market in almost everything. If it isn't a bear market, obviously something has gone wrong with your judgment. Get out. Take a rest. Try not to look at anything for a period of a few months. Then go back with a new look and a new appraisal. But most important, when everything is going bad, STOP!

When you've run out of investment ideas and good ones, it's time to quit. Likewise, when a writer has run out of good ideas on a series, it's also time to stop.

Market Philosophy
A Sure Thing

A sure thing is a dangerous thing. It is dangerous because it is so sure. Being so sure, you rely on it with a certainty. Having relied upon it completely, alternatives are discarded and any opposing notion to the sure thing is rejected out of hand.

If, just by chance, the sure thing turns out wrong, the result isn't just a set-back; it's a catastrophe. The surer a thing is in your mind, the greater potential for disaster if it fails. The greater the following of a sure thing, the more massive the disaster if it fails.

For example, in 1929 continued expansion was universally expected. It was expected to the degree where people were borrowing to the hilt. Developers were developing to the limit. Some of the biggest structures in North America went up in 1929, built on the certainty of continuing prosperity.

171

The initial market picked up pretty fast. Soon everyone was on the bandwagon to grab those bargains. How stupid we had been to think that this market break was anything but a passing phenomenon. The sure thing we had believed in before the crash became even surer as the rally soared.

Then the collapse — the daddy of them all. Here was the disaster. Those who had weathered the initial fall sealed their fate when they returned for the bargains. The fall of the market did not finally conclude until the DJ had retreated to a mere 10% of its former stature. That we would be overtaken by a depression that could last a decade — unthinkable! Except for a very few intensely perceiving minds, it was unthought of.

If you take a measure of the thinking in the world across the spectrum of bankers, economists, governments, investors, and even the mass of the men on the street, you come up with the discovery that there is one immensely SURE THING. That sure thing is CONTINUING INFLATION.

To my mind, inflation, if for no other reason, is suspect. How can it be that the masses will make money by accumulating debt, by buying material things and then paying them off in cheap, cheap dollars? The result is that the masses continue to accumulate wealth upon wealth. You and I know that cannot be so. Something is going to happen!

A good example of "something" is the real estate game, where one real estate property is leveraged by another; then both are sold and these are leveraged to buy some more; and so on. Self-styled millionaires today are floating high on this theoretical wealth. But a deflation could make them paupers.

People tell me it is a sure thing that gold is going to $1,000 an ounce. And I have, in the past, said it is a likely thing. But I have never said it is a sure thing. And if you listen to the masses who believe that inflation is going to burst into flame faster than ever before — you would almost be forced to believe that gold at $1,000 is a sure thing.

The second problem with a "sure thing" is the development of a certain loyalty; loyalty can lead to fanaticism. When fanaticism enters an investment decision, the subject is blind to reality and stands thereafter in great danger of disaster.

Many people take newsletters to know what is a sure thing. Our position has always been to try to point out what is a highly likely thing, to the point sometimes of being very close to a sure thing. But times change. Sometimes there is enough concrete reason to come to a wondrously strong conclusion. At other times, there are too many clouds.

It would be as much a mistake to be sure that we are facing an inevitable nearby deflation as to be dead certain of raging inflation. We can only say that if the cuts of the Reagan administration go through, and in view of recession developing in Europe and around the world, and in view of the threatened bankruptcy of Poland and others, and the massive illiquidity in the United States, deflation is a very likely thing. But we must be aware that if the Fed should throw billions into the fray, another surge of inflation could overtake us.

So, this is a time to be acutely aware that loyalty is out of place in the investment mentality. There ought to be no loyalty to gold; if you find you are "loyal" to gold — get out of it; your judgment is clouded. If you find you are "loyal" to a stock — get out of it. It's a danger to you. The most successful speculators are fantastically aggressive when they believe they are right, and the fastest-running cowards at the first smell of danger.

Market Philosophy
Number Psychology

Over the course of a long time, I have noticed a general fixation with numbers. There seems to be a psychological preference for certain numbers. And this tendency seems to me to be universal.

If true, it is a tool for the stock market investor and one that I have never seen mentioned by anybody. I have used it a lot and it has been quite helpful to me.

There are stable numbers and unstable numbers.

Did you ever see anything in a store priced at 8 cents, 18 cents, 48 cents, or 90 cents?

Now use all those figures in dollars. And have you seen many items priced in the store in dollars in the same numbers? I have not. And I call these the "unstable numbers."

That means that if a stock or a commodity is priced at 8 cents, it will soon move one way or the other to a more stable area. On the upside, it will usually move to languish between 10 cents and 12 cents for some time. If it is in an uptrend, it will not again go down to 8 cents. Rather, it will advance probably to 18 cents and then maybe fall back to 15 cents or even 13 cents, but it also will not stay there for long. It can stay at 17 cents to 18 cents for awhile because 20 is a stable number. There is a great resistance to paying 20 on something that has been priced at less, whereas there is hardly any resistance at all to paying 18 cents for something that has been priced at 16

173

cents. This applies to cents, to dollars, and to a lesser extent, to the hundreds of dollars.

You have seen in the past countless folders advertising store goods for their $1.49 day, or their $1.99 day. In earlier times when a dollar bought more, they used to stage 99 cent day.

A huge barrier on the road upward of any price is $1. And if it breaks a dollar, it will stay at a dollar for only a short time, going from there to $1.10 to $1.12 or from $100 to $112. Then, the action will be the same as the stock action from 10 cents to 12 cents. It is found that the stock will not go back down below 100 by very much or for very long. It will continue to advance from $110 to around the $120 level. All of the stable areas are barriers on the way up. Thus, you have the following barriers in either cents or dollars: 20 in either, 25 in either; 35 in either; 50 in either; 65 in either; 85 in either; and 100. You always have barriers at the uptrend. For instance, gold in the first place had an enormous barrier to overcome at $100 which also acted as a floor on the down side when it came back in 1975. Also, $185 and $200 were barriers, although not as strong as the $100. The $300 number is a barrier and also the $400, but not nearly as strong as the $500, because $500 is half of a thousand.

My observation is that the strength of a stock or commodity can be judged by what side of the barrier it plays on. For instance, if gold were to fluctuate between $350 and $380, I consider that a sign of **inherent** and underground strength. If the commodity or stock plays below the barrier line, I consider that an indication of a lack of enthusiasm of "wanters." To me, that means that some new element would have to be introduced to cause the "wanters" to get excited about it and thereby create an important advance. When the "wanters" are lethargic, a stock is almost bound to deteriorate because there are always some sellers, and in the absence of "wanters," the price has to weaken. But if it plays too long in any area, the tendency will be down.

Gold playing around in the area below $450 gave me the impression that the psychology for gold in the marketplace was weak. This is by no means a foolproof tool, but it is one of the tools which can help tip the balance in favor of a purchase or in favor of a sale.

Another reason to suspect weakness is if a stock plays on the lower side of the psychological barrier and in small volume. You know that the holders are hanging on with hope that the price will return to previous balances but there are very few buyers in the woods.

It depends on how the price acts on either side of these barriers as to whether you can expect lower bottoms or not.

I have used this with some success.

This level almost worked for gold. Long-term subscribers will recall that after gold fell to $103 I refrained from any buy recommendation until $132. With gold playing at $132 to $135, and refusing to come down below $130, I felt we had a new underground strength and then recommended that 50% of all your assets be placed in gold.

When this strength was confirmed by an upward movement toward the $150 barrier but pressing against the barrier, we went into the other 50%.

I'm sorry I can't explain it better. It's kind of a feel you get after a long time. **If the price continues to press toward the lower end of the barrier, the indication is that the stock will go down through it. If it continues to press hard against the upper side of a new barrier, the odds are that it will go up through it.** On which side of the barrier does the stock press?

You might not make any money with this but you will have fun with it.

Market Philosophy
Bottom-Picking

If you are a diver sent down to find the depth of a lake, when will you call the bottom? You might be expecting an 80-foot lake. Will you think you are deep at 70? Will you relay a message to shipboard that you are near the bottom? What about at 100 feet? Will you relay a message that now you are certain you are near the bottom? What about at 200 feet? What about an incomprehensible 300 feet — and you have still not hit the bottom?

Well, it really isn't for you to know, is it, until you get there. That is your mission. If you knew where the bottom was you wouldn't have to dive.

And this brings out a broad truth. You never know the bottom until you have been there.

This truth is not limited to lakes. It also applies to the stock market. It applies to any particular stock and any particular commodity that has been set in motion. Gold furnishes an ideal example of the folly of predicting bottoms. When gold fell from $800 to $700, there were plenty to proclaim that the bottom would be $700. But when the bottom was not $700, there were plenty — though a few less — to proclaim that $600 was surely and forever the bottom. But $600 was not the bottom.

The same applies to tops. Again, gold is an ideal example. When $35 gold went to $70, a lot of people thought that was high – and they sold. When gold passed $100, top-pickers were a dime a dozen and they included many newsletter writers who had been gold-bugs. But when $100 fell aside and gold reached $150, the top-pickers became fewer. By the time gold had reached $200, there were hardly any top-pickers left. People were coming in and they began to believe there was no top.

That was just when gold turned around and LATER proved that $200 had indeed been a top.

But the true professionals were never part of the crowd of either top- or bottom-pickers. The surest sign of an amateur is his frequent prophesies on tops and bottoms. Some of our newsletter writers do this.

In the high 300s, one of the best known but least experienced writers thought this must be the top because it was so HIGH, and he told everybody to get out – only to find out much, much later that the top was really hundreds of dollars ahead of that. By the time they got back in again – those who did – were in at very high prices.

I was surprised at a veteran newsletter writer who now ventures to guess that $312 is probably the bottom for gold.

I don't disagree with him – and I don't agree with him. I simply don't know, and I don't think there is any basis at all – technical or fundamental – to claim a gold bottom.

The fact is that in gold we are in a "no man's land." The best that I can say for gold is that I expect strong resistance at $250. Whether this will hold I do not guess. In any case, the bottom is academic to all MFE subscribers who have been gone a long, long time.

I want to expand it to the DJ stock market.

You can find bottom-pickers on Wall Street Week every Friday. New York is lousy with bottom-pickers who are economists/stock brokers. Whenever you are tempted to listen, remember how stocks like West Driefontein rose from $13 to $70 and fell all the way back again to $13 in 1975. Tops and bottoms can do the absolutely unbelievable, and they often do.

I want you to apply this to the DJ which, falling from 300 in 1929, did not eventually reach botom until DJ 30, thereby confounding every bottom-picker that ever showed up.

176

Market Philosophy
The Dow Jones has a Problem

Great numbers of analysts will tell you that the DJ is the infallible prophet of what is coming up in the economy. This is another one of those axioms that is accepted without much thought and with practically no analysis.

The idea ought to be examined from three standpoints. What happened the last time the DJ predicted a booming economy? Just what is the DJ? What are the components of the DJ?

The rising DJ of 1929, according to its disciples, had to be predicting that they were running into a greatly accelerated economy — that the decade of the 1930s would be the economic bonanza of all times.

Well, it didn't happen. In fact, the opposite happened.

What is the DJ made up of? Well, it is made up of 30 so-called industrial blue chip stocks. Those are the companies that produce the industrial guts of America. They are giants in autos, steel, computers, chemistry, appliances, etc. All of the quotations of the price value of these corporations are worked into an index. This index changes daily as the prices change and the index is a composite of what all of these corporations are doing collectively on the free marketplace.

What are the component activators of the DJ average?

The components are the buyers and the sellers of the marketplace. John Jones is selling. Jack Smith is buying. One bank is selling. One bank is buying. A mutual fund is jumping in. Another mutual fund, observing that, also jumps in. After three or four have jumped in, the entire flock of sheep is jumping in. That is part of the components of the Dow Jones.

The DJ is composed of buy-and-sell orders around the world from Zurich, England, France, Itahly, Saudi Arabia — everywhere. It is a huge composite photograph of every transaction ventured on a particular day.

To come up with the infallible prophecy, the chartists now transfer these daily actions onto charts. After awhile, the charts begin to make a pattern. Eventually a rising DJ, covering an unspecified amount of time, but climbing fast enough to create excitement, begins to convince all the followers of the DJ that a bull market is underway.

Now, the astute observers apply the inevitable logic. If the DJ by the rising quotations on stocks is predicting a great advance in the economy, that naturally means that the earnings of these companies are going to be perhaps dramatically higher,

177

and therefore, if one buys the shares today, he will be able to sell them at a very much higher price later on because the new increased earnings will naturally justify the new price. And there you have it.

But there is a very naughty question involved.

First of all we must ask, did any one of those buyers on a particular day have any real knowledge of a particular stock which he bought that was anything more than a guess? Now when this fellow bought, there also had to be another fellow who sold. Now was this seller a bit wiser than the buyer and did he have real good reasons to believe that the earnings of that particular stock were going to go down?

In other words, if you took all of the activators of the DJ in a single day, could you pick out any single one of them and say that he knew what the hell he was doing any more than his counterpart (buyer or seller) knew what he was doing — or any group or groups?

In other words, did these components in total know any more about the future than you know?

Now if there was no great wisdom in the majority of the components who acted to buy or sell, then how did it come that taken collectively they produce a gem of wisdom?

Taken individually, they know very little. But taken collectively, are they sages?

Does that make sense?

Since 1966 the DJ had been fluctuating through an area of about 300 points — 700 to 1,000 — in wave after wave. Each of these was called a new bull market. Yet not one of these over the course of 16 years produced a market that was noticeably higher than it was in 1966.

Now I don't claim to be any wizard. But I have been around and involved in the market in various ways since 1945 — 40 years. I've looked at a lot of charts. I've listened to a lot of brokers. I've read a lot of economists. I've seen some fortunes made, but I have seen more smart guys get their comeuppance in the market than anywhere else. Mostly, they get it because they accept one or another line of thought as being a reliable gauge of what is going to happen. The worst of it is, it sometimes works. That is usually unfortunate for the novice. This initial success gives him confidence. But the next time he plunges through a door that he opens with this key, he finds himself falling down an elevator shaft. He never thought a single key could lead him into two diametrically opposed positions, the one door going up to fortune, the other into an abyss.

Now in 1928, and especially the first eight months of 1929, the DJ charts were registering the action of the greatest bull market in living memory. Was that chart foretelling the great economic gains of the future? Almost everyone thought so.

In 1983 the DJ turned into a bull, fully as fierce as the 1929 bull. And people went for it hook, line and sinker. Hardly an analyst remains bearish today.*

Well, as the 1929 bull turned out to be nothing more than a huffer and a puffer, is there great reason to believe the fierce bull of 1983 was a more awesome prophet of a great economy now building?

The debt under-structure of 1929 and 1983 are highly similar.

I think it is very poor business to take any one theory very seriously. Even when you get a number of reliable theories all saying the same thing — fundamentals, charts, economic analyses, political considerations — your investment is no sure thing. If it does have heavy odds in its favor and if you make enough investments when the keys all agree, you will be successful. But whenever you begin to rely on a single key — don't. There is nothing inherent in the DJ that makes it an infallible prophet of the economy. Since none of its individual components by themselves have any special knowledge, surely the sum of the components by themselves has no special knowledge. Surely the sum of the components cannot be relied upon for more intelligence.

Could it be that almost everyone gets seduced by the tune of the Pied Piper — marching on a childish faith to oblivion?

*   *   *   *

I believe that at one time the DJ was a much better indicator than it is today. In the olden days when the tycoons practically ran the market, they knew ahead of time what they were going to do. They probably knew also what a lot of their friends were going to do. They were insiders. Their buying was a tip-off to what was going to happen. And their selling would have been a tip-off to what was going to happen. In other words, the leading wizards were also the leaders of the market. Things

*Most of the staunch bears, one by one, in 1983 became bulls. Even those who did not actually become rampant bulls, nevertheless, renounced the bear for the foreseeable future. Of the letters I read, and they are many, only three others remain unqualified bears — Holt, Granville and Weiss. Former snarly bears, but 1984 bulls, were Dines, Russell and Wellington.

don't happen that way anymore. The marketplace today is the sum of every brain and also every numbskull who entered a transaction on that particular day.

Market Philosophy
The Herd Instinct

Witness the crazy buying of gold as it grew from $700 to the $845 peak in only about two days. All the while, from $500 it had been gaining momentum. We know now that $500 would have been a reasonable top. The crowd was streaming forward.

Did you see the wild plunge into the stock market in the fall of 1982? The herd instinct took it up over 400 points which was mostly unjustified, as we shall see.

When it comes to getting out of the market, we will witness the same kind of stampede.

Witness the record volume days of January 5 and 6, 1984, with huge volumes of 160 million and 138 million. It was much ado about nothing because the overwhelming volume of a total of 928 million shares raised the DJ a measly 16 points after which it promptly started down — the crowd having picked the peak as it did in the case of gold.

The herd instinct is not a good reason to buy anything and you should be careful of it. A herd movement is more likely to be wrong than right.

In the market the most successful people are individualists and even non-conformists.

Market Philosophy
Dead Certain May Mean "Dead"

It is a very dangerous thing to adopt a viewpoint as unyielding as is indicated in the words, "**dead certain**." Dead certain implies that a thought has been turned into stone. It is no longer alterable.

I was greatly impressed by the danger of "dead certain" when as a boy in grade school I read the story of *"The Gold and Silver Shield."* It was in the McGuffey Reader, and they probably don't have it in schools anymore.

Two powerful knights happened to meet at the top of a hill where a large shield, placed in a stone monument, gleamed in the spring sun.

Said the one knight, "This is the most glorious shield I have ever seen. Never has silver been so beautifully burnished."

"I agree. This must be the world's most beautiful shield, but you mean, of course, — gold. It is a gold shield."

"Sir, do you mock me?"

180

"I mock you not. I correct your description of the shield. It is a gold shield as you must surely see."

"Your statement is so outrageous it must be meant to insult me. Please tell me you are joking, Sir, and I will not press the matter. Let's not be foolish."

"Joking, joking! **You** must be joking! You would have me agree to a lie to satisfy your arrogance? You would make me denounce what I see with mine own eyes? Surely, you must know the shield is fully gold."

"You make a mockery of my knighthood — **for** what reason I do not know. But repent; withdraw this insult; or prepare for combat."

"Of all the absurdities known to knighthood, this must be the worst. Draw your lance."

So the battle began: Broken lances, unhorsed riders, broken swords, slashed armor, the men sweating and bleeding on the ground beside the shield they both admired — until finally, one was mortally struck and the other died from loss of blood — the two great knights lay dying in their own blood up there on the top of the hill by the shield.

What a passerby noticed the next day was very strange. The shield was gold on one side and silver on the other side. Both knights were right, but both were dead.

*   *   *   *

In all my opinions during my life, I've always tried to stop short of "dead certain." There are times when "dead certain" is justified. But I've also seen times when I would swear upon my life that a certain thing was true, only to find out afterwards that there was a loophole in the background — absolutely concealed — which changed the whole picture and made "dead certain" nothing more than dead.

We still have to move along according to our best knowledge and our best reasoning and on the basis of the amount of certainty we can muster. That is one of the reasons why circumstantial evidence never quite satisfies me. We have found in many cases that men have been put to death on evidence that looked "dead certain." But later on, something else had come up to show that the verdict was wrong. A fundamental had been missed. "Dead certain," in truth, came to mean "uncertain."

*   *   *   *

181

In the market, you see a lot of this. Most notably in the 1970s and 1980s when the religion of the goldbugs had swept out any vestige of a possibility that gold could go down. They were just "**dead certain.**"

The fact that they wouldn't look at the other side cost people millions.

I was one of the gold religionists until 1980, and luckily for me the market caused me to take still one last look all the way around to the other side. It made the difference between subscribers having a fortune and losing one; today we have those who are "dead certain" that there is going to be a massive, destructive inflation that will ruin the currency. And I have to give them credit for a lot of good arguments. But I have walked around to the other side of the shield and I no longer believe, as I once did, that such an inflation is inevitable, or even indeed that it will come again.

Now, I'm not "dead certain" about deflation, but as I've walked round and round the shield, I have come to believe that if indeed there is to be an inflation someday, it will surely be preceded by a ruinous deflation. If it is, those "dead certain" people will surely come to think of the two knights dead at the top of the hill.

XVIII

ROLLOVER IN GOLD

In all of our recorded history, it seems, gold has been money, and the three greatest powers on the face of the earth, Rome, Great Britain and the United States, have used gold as their standard of money and, since it has been the standard of these powers, it became the standard of money throughout the world.

Gold served as the foundation of the British pound, and the British pound served as the foundation of international trade, and other currencies that were converted into the British pound could be reckoned in terms of gold.

In the commerce of the last few hundred years, gold's place as a circulating medium was largely taken over by paper money. As the world populations increased, as trade doubled and quadrupled, as market places developed all over the world, there simply was not enough gold to be traded by the average population. At first, certificates guaranteeing the ownership of gold were used instead of the metal. It was much more convenient that way. It was also a lot safer. The gold could be locked up in tight vaults while sending its emissaries – that is the paper guarantees – scampering all over the world. And there was nothing wrong with that.

The world enjoyed its most prosperous period and its most prolonged period of prosperity for over 200 years while Britain was on the gold standard.

But there's a great risk inherent in the gold standard. All of these pieces of paper representing gold, scattered far and wide, may add up to more gold than the issuer has. Indeed, that is the hope of the power that issues the paper. But if it ever reaches the point where people suspect that the power that issues the gold has far overspent its substance, and if a run ever develops, if creditors begin offering mountains of paper in demand for exchange of gold, the power that issues the certificates faces bankruptcy. Its credit around the world is drastically reduced. It suffers a loss of prestige, respect and trust. An economic defeat of this kind can produce results almost as bad as a military defeat. The country's currency loses value and imports from other lands become expensive, if not prohibitive. The general population takes a beating that can last a long time.

Therefore, the gold standard is great for the power that is able to run it because of its vast reserves of gold and its strong economy, when the gold standard is getting started and as long as it runs smoothly and as long as the credit of this power is not overdone. But the other side of the coin is that in all history every power has eventually, by one means or another, lost its preeminence, lost its gold and, with that, its economic prestige.

Through hundreds of years, people became so accustomed and so awed by the power of gold that it became practically enshrined as the fountain of money and as the only good money in the world. All currencies were, in one way or another, related to it, and all commodities were being constantly related to the money, which was related to the gold.

Sometimes idols stand a long time. As long as an idol is not challenged or tumbled, the worship of the idol can continue unabated. But the point is that an idol is still only an idol and remains an idol only as long as the people think it is. Gold actually holds that position.

And that raises a big question, a question as to whether gold is inherently as imperative as it is thought to be. The question has to be asked, "How does the country which is the great gold power get the gold?" Surely nobody gave it to them. In nearly all cases, the gold is not mined in the country that has the great gold power. Well, then, the country must have earned the gold. The country, in fact, must have had an economy so superior that in its trade with the rest of the world it was in surplus. Continuous and continually increasing surpluses of a great economic country net gold. The debtors are required to pay in gold. The accumulated wealth of the great country, by itself, attracts business, attracts confidence. So the economic power that has managed to get the most gold manages to become ever stronger, and gold from around the world tends to flow to this power, as filings to a magnet.

When Britain had to go off the gold standard because she could no longer meet the claims, she lost her position as the number one economic power in the world. A great deal of gold left Britain.

Now when gold leaves somewhere, it has to go somewhere. So where do the owners of the gold take the gold when they withdraw it from a weakening power center? For a large part, they are inclined to deposit the gold in the safest known place, that is in a country which had previously been the second-greatest power.

In our recent history, gold left Britain when it went off the gold standard and gold flowed into the United States. When World War II became increasingly imminent, the flow of gold to the United States increased. The warring countries chalked up ever-enlarging trade deficits and all of these deficits were countable in gold.

By the end of the war, the United States had over $36 billion in gold at $35 per ounce. In other words, they had nearly a billion ounces. But in all the world, there was less than two billion ounces, so the United States had more than half the monetary gold in the world, because individuals have a good part of it socked away, too.

But notice that gold was still the ultimate money, before the war, during the war, after the war, moving along its imperial path, without ever once arousing a question of doubt.

No one even thought to ask if the gold was necessary to the leading economic power. Was the leading economic country rich because it had the gold, or did it get the gold because it was inherently successful, and thus inherently rich?

People never questioned whether gold was actually a necessity. The countries that had it naturally wouldn't question that. And the countries that did not have gold didn't have enough influence even to get the question heard — if they had by any chance thought of it.

The gold people around the world tell us that gold has been the money of the world for thousands of years and that it always will be. We never seem to question that, although plenty of questions can be asked. In fact, after being off gold for 13 years, one may wonder whether gold, itself, the real stuff, was more than an idol that lived mainly in the admiring eyes of those who viewed it, and that amounted to most of the people of the world.

Certain gods in past history have occupied this position. Where the worshipers of the idol really believe in the idol, it is

185

very dangerous to question them. Only when the idol tumbles does this urge of realistic comprehension overtake the populace. And when an idol has crumbled, the disillusioned, because of the previous blind belief in the idol, usually smash it to smithereens.

The question we need to answer is whether gold was absolutely essential in the advancement of industry and our way of life throughout the glorious reign of Great Britain and, later, the glorious economic reign of the United States. Or did we just think so? And was it necessary for the success of the Industrial Revolution? Or did we all just think so?

At any rate, a dramatic thing happened on August 1, 1971. The foundation of all of the money in the world had been excommunicated overnight, and world money was totally without gold. Nixon had closed the gold window. He effectively eliminated gold from the role of money, knocked the foundations from under a concept held by society for thousands of years. Gold, thereafter, bore no relationship to money. It was a commodity, like copper or wheat.

Easier said than done. People don't get over an idea so engrained by a mere pronouncement of a politician or even a world leader, or all world leaders. The concept of gold as being very valuable hung on, and since there was no further official bridle on the price of gold, people began to buy it for they knew now it could be bid to any price.

The first gold movement, rising toward the $200 mark and falling back to $105, was related to the money concept which had been alive these many millenniums. The second movement of $105 to $700-$800 differed little from the wild bidding that went on during the tulip bulb mania of Holland in 1634, or the Mississippi bubble in real estate of 1720. Gold had been set free and it was a willing gambling vehicle.

This tells us a lot if we want to think about it. The character of gold on the marketplace has been transformed. The price of gold is now a function of **psychology** throughout the world. No longer is it related by any common sense, related to need or use, to the value of the U.S. dollar, the French franc, or any monetary function. The price of gold is just a function of **what people think the price of gold will be on some later date**. Whether the price is $400 an ounce or $200 an ounce is immaterial as the commerce proceeds independently on gold.

The price of gold will remain a function of the collective imagination, the collective greed, the collective fear, and the collective nervousness around the world. The price of gold needs

186

neither rhyme nor reason with the general economy. In the spring of 1984 it was holding around the $380 mark because the consensus of gold watchers was that a great new surge of inflation was coming and this inflation would somehow cause future buyers, Johnny-come-lately's, to pay higher prices.

Thus, gold having been cut loose from the monetary stream is condemned to remain a speculation until such time an authoritative, although arbitrary, price is set.

The people who bought and held gold in 1984 have no idea of specifically how gold can be brought into the stream again. Can that be brought about? That is something we ought to examine very carefully before we either hold or buy gold on a substantial scale.

*   *   *   *

Now you see what we are talking about here is ROLLOVER on a big scale — a change that reaches back to the economic roots of civilization. Gold always having been enthroned as money is assumed to have the divine right to remain the sovereign of all money. Therefore it is not surprising that we see large masses of the people around the world confident in the future of gold as money. Can it be taken for granted?

All the people around the world were almost unconsciously confident that the only way of life was tribes of wandering herdsmen. But it turned out that that was not true. Then there was universal confidence that agricultural settlements, and towns arising from agricultural settlements, and a society built around the local churches, were the way of life for humanity and would always be. Who thought to question it? But then it turned out that that was not true. During the course of the Industrial Revolution, gold came more to the forefront of the money than ever before, as highly organized states used it as a vehicle for the trade of the vast amounts of products that were being made and produced by mankind in different parts of the world. And it was considered that the way of the Industrial Revolution was the way of life for civilized man. But now it is beginning to look like that is not so. For the seeds imbedded in this way of life inevitably project its decadence, and a new way of life of the human race is germinating. And bound up in this new way of life — a principal component of it — is money. So, if all of these other phenomena were regarded as immutable and eternal, and if each has given way, one by one, to an unforeseen successor, is it possible that gold, the dominant symbol of money for thousands of years, will not also give way?

That has to be examined.

In the first place, gold's scarcity was an important factor in its function as money. Money has to be scarce. In a country filled with outcroppings of coal, the very abundance of coal would prevent coal from any useful function as money. Money is the distilled concentrate of huge amounts of effort by mankind. In small amounts, it represents very large volumes of the commodities. For example, a warehouse full of wheat can easily be carried in a suitcase of hundred dollar bills — or even on a single piece of paper as a guaranteed, note or in the form of gold where a tiny single-ounce bar can take the place of a hundred bushels.

Money is the distillation, highly concentrated, of all of our sweat, tears and efforts, and of all that has been produced from these efforts. Money has greased commerce throughout the world, and until 1971 its basis was gold. Is it possible that this will never be so again?

First of all, how do you get a gold standard? A gold standard is a condition where an economic power offers to buy or sell gold at a given arbitrary price. The country must have so much gold that it can stand behind its commitments to purchase any amount. Of course, it realizes that a lot will depend on the belief by other countries that it has this great amount of gold. And then when the test comes, it must pay out the gold unflinchingly until all become satisfied that there is no real reason to convert the paper promises of that country into gold. Then the gold comes back.

The great reserves of gold in the world went from Persia to Greece when Alexander the Great conquered Persia, from Greece to Rome, and gold took on through custom a certain value in regard to other things and other monies that were generally accepted through some hundreds of years, but the mass of new gold came from discoveries in the new world and fell into the hands of Spain.

The gold standard grew out of the power of the British, which had been able to conquer the Spanish and which, as a result of the Industrial Revolution, became the greatest economic power. Britain was able to set a price in British money on gold.

We are asked sometimes, "Why don't other countries give the United States the power to issue money on gold at a certain set price, and all countries support the United States in this offering?" But that is a very simplistic view, since support would mean adding the gold pile of other countries to the American

188

gold pile. Actually **gaining** reserves. What country is that cooperative?

Power, it must be remembered, is not given in any case. Power is taken. When England had the mass of the world's gold and the greatest economy in the world arising from not only its own production but from its colonies, who could challenge England in its proclamation of a fixed price for gold in terms of British pounds? When other countries traded with England and earned pounds they could trade the pounds for British gold. Or if gold was discovered or declared for sale elsewhere it could be turned in to England for British pounds. The power to handle this situation was inherent in England's military and economic power.

By the time England went off the gold standard in December 1931, the United States was the number one power in the world. The Industrial Revolution had received its final impetus in the United States. The vast storehouse of natural resources in the way of petroleum and most of the minerals, and the rich soil for the production of grain, cotton and livestock was the United States, an economic power unsurpassed. Thus the United States was the natural beneficiary of the vacuum of monetary leadership, abdicated by Great Britain.

In all the post-war years, the power of economic and military might rested with the United States and no one ever rose to challenge it. What beast of the forest will challenge the lion?

Where can we find in history that a government has suddenly come up and declared a price for gold which it was prepared to put back on the marketplace worldwide? Where can we find in the world today the country that can do this?

For example, as stated earlier, when the claims against the American dollar exceeded the store of gold by 300%, world confidence ran down until the demands on the gold began to be made, and the gold began flowing out in an ever-widening stream. The U.S. dollars sent abroad had become a claim on our core of wealth. The United States went off the gold standard because it didn't have enough gold to pay off the claims. In a strictly gold relationship, the United States was broke!

Now we find that our trade deficits are continuing to grow and it has been calculated that the trade deficit of 1984 was $123 billion. Even if we were to have started out on January 1, 1984, with a convertible pile of gold, we would have a $123 billion debt against it by the end of the year. As long as our economy generates a deficit instead of a credit, the gold pile would continue to shrink. Shrinkage brings on added shrinkage which causes the loss of confidence, which brings on increasing shrinkage.

In other words, the United States is off the gold standard now because it was forced off the gold standard because it could not pay. Now, how in heaven's name under the present circumstances can it re-enter the world market at an arbitrary price for gold, when the process of losing gold and when the process of accumulating claims against the gold pile are rampant, even from the beginning?

It is, as a matter of fact, literally impossible for the United States to declare an arbitrary price for gold, buy or sell, come what may. There are those who claim that if the price were set high enough the United States could do this, but could it? Remember if it sets the price of $2,000 an ounce on gold, it sets that price for the world. The United States has something over 250 million ounces, but the Common Market of Europe has more than 435 million ounces. Immediately the gold reserves of the Common Market start out exceeding the U.S. gold reserves, and deficit claims are building up against the United States.

Moreover, such a high price for gold would provide monetary reserves far in excess of what is needed in the world and would, therefore, of itself, start a vast and ruinous inflation. Raising the price of gold to a fantastic level would be tantamount to making coal the official money in a country where coal is plentiful everywhere. So the whole purpose of the gold standard would be defeated.

The gold standard can only work where a huge economic power has the muscle to set a price and hold it. If its economy is such that it is in a net earning position with other nations, that means its gold pile is year by year increased. And that means that all nations will respect the price that is arbitrarily set by the leading power.

There is no other way for the gold standard to work.

If the Common Market and the United States were to come together with 500 million ounces of gold among them they might commit the world to a gold standard. But who is going to take it in the neck when the claims come in against the U.S. deficits — or against French deficits — or against Italian deficits? As you can see, such cooperation is not decades away; it may be centuries away, if ever. Such a standard is unworkable and therefore unthinkable.

Also, what would they do with a great economic power like Japan which has hardly any gold at all? Would each one of

190

them divvy into his pile to give Japan some gold? Or would Japan be condemned to live on the periphery of the gold nations? And how would this affect world trade?

One doesn't have to think very far in this situation to realize that the gold standard at present is at least unforeseeable. None of the circumstances support it. The biggest reason we cannot get back to a gold standard is: **The wrong people have the gold!**

Who Has the Gold?

Below is the list of main gold-holding countries of the world, and a projection of the gold reserves of the various countries if the United States were to declare a price of $1,000 an ounce. Notice that the United States would have $264 billion worth of gold, but that West Germany, Switzerland, France, the United Kingdom, Italy, the Netherlands, and Belgium would have a combined 432 billion ounces and therefore $432 billion worth of reserves, far exceeding that of the United States. Notice that reserves of Japan are relatively small at 24 million ounces, or $24 billion. Notice that the United Kingdom would have only $19 billion in gold reserves.

Holder	Ounce of Gold	$ Per Ounce	$ Reserves
United States	264.0 Million Oz.	$1,000/Oz.	$264 Billion
IMF	103.0 Million Oz.	$1,000/Oz.	$103 Billion
West Germany	95.2 Million Oz.	$1,000/Oz.	$ 95.2 Billion
Switzerland	83.3 Million Oz.	$1,000/Oz.	$ 83.3 Billion
France	81.9 Million Oz.	$1,000/Oz.	$ 81.9 Billion
Italy	66.7 Million Oz.	$1,000/Oz.	$ 66.7 Billion
Belgium	44.2 Million Oz.	$1,000/Oz.	$ 44.2 Billion
Netherlands	44.0 Million Oz.	$1,000/Oz.	$ 44 Billion
Japan	24.2 Million Oz.	$1,000/Oz.	$ 24.2 Billion
Austria	21.1 Million Oz.	$1,000/Oz.	$ 21.1 Billion
Canada	20.2 Million Oz.	$1,000/Oz.	$ 20.2 Billion
United Kingdom	19.0 Million Oz.	$1,000/Oz.	$ 19 Billion

This amount of fresh monetary reserves in the world created by the stroke of a pen through arbitrarily raising the price of gold would result in a tidal wave of inflation, impossible to control and which would be the ruination of the world. That is probably the biggest reason that such a price for gold, in these times, is out of the question.

Now, some adherents of the revival of gold in money point out that the people of the world have about as much gold as the governments and the organizations — that is, about 1,000 million ounces each. These economists believe that the people of the world would sell their gold to the United States. But that is a totally unmapped jungle. It would depend on the price. Who is smart enough to say what the price of gold would have to be to cause the people to turn in their gold for paper money? And what country could be prepared to take such a gamble?

No matter how you slice this tomato, it's always the same. A gold standard is simply unforeseeable. It was easy enough to hang onto as long as our preeminent position in economics could be held. There was no trouble in keeping the gold standard. But once the gold standard has been smashed, you can see quite readily that putting it back in operation again is a task that has never been faced. But, frankly, I do not think Humpty Dumpty is going to get back up on the wall.

The people who see gold soaring in the event of a credit crisis in the world may be right in the short run, but on the other hand they may get a nasty surprise. If you think about it, you know that a credit disaster means that credit is short everywhere. Everyone is scrambling to pay his creditor to avoid foreclosure. Every last dollar is being called into use. In this kind of an atmosphere small business is calling on its savings and on all its resources to keep going. Unemployed people are trotting out their disposables to get dollars.

Think of it. We don't go to the grocery store with gold. You go with dollars. If you have gold, you sell it to get the dollars. It seems to me the gold holders will be selling gold rather than buying it. Now I believe that in the first few days of a dramatic bank closing around the world, some people might buy gold. But I believe that they would find that gold has taken off in exactly the wrong direction and that, in a few days the sellers of gold would overwhelm the buyers.

That's because gold is not money. It has to be transformed into money before it can be used. And for this very reason, gold would be massively for sale. In past crises, gold has been money. It has been the ultimate money. And it was usable directly. You could go in with gold coins and do your direct buying from the grocer or the dry goods store. Nothing is transacted in gold these days. No merchant wants to take gold for his merchandise because he doesn't know what the price of gold will be tomorrow and he is not in the business of speculating. He is in the business of selling goods.

The fact alone that gold is no longer money and cannot be relied upon for any quoted value tomorrow makes its usage in the case of a national credit disaster strictly limited.

The fact that people may have done so in previous deflations isn't a reliable guidepost today. In all deflations, for hundreds of years, gold was a well-known vehicle in the marketplace.

And now we come to a very nasty part in the projection of our logic. If gold is not money, quickly and readily exchangeable at a set and stable price — then just what is gold? No matter how much of a gold bug you may be, you will have to admit that it is nothing more than a commodity. A rare commodity it may be, a treasured commodity it may be, but if it is not used **directly** in buying and selling, it is a commodity.

The price of other commodities is regulated in the marketplace through the forces of supply and demand. They get out of whack every once in awhile, but they always come back to reasonable prices in relationship to all other commodities. And they respond to the laws of usage or disuse. If a large new demand develops for lead, the price of lead would go up. If manufacturers found a substitute for copper and its usage began to drop off, the price of copper would sink. But where do we stand with gold?

In the first place, we still have most of the gold ever brought out of the earth by man; about 1,000 million ounces in the hands of the official authorities and about the same in public hands around the world. The usage of gold is only minuscule compared with the amount of overhang. If gold is not money and if no power will set a price on it that it is prepared to enforce, where is the demand for gold to come from? For some extended time it will be a psychological price, but it will be ranging high and low as the emotions of people sway in the marketplace. At that time it becomes a speculating proposition because the need for gold would not be used as an indicator at all. Only the greed for gold. But then who would there be to evaluate the greed if gold was no longer money?

Well, I'm not making a prophecy, but I can see the possibility at some distant or semi-distant date where the

193

amount of gold in the treasuries would be a drag on the market of the world. We have been without gold in the money system for 13 years. In another five years chances of that recovering will begin to look tarnished. And that could be the beginning of a long slump in the price of the yellow metal, for who would there be to buy it except some countries that would wish to enforce the gold standard? So what would it then be worth an ounce? First of all, there is the psychological price throughout the world, and then the demand and supply price.

World uncertainty might tend to put some backbone under it, but not enough to command a great premium as it now does.

And then gold's identity in the world would take on a different image. A store of value would still be in it – no one would know how much; but as a medium of exchange it would be unusable exactly because no one would know how much.

I don't want to shock my readers, but if it once became an accepted fact that gold was not to be officially used as money by the treasuries of the world powers, I could not see any reason why anyone would want to pay more than $150 an ounce, maybe $50 an ounce, maybe $25 an ounce – who knows?

Only if gold becomes crucial to the treasuries of the world, in the manipulation of world money, will it ever come back to the price it now enjoys. In fact, it is hard to see how it is even possible to construct gold-structured money again.

A lot of people may say that the United States may just have to go back to gold to at least at $1,000 an ounce. And I will answer if it will pay $1,000 an ounce in the U.S., then it will have to pay $1,000 an ounce on the world market and we'll have to be prepared to dish out $500 billion to Germany, Holland, South Africa, Russia, etc.

If anyone can see through this maze as to how to put gold back on the pedestal, I would surely like to examine the reasons.

Who Owns the Gold?

And this is what lies behind the concept of the ROLLOVER IN GOLD. It is at the junction of the dying phase of an ancient concept, and at the phase of a new one, where gold takes on an entirely different position and is finally divorced from the arbitrary authority of government to what its price should be.

Does this mean that you are helpless in the path of a devastating wave of inflation? You know, I don't believe in that. But assume for a moment that it might be the next move. Can't you do anything about it? You certainly can.

194

If you are one of those who believes (and I don't quarrel with you) that your money or at least a large part of it should be contained in items of VALUE, contained in something REAL, contained in something you can POSSESS, you can still accomplish that by a different route. Gold is the only one of the commodities that could suffer a disaster because of a failure of a gold standard to get started again. But there is a way you can avoid that disaster and still be as well positioned against an inflation.

Gold Caveat

Although I have given you a massive argument against gold, and though I believe in the validity of every argument I have put forth, I still have to warn against "dead certain" conclusions about the metal. It is virtually impossible to measure gold as an investment by the ground rules used for almost anything else.

As far as I can see, gold will not be able to get into the official monetary stream for a long, long time. That being true, in times of great stress, gold is not the money of last resort. But there's one factor I have not taken into account and that is the money of last **emotion** resort. Will people bid high for gold just because there are revolutions around the world? And, for the people who obtain gold, how will they spend it when really it is not money?

Nevertheless, there may be answers to questions like these I cannot know. This is a caveat on my prognosis on gold.

I believe that because of its emotional background with the human race, it will never sell for less than its price in relation to average commodities during a stable period of some 40 years. So if gold was $35 in 1935, then you might, as a horseback figure, take a guess that gold ought to be worth $250 to $350 under present commodity price averages. And I don't think that's too bad a figure to come to terms with, plus or minus.

Now that can have a meaning, from an investment standpoint, that must be brought forth here. Gold can be bought without being a speculation. It can be bought as simply a store of value — as a hedge against others.

In the 1980s, we have come down to a place where no monetary instrument can be fully counted on. You can't count on cash 100% because you don't know for sure that an inflationary period might not re-develop and depreciate your cash. You cannot count on corporate bonds because the companies may go bankrupt. You cannot count on the government bonds over the long haul because, if interest rates go up 3% or 4%, the value of the government bonds might deteriorate by a third or more on the marketplace.

Then you have to look at gold and assess the chances of stabilization around $250 to $350 — and if you like to have something you can actually feel, gold coins as a physical assurance may be important from that point of view.

MFE readers have gold survival coins which they have held for a long time. I never recommended the sale of those, nor do I now.

XIX

PLATINUM & SILVER WON'T ROLL OVER

Platinum and silver are two precious metals that will not roll over because, no matter what happens to our money, they are in scarce supply; we continually use more silver than we produce and all that keeps us away from a silver crunch are the rather large stores of silver above the ground. It was so plentiful a century ago that hundreds of millions of ounces were minted into United States currency and vast amounts of this currency are still around, a potential for industrial use, always meeting, to this time, the imbalance between production and consumption.

The platinum story is similar. It is in extremely scarce supply in the world. Usually it has been a higher price per ounce than gold. Although it has nothing to do with the monetary picture, for the last 10 years it rose almost on a parallel plane with gold. Platinum reserves in the United States are known but they are, to date, so expensive to produce, that they cannot be seriously considered for production. Loss of platinum shipped from South Africa would hamstring the U.S. military efforts as well as its industry. Russia, rich mostly in palladium which is a sometime substitute for platinum, could not be counted upon to help us out of our strategic hardship if we were ever cut off from South Africa by action of that government or as a result of black revolution.

These metals have a different base than gold and a different base than money and they will not roll over no matter what.

In late spring of 1984 I recommended that our subscribers should devote 20% to 25% of their investable funds into platinum. I wish to demonstrate to you how I finally arrived at that conclusion after much soul searching and internal debate with myself covering a period of some months. I do that because I think if you know how I arrived at that conclusion, you will find the conclusion more credible. I believe you will agree with it. And you may even act upon it.

Arriving at a Strategy

No strategy is complete or even trustworthy unless it has taken into account the enormous federal debt, the increasing expenditures by the military and the failure to reduce social payments. Of these, the debt is the most frightening because it grows like an uncontrollable monster, once it has been created. The debt now eats up about 23 cents of every tax dollar collected. All of us are bogged down by this enormous albatross. The albatross is growing, and growing, and growing.

The talk about reducing the budget deficit next year is hollow. They have already announced they expect to increase military spending. They have already shown their inability to trim social spending. They never had a chance to trim the interest on the debt. Deficits which were absolutely shocking at $100 billion a couple of years ago are now estimated to grow as high as $500 billion. In about four years the interest on the debt will devour 50 cents of every tax dollar. Out of every dollar you and I pay in taxes, 50 cents will go for interest on the U.S. debt.

But that isn't the end, of course, the monster keeps on growing. The albatross around our necks becomes heavier. What is the end? Is it 90 cents from every dollar, 95 cents, 103 cents?

I do not know of a single politician or economist who will even take a guess **or even mention** the end.

Nor does anybody have even the faintest idea of how he will deal with this Frankenstein. Did Reagan ever mention this horror moves inexorably forward? Inexorably it will grow until it becomes a panic. But panic is not the end. What happens after the panic?

Each increase of interest because of increased borrowing demands further borrowing. Every increase in borrowing means more increase on the interest.

These payments will become so punitive that business will be gradually strangled. Individuals will have to cut their spending. These two elements will reduce the availability of tax dollars.

Something Has Got to Give.

There's a wide school of thought that believes we will solve this by inflation. The same school believes that the foreign

198

debt problem involving the banks and the Third World countries will be solved by inflation. If they are serious they are talking about the pure manufacture of a trillion dollars of unsupported money — thus destroying the currency.

In these circumstances, the only thing that would do you any good would be what you own. And the most important thing you could own would be your home. But as for the rest of it, you know if the inflation got that bad, ten-fold, twenty-fold, fifty-fold — what would it matter how many dollars you could get for a piece of commercial property — or a hundred-ounce bar of gold? Even these dollars would be like straw in the wind.

I have no reservations about the scenario I have painted here up to the point that an enormous economic and monetary disaster will befall us. UNLESS — somebody gets a handle on this thing and very quickly, it will take nothing less than a military dictator to handle the situation.

Fed Lacks the Power

Meanwhile, however, I disbelieve that the Fed is in any position to issue the unimaginable amounts of money that would be required to save the banks, the countries, and the economy. It is therefore my view that the first tremor of this violent earthquake will be a deflationary tremor and this, in itself, will wipe out debts in gargantuan amounts. The wiping out of these debts will bring on the deflation which will make government tax payments shrink. It will be necessary for the government to introduce measures now unthinkable.

One of these measures could very well be that from each paycheck a forced loan to the government would be taken in the form of a bond, the promise, of course, being to repay the bond. The only difference between it and liberty bonds during the war is that they were voluntary and this will be involuntary. It will take a dictator to enforce it. Before we reach that stage, there will be enormous unrest in the streets. I pictured it all in my 1976 book *The Coming Deflation*. The events are unfolding just as they were outlined, only they have been unfolding more slowly than I thought. Nevertheless, right now there are lots of signs that we are approaching the climactic phase.

Now this initial deflation will provide an opportunity for those with ready cash to acquire lots of real property. It may be raw land. It may be some of the commodities, oil-drilling rights or whatever.

I am in agreement with those who claim the Fed will do everything on this green earth to save the banks. But I have a small difference with those who prophesy it. This difference is

199

that **they believe the Fed has the power and the ability to stop
the avalanche. I, on the other hand, do not believe the Fed will
have the power or capacity** under the present government, or
the know-how to halt the crumbling avalanche of debt. It will be
about as effective as a hand raised to stop the hurricane.

Rollover Coming

But when this phase has passed, and it might last only a
year or so, we will witness a transformation in the govenment of
the United States. We will witness then what dovetails into my
belief that civilization is approaching a complete **ROLLOVER** —
when our social order changes, and the Orwellian scenario begins
to materialize only a few years late.

At that time, we may very well see the end of currency.
The government is trying to get rid of cash now. Your paycheck
may be simply issued to a central agency which will deduct first
your taxes and then your forced loan to the government. The
rest of it will be credited in that account. When you spend, it
will be deducted from that account. It's likely that an effort will
be made to strain hard cash out of the system. Certainly its
possession in large sums will be frowned upon. How far away is
it?

I believe we cannot escape the present crisis without
bringing on a crashing deflation within a year or two. That will
be the period of low prices. That will be the time to anticipate
inflation as unlimited power falls into the hands of an
authoritarian government rising out of the military.

Can you imagine a better man — seriously — to take this
post and one more able to handle it than Alexander Haig? Or
one more anxious?

To Summarize

Our search for a strategy leads us to get ready first of all
for the deflation and seriously falling prices in all things, and to
endure that for a limited period, maybe for a couple of years,
and during those years to prepare for the final inflation. And
during that period of a couple of years of the most fantastic
inflation in the world, the rise to power of a military
government.

Therefore, our search for a strategy tells us this:

For the present be in cash, be in U.S. treasuries, be
absolutely safe. A certain amount of precious metals in coinage
and especially silver coinage would be a valuable part of the
strategy. Be ready to use the cash to buy up reality once the
deflation has struck.

200

For those who feel naked for the present time without the precious metals — and I know it's a natural feeling — I have pursued the matter further and the analysis of that is contained in the following:

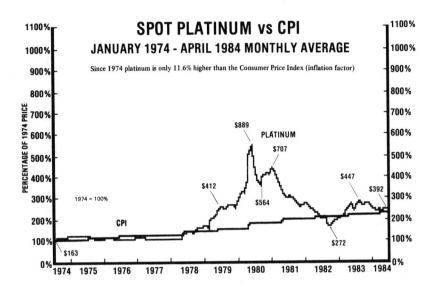

SPOT PLATINUM vs CPI

JANUARY 1974 - APRIL 1984 MONTHLY AVERAGE

Since 1974 platinum is only 11.6% higher than the Consumer Price Index (inflation factor)

Platinum—Gold—Silver

We are here assuming that while the odds **heavily favor** deflation in the near run, a danger of inflation could develop later.

The forces building toward a monetary disaster are getting worse. The consequences of such a disaster are horrible, and because we don't know just what shape the consequences will take, the most confident of prognosticators have to yield to a growing doubt. In its end the collapse of the credit pyramid, the greatest in the history of the world, will shake governments as well as their banks.

The condition which produces just a pinch of panic already is the fact that neither bankers nor politicians have the slightest idea of what to do about it. Let it be said in their favor

201

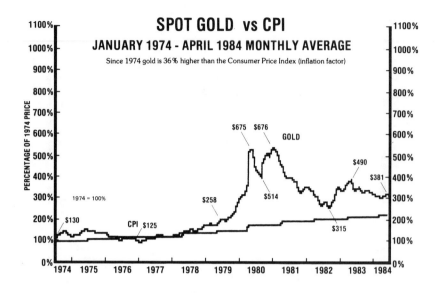

SPOT GOLD vs CPI

JANUARY 1974 - APRIL 1984 MONTHLY AVERAGE

Since 1974 gold is 36% higher than the Consumer Price Index (inflation factor)

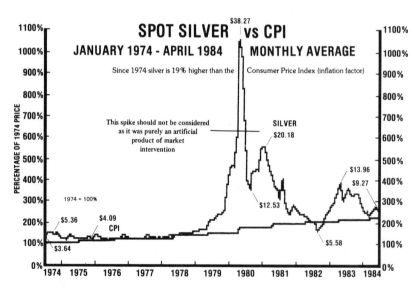

SPOT SILVER vs CPI

JANUARY 1974 - APRIL 1984 MONTHLY AVERAGE

Since 1974 silver is 19% higher than the Consumer Price Index (inflation factor)

This spike should not be considered as it was purely an artificial product of market intervention

202

that, by now, numerous economists and bankers see it coming. The politicians seem to remain oblivious.

I am beginning to wonder whether the government can be stabilized. And if it cannot—how do I know what steps panic-driven men may take?

The magnitude of the consequences prescribes, therefore, to me that one should be hedged against both deflation and inflation. Those who believe we are to be overtaken, first of all by a wave of inflation, ought to be hedged against deflation and should own cash and treasuries. Those who believe (as I do) that the first wave will be a deflationary wave, ought to be hedged, too.

To make it clear, I shall examine here the three precious metals, gold, silver and platinum.

Viewing the charts — clearly these metals have traveled an almost parallel path in the last 10 years.

The bar line in each of the graphs is the Consumer Price Index at 215. That means that it takes $2.15 today to buy, on the average, what you would have bought in 1974 for $1.

The price of gold (April average $381) is 293% of the 1974 dollar value. It is **36% higher than the Consumer Price Index**, which is the inflation factor.

The price of silver (disregarding the enormous spike caused by the Hunt battle to corner the silver market) shows a highly similar pattern to platinum and gold. Silver ($9.29 April average) stands at 255% of its early 1974 price compared with 215% for the Consumer Price Index (inflation factor). The silver price then is **19% higher than the Consumer Price Index** as of now.

The price of platinum (April 1984 average) is 240% of its cost in January 1974 compared with 215% of the Consumer Price Index, which is the inflation factor. Platinum as of May, 1984, was only **11.6% higher than the Consumer Price Index.**

*   *   *   *   *

It will come as a great surprise to many readers that all three of the precious metals have not appreciated a great deal above the **average** prices in the last 10 years; gold only is 36% higher. Silver is 19% higher. Platinum is 11.6% higher. It's quite clear that money invested at even a modest amount of interest would not be far behind the precious metals.

*   *   *   *   *

Probably the second most outstanding feature of these graphs is the almost parallel positions of gold and platinum. The only difference is in January 1980, when platinum went up

203

quite a bit faster than gold and this well may be attributed to the Iranian crisis and the fear of a war. And we might conclude that the strategic value of platinum is a substantial plus over gold. We could fight a war without gold. But we could not proceed with our industry, and especially our military, without platinum. That's terribly important in any comparison of the two.

But perhaps the most important truth arising from this graph is that if gold appreciates, platinum also appreciates and most of the time to a fairly equal degree. The fact that platinum is not related to money, whereas gold is almost completely related to money in people's minds, was no drawback in the price advance of platinum versus gold over 10 years.

In fact, the graphs are so much the same that I had to abandon my original plan of showing them both in two separate lines on the same graph. Most of the time it was one line. Remember, all the graph points are percentages.

*   *   *   *   *

Thus you arrive at the position where: (a) the platinum price appreciation is almost a dead ringer for the gold price appreciation; (b) platinum avoids any risk of demonetization and a resulting devastating plunge; and (c) platinum enjoys the twin advantages of scarcity and mandatory necessity.

Weighing Gold Against Platinum

You know that my reservations about gold are three-fold:

One: The signs of increasing government intervention.

Two: There is certainly the possibility if not probability that gold will not be officially connected to money, at least for a long, long time. During that interval it would be subject to great psychological swings in price, according to what the world population thought of its chances. That makes it far more speculative than platinum—and more dangerous.

Three: If gold does not get an official position again in the monetary system, we have a surplus of two billion ounces that we have no use for. Gold's principal use is connected with monetary meaning.

Platinum avoids all three of these drawbacks. In terms of surplus — there isn't any. Each year the world produces about 10,000 tons of silver, 1,000 tons of gold and 175 tons of platinum. While gold and silver are produced in numerous countries, platinum is only produced in South Africa and Russia. One might say that platinum is produced only in South Africa because if we were ever cut off from supplies there, it would take a fool to believe we would get some help from

Russia. Our whole industrial machine could be stalled, hamstrung, by the denial of platinum. **Think of it!**

Next, we don't have any surplus above-ground stores. The U.S. reserve position is said to be from six months to one year, and probably more like six months.

Since the U.S. Congress wants to ban the importation of Krugerrands and lay down heavy duties on South African goods, why wouldn't South Africa ban the delivery of platinum?

South Africa doesn't have to worry about a world cartel in platinum, it **IS** a world cartel, when you consider that Russia couldn't be relied upon in the slightest to fill our needs if we were in a bad spot.

Since we can't get along without platinum in oil refining, in automobile exhaust systems as a catalyst, in fiberglass and plastics; since it is essential in most high-tech productions; and since it is used heavily by the military in satellites, missiles and airplanes, what a horrible thought to realize that our industrial life – and that means life itself – is dependent on only two countries, one which is our sworn enemy, and the other one which is our friend but which we are alienating and who would be foolish – in a pinch – if they didn't use their platinum power to scare some sense into us – either by large increases in price or complete denial for a period of time. Well, that doesn't have to happen for platinum to weigh in quite a bit heavier than gold on the investment scale. They have now begun to install catalyctic converters in cars in Europe. That means greater demand for platinum and some platinum coinage is beginning to be manufactured in South Africa and on the Isle of Man.

CONCLUSION: The point is that platinum avoids all of the negatives piling up against gold. More importantly, it is scarce, it is strategic and a constant supply is mandatory. Additionally, we have a 10-year record which shows that the platinum price kept pace with the gold price at the time of the greatest gold advance in history.

*   *   *   *   *

Picture on Silver

If you're going to buy one or the other, there is my considered opinion on that that.

If you place the silver graph over the platinum graph or the gold graph on a light table, you will find almost identical lines – **EXCEPT** – that during 1980 the silver price shot into the stratosphere, but I believe I am right in contending that this should not be considered in a comparison among the metals because the silver spike was a purely artificial product of market

205

intervention when the Hunts made their big effort to corner the world's silver market. As soon as that effort collapsed, the silver price picture fell back into line with both gold and platinum.

The percentage advances and declines of all three metals remain very close throughout the period 1974 to 1984.

An investment in silver avoids the danger of gold in that it is finished on the marketplace unless it remains an essential part of the world monetary system, until such time as gold's price might be backed by the authority of a huge and powerful national economy head and shoulders above all the rest. So from that standpoint of surplus, silver is out ahead of gold. By avoiding the dangers that gold has, it is stronger. Through the fact that the world continually produces less silver annually than it uses, it avoids the big overhanging surplus danger in gold.

But we are not likely to be put out of business by a shortage of silver. There is still an unknown but huge supply of coinage. The above-ground reserves are certainly enough to get us safely over any emergencies, even if they should be long ones. Since there is a surplus of above-ground silver, and since reclamation has come into the picture, it seems we could expect silver to rise only according to the inflation factor. In the event of deflation, its price would fall, along with platinum and gold. In the long run, the silver shortage will make itself felt and then the price of silver should outpace gold.

CONCLUSION – **silver investment is preferable to gold because it avoids the pitfalls in the gold investment** and if gold enjoys a healthy advance due to deflation, silver will be right there along with it. Eliminating the disadvantages of gold, its eventual shortage predicts that it will trim down the silver/gold ratio of 40 to 1. That means it will appreciate further and faster.

Its only disadvantage is the storage problem.

Numismatic Coins

While the rarity of coins is unquestionably a big factor in their quoted value, it is nevertheless a highly variable factor from the coins bringing the highest premium to those at the other end of the spectrum. That means that the biggest part of the value of most numismatic coins is bound up in the price of gold. In some coins, the premium is only a small percentage, such as 10% to 20%. In buying numismatic coins, you are dealing with two variables, both of which are psychological. But broadly speaking, the gold price is the key. So, to a large degree, you are taking the same risks if gold goes down as you are with gold. But I'm not sure whether there would be added profits for rarity if gold goes up – just for the gold.

I've claimed that the gold standard will probably not return to the world in this century, and without expounding on the reasons I have given, there is one overwhelming reason that no one has been able to deal with. It is this:

THE WRONG PEOPLE HAVE THE GOLD.

The gold standard must be enforced by a super-strong economy. I don't think, in history, it has ever been artificially produced.

So numismatic coins, for the most part, carry similar risks to a plunging gold price as the metal itself.

Benchmark Prices
A Point of Reference

Few realize that the prices of three key commodities are almost the same at the beginning of 1985 as they were at the beginning of 1973.

At the beginning of 1985, gold is just about back to that plateau.

This graph should be valuable to you at future times because, by keeping up with the commodity price index, you can tell at any time in the future just where gold is priced in relation to the beginning of 1973.

This gives us something to go by when we are judging gold as an investment or a buy or a sell. And even more so if we consider the history prior to 1973.

Gold had been $35 an ounce for many, many years. The commodity price index since the 1940s had about tripled and I recall that my belief was that gold would go to $100 or $105. And that that price would be about right in keeping with inflation as of 1973. Gold did exactly that and I believe that it was then about a fair price and since it is now back to that same price in constant dollars, I believe it is not too far off a fair price at $300. There is nothing in the markets to guarantee that they will be fair, but there is something to say that eventually they always become realistic. Gold may well go down to $250 or even less. If it did I would think it unrealistically low in comparison to everything else. Nevertheless, a downward movement usually exceeds the realistic range. Afterward, it works its way back up again. The net result is that I think gold is not a good speculative vehicle no matter which way you look at it now. It hasn't got far enough to go. It hasn't got it on the upside and I doubt that it has it on the downside. It's not good enough to get into a commodity that might fall by only a fifth or a sixth. Such risks demand more potential.

Those people who hang onto the idea that gold in the 1980s will give a repeat performance are, I think, whistling Dixie. You just don't get that. One of those deals in a lifetime where the investment multiplies several hundred percent is about all you can expect. You may expect that in something else, but hardly in the same investment a second time.

At any rate, there is your basemark. It will be important for you to keep this book around in the future to keep up with the consumer price index and watch where the gold price is going in constant dollars.

*   *   *   *

Silver shows pretty well the same position. Silver is back now again to just about where it was at the beginning of 1973. At $6.20 per ounce, it is worth $2.58 in 1973 dollars. You notice the same long plateau. You notice the same fantastic rise and repeats once again to the same plateau. I think the plateau is a pretty good horseback guess at what silver will be worth for quite some time in constant dollars. Once again, it's not an investment that should be attacked on either side of the market.

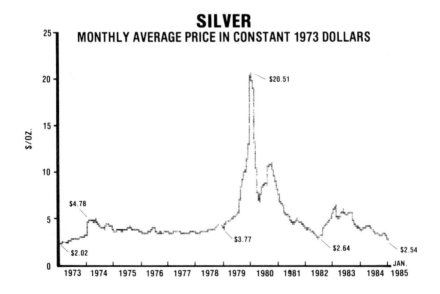

SILVER
MONTHLY AVERAGE PRICE IN CONSTANT 1973 DOLLARS

GOLD
MONTHLY AVERAGE PRICE IN CONSTANT 1973 DOLLARS

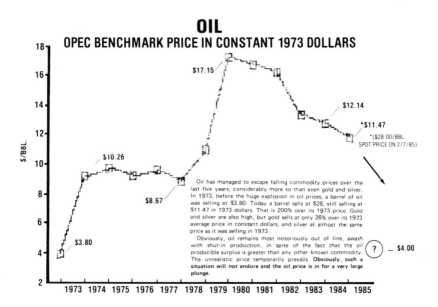

OIL
OPEC BENCHMARK PRICE IN CONSTANT 1973 DOLLARS

Oil has managed to escape falling commodity prices over the last five years, considerably more so than even gold and silver. In 1973, before the huge explosion in oil prices, a barrel of oil was selling at $3.80. Today a barrel sells at $28, still selling at $11.47 in 1973 dollars. That is 200% over its 1973 price. Gold and silver are also high, but gold sells at only 26% over its 1973 average price in constant dollars, and silver at almost the same price as it was selling in 1973.

Obviously, oil remains most notoriously out of line, awash with shut-in production, in spite of the fact that the oil producible surplus is greater than any other known commodity. The unrealistic price temporarily prevails. **Obviously, such a situation will not endure and the oil price is in for a very large plunge.**

209

Oil is a little different picture. You see that at the beginning of 1973 it was $3.80. We then experienced a marked increase in price to the end of 1974. Here we ended the plateau until 1979 when the explosion took place in the price of oil. However, as the graph shows, the explosion was not as great in terms of 1973 dollars as one might have supposed. Nevertheless, the oil price seems to have exceeded reality. It has been weakening since 1981, both through disinflation and lower bids due to the oil surplus. Saudi Arabia, alone, by withholding over 4 million barrels per day from the market is not able to hold the oil price firm. And this is an indicator that we shall see further weakening. Again, if we use a price of about $26 a barrel in February of 1985, it is equivalent to $10.83 back in 1973. It's not an unreasonable guess that oil, like silver and gold, will repeat that 1973 value. Certainly, with the great surplus in the world there is no reason to keep the price inflated except to the arbitary ruling of a cartel. But this cartel has already shown its great weakness and shows every sign of coming apart. **So the outlook is that oil will go back to somewhere around the $3.80 per barrel price in 1973 or $9.12 in the current inflation adjusted price of 1985.**

Since oil is a chief commodity in the world, its price will be an important indicator as to whether we are proceeding in an inflationary or a deflationary trend.

These graphs may look like duplications of other graphs we've published, but they are used here from a different point of view, related to a stable base point, and with a beginning year of 1973, at which time important corrections in world prices had already been made.

*   *   *   *

It's clearly indicated now that none of these three blazing phenomena of the 1970s will see even a resemblance to the price action they enjoyed then. That's all over.

XX

ROLLOVER IN ENERGY

Oil was formed over the course of millions and scores of hundreds of millions of years. Abundant life of the sea sank into the muds and the sand, and as the ocean encroached upon the land, they were buried in layers and under layer upon layer of further sediments to the depth sometimes of many thousands of feet. Through heat and pressure nature distilled this brew, mixed as it was with the salt water also contained in the sediments. In the course of time these sediments ended up in the deep water as the sea moved further inland, and so a shale (the deposits of deep water) was laid down upon these hundreds of thousands of feet of sediment. This shale is an impervious layer.

During the course of time, the seas receded and advanced in other areas of the globe, or as an alternative the land was raised above the level of the seas. Further down the line, great folding movements occurred in the crust of the earth and often these foldings resulted in the formations of dome-like structures. This is what is known as an anticline.

Now as the eons passed, the oil of course ever strove to be higher than the water, moving up the sides of the anticline through the water. Since this dome, or anticline, was covered by a seal of impervious shale, the oil could not escape. Indeed, if there was enough of it, it kept moving forward and even past the top of the anticline and down the other side, against the water coming up on the other side. The water and oil were fulfilling their fundamental nature just as can be shown by placing water and oil together in a cup.

If there was a lot of oil, the sides of the anticline containing the oil were very long. That meant the oil field covered a large area. It also meant that the oil on the other side of the anticline went to an equal level. The oil-water interface is always the same in this kind of a container or field. As a result, the driller knows the level of the water below sea level – and he knows that all of the anticline to that certain level will be full of oil.

After the discovery well, the oil company will try to define the limits of the field by deliberately stepping out until it hits water.

Now this layer containing the oil, often a porous limestone layer, provides the tiny receptacles for the oil. By taking cores from the well, the geologist can figure out the percentage of the volume of rock containing the oil. He can then calculate how much oil is in the entire oil field.

This is the way you arrive at proven reserves. It depends absolutely on the delineation of the oil field by actual oilwells drilling to the water level. There's no other way on the face of the earth to know the size of an oil field until the field has been delineated.

And right here is where the person with only a small amount of knowledge about the nature of oil and the genesis of oil can pick out the charlatans who shout "billions of barrels," and who shout "suppression of production," and who talk about streams of oil under the earth and who talk about veritable oil lakes under the earth. And here is where you can spot the utter nonsense that gets bandied about.

For instance, three or four years ago a preacher visited the Prudhoe Bay area and some of the projects of Atlantic Richfield. He wrote a book pertaining to the vast amounts of oil in Alaska, enough to do the United States for a hundred years and then some – if only the companies would let loose of it. He claimed to know a powerful "Mr. X," an executive, so he said, of the big company, an executive he could not name. He told about how Mr. X took him to the top of a hill and showed him a huge area where all of this oil lay abundant under the Alaskan tundra and even out into the sea. But just the little bit of background I have given you here shows that the preacher didn't have the faintest idea of what he was talking about, and if Mr. X indeed told him about these vast volumes of oil as yet untapped, he didn't know what he was talking about either. The seismologist can discover these domes. In Alaska there are some tremendously huge structures. If they were full of oil, they could be rated as vast reservoirs. When a field is discovered, it has that possibility. However, when the wells are drilled on all sides, then the size of the field can be known and published. Until the wells have actually punctured the structure, no one knows if there's any oil in it at all. The famous Mr. X apparently did know of huge structures in Alaska. But already some of these monsters have been found to be vacant of oil.

And the amount of oil that will accumulate in a structure depends entirely upon how much oil there was in the first place. It has seeped up from the sediments and it may come from a few miles or it may have permeated hundreds of miles to find its way into the top of a vast reservoir. This is the nature of Prudhoe Bay.

But when seismologists find other large structures, no one on earth can say there is oil in them until the bit has told the story, and even then no one can tell the area of the oil field until many bits have told the story and dry holes have hit the water line. The diagram below illustrates, in a general way, what happens.

Genesis Tremendously Important

In a little over one hundred years, man has managed to deplete the earth's crust of most of the distillation of nature. There is no longer any doubt about this to people who know.

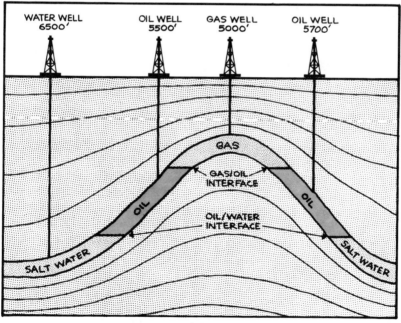

STRUCTURE OF A DOME

We are constantly told that all it takes is drilling a little deeper and it is true that deeper drilling will discover further fields. But, by the very nature of the movement of oil, the tendency has always been to reach as high an elevation as possible. It will always rise until it hits a barrier, usually a layer of shale or slate, or any non-porous rock. Because of this, the largest oil fields, the most prolific, have tended to be those nearer the surface. There are tremendous fields down to 10,000 feet or more, and we will probably run across others deeper than that. But the great majority of the oil, the mass and the bulk of the oil lies at shallower depths.

That's natural to expect because the earth is always in some state of flux. This causes fractures to occur in the rocks. So when such oil-bearing formations are fractured, the oil will rise along fractures until it hits the next porous formation and then it will continue to move up until it hits impervious rock.

Sometimes there is no seal and the oil spills out onto the surface. Sometimes there is a seal but, in time, the surface of the earth has eroded and the oil is released and seeps upward to the surface.

Fort McMurray, Alberta, is a sample of oil from great depths having reached the surface and seeped up into the sands which were the estuary of a great river system. And so the oil has been dissipated and mixed with millions of tons of sand. As time has gone on, the lighter of hydrocarbons, that is the gases, have all moved off into the atmosphere. As time progressed, more of those components moved and the original oil has consequently become thicker. Today at McMurray it is a heavy black, tar-like substance. Extraction of this, the greatest oil field on the face of the earth, is immensely expensive because the sand has to be mined. The sand has to be thrown into great vats and various processes of hot water and steam have been used to extract the oil from the sand. This oil has difficulty competing with conventional oil even when conventional oil sells at $30 to $40 per barrel.

There are huge oil/sand deposits in Venezuela and in Russia. It's all something to fall back upon, but it is no great bonanza for a society that uses oil like water, and where no better care has been given to the most economical ways to produce the oil.

For instance, go back to the illustration of the anticline. In order not to confuse you there, I left out the subject of gas. Now, gas is lighter than oil and it will be found in the top of an anticline. If the oil has been very light, which the highest quality oil always is, the gases and light liquids have risen to the top, and this is called the gas cap. This gas cap is under tremendous pressure and it will push the oil through the boreholes of the penetrating wells with great force. But production has been greatly limited to the pressure available to force the oil up. When the gas is flared − that is, burned into the atmosphere − the power to produce the oil is dissipated, and to the extent that it is dissipated, the oil it would have produced will never be seen although it may remain in rich quantities a mile below the surface.

Turner Valley, Alberta, is an example of an enormous oil field where the gas and the light ends were dissipated. Moving down the anticline from the gas cap, the oil was very light, containing a high percentage of naphtha. And as it was produced, the gas had to be produced with it and the producer simply burned the gas into the atmosphere. Of course, this was long* ago before the true nature of oil fields was known, and before it was generally known that oil was finite; that is to say there is only so much of it, that there will never be more of it, when it is used up it is gone forever.

People have tended to think oil is something like water, that there will always be more. But the great difference is that water is constantly being evaporated from the earth into the atmosphere and then dumped elsewhere on the earth from the clouds and thence evaporated once more then dumped once more. So actually water in its total quantity goes through a process of regurgitation.

So the Turner Valley oil field had to be abandoned when less than 25% of this terribly high-quality oil had been produced.

Some other anticlines were found in the foothills of Alberta but only a few were found to bear petroleum.

The Leduc field which started a search for Devonian oil in Alberta was a reservoir that was made by corals. The oil was contained in the cores of huge coral reefs built up in Devonian times.

The structures that are apt to contain oil are much easier to find than they were 40 years ago. Great improvements in seismic methods have facilitated the accurate mapping of underground structures, even if they are a mile below the surface. Sometimes all the oil of a vast area will find its way into a single huge anticline or stratographic trap.

The stratographic trap is a second kind of structure where the sediments are sloping upward and the oil has accumulated usually in a limestone or sandstone sediment. Like the anticline it has to be sealed on top. The oil has moved upward in the porous rock toward the top seal. As the gases have come off the oil, they occupy the highest part of this trap. When they have made room under great pressure for all of the gas, you find the oil-gas interface. If there was a lot of oil in the first place this oil column might extend several miles.

It might have a thickness of a few feet or it might have a thickness of 100 feet or even more. It all depends on how thick the structure was in the first place but even more on how much available oil there was in the first place. If it was easier to move into this structure than into some others maybe 50 miles away we may find that there are not a lot of oil fields around this structure. We may find that this monstrous oil field has been a depository of all the available oil over a wide area. We do not know or never will know how wide an area.

The giant oil fields of the world have mostly been discovered. The discovery records and the discovery rate all show these facts to be true. We are drilling more and more and finding less and less. Still, some of our biggest fields have been deep. The four giants of the world, the Safaniyah field of Saudi Arabia, discovered in 1951, struck an 18 billion barrel reserve at 5,100 feet; the Iraq Pamaila field, discovered in 1953, struck a 14 billion barrel oil field at 10,800 feet. In Russia, the Sanatorskoye field was discovered in 1965 and hit a reserve of 15.5 billion barrels at 7,300 feet.

The newest giant in the world is Prudhoe Bay, discovered in 1968 at a depth of 8,200 feet and measuring 10 billion barrels of reserves. Producing half a billion barrels a year, and with remaining reserves of 6.5 billion barrels, at the current rate the field would be exhausted in 13 years. Of course, it won't happen that way. In its later years the field will begin to decline and will be producing some oil long after 1997 and its importance as an oil reservoir, however, will be gone. Throughout the land, of course, there have been all different sizes of oil-bearing anticlines, large, small and medium. Mostly only the smaller ones are left. You might call them "pimples." The most promising exploratory territory is offshore along the continental shelves.

* * * * *

I think you can see from the above how it is possible for oil scientists to conclude that the best has been found. And it is no idle guess, it is knowledge from experience. It is knowledge that arrives from the fact that it takes more wildcat footage for every barrel of oil almost every year and there are fewer results for the effort. The average producing well is constantly getting deeper.

So now when you hear some geologist or oil company claim that the world is running out of oil you will not be so inclined to call them prophets of doom. It is a fact. An indisputable fact. We know what reserves there are in the world and we know the rate at which they are being consumed and we can calculate how long this would take.

We do not know how much more oil will be found but we know that it will be very much less than has been found unless we drill terribly increased footages at terribly increased costs, and that must mean a thirst for energy in this industrial society, and a more costly living standard which is to say a lower standard of living.

Man has been riding the clouds for a hundred years. Think of the energy in a gallon of gasoline.

A dozen men might push an automobile a mile in a couple of hours, and then fall down exhausted. A gallon of gasoline weighing less than eight pounds will push that same car 20 miles in 20 minutes. A dozen men would have to labor prodigiously, sweat profusely, strain every muscle to its limits, to lift a ton a hundred feet, but a gallon of gas could lift a ton a hundred feet 20 times, or maybe 40 times, in a few moments — effortlessly. The progress of civilization, the living standard, the fast and ready transportation, are all traceable to the **magic power of petroleum**. We owe most of our progress to a cheap and abundant supply of oil.

In little more than 100 years, man has discovered and nearly exhausted the global supply of this elixir. Now that we can foresee the day of its virtual disappearance, we must find substitutes.

Right now, we have an oil glut. We are not yet aware that, up to now, it has been a case of merely rubbing Aladdin's lamp and producing the genie. The whole world has danced and celebrated on a bonanza of cheap and abundant energy.

In the next 20 years, or less, it will become very apparent that the age of petroleum is nearing exhaustion.

Of course, we will never be completely without oil. My favorite analogy is going in to pick a virgin berry patch. We used to do that in the wilds when I was a boy in Alberta. And when we could find a new one that no one had discovered, we could fill our pails in a few minutes. As we continued to pick, we found that it took a little longer to fill the pails. If we went away and came back in a week or two, we usually found that, by that time, someone else had also discovered the patch. And finally it became so difficult to fill the pails and was so tedious that we had to go elsewhere, although there never was a time you could come back and say we had run out of berries. You could always get a cupful in ten minutes if you wanted to spend the time.

And it will be that way with oil. We will have oil far into the next century, but the quantities will be constantly more expensive and constantly shrinking.

Oil Reserves
(See graph Page 221)

Total oil reserves of the world amount to 670 billion barrels. The non-communist world has 585 billion barrels, and the communist world 85 billion. The chief oil countries are the USSR with 63 billion barrels and China with 19.5 billion barrels.

In the free world, the Middle East has 369 billion barrels. The Western Hemisphere 115 billion barrels. Mexico has the giant's share in the West with 48 billion barrels, while the United States has 30 billion barrels, and Canada 7 billion barrels. Less significant oil areas like Argentina (2.6 billion barrels) make up the balance.

Biggest oil sources in Africa are Libya, 21.5 billion barrels, Nigeria 16.7 billion barrels, Algeria 9.5 billion barrels, Egypt 3.3 billion barrels, and Tunisia 1.9 billion barrels.

The major reserves in the Asia Pacific area are Indonesia 9.5 billion barrels, Malaysia 3.3 billion barrels, India 3.4 billion barrels, and Australia 1.6 billion barrels.

XXI

NEAR TERM FOR OIL

This is the big picture. But the marketplace does not price itself out according to the big picture. They don't get the big picture until it is fully upon them. Silver is running out, too, and we have known it for a dozen years; the marketplace doesn't pay much attention. When supplies get tight they will wake up all of a sudden.

And that's the situation with oil. Currently we have a glut of oil on the market. We have a capacity to produce 12 or 15 million barrels a day more than we are using if we include the demobilized capacity right now in Iraq and Iran.

Unfortunately, this tends to lull us into complacency about the future supply. It is very certain that, for the next few years, the price of $28 per barrel is an unrealistic one. It is arrived at via the OPEC cartel. They erected an artificial structure and cut off the oil to the western world. Since then the following developments have stopped OPEC in its tracks.

Conservation in the western world reduced consumption from 60 million barrels per day (mb/d) to a little over 40 mb/d. Prudhoe Bay in Alaska, and Great Britain's fields in the North Sea came on full steam. Consequently, we were suddenly faced with a glut. Saudi Arabia with the capacity of 12 mb/d — even more — cut down to the neighborhood of 5 or 6 mb/d. We have a huge shut-in capacity at present of at least 10 million barrels daily and there is no evidence of a change in the near future. Peace in Iraq and Iran could yield another 5 mb/d. The price of oil, therefore, is preposterously high.

The following graph shows the increase in price of the average commodity as a result of inflation rated by the

Consumer Price Index. Notice the two commodities most out of line are gold and oil, and oil is far more out of line than gold, having risen about 27 times its 1967 price while gold has risen about 12 times its 1967 price.

AVERAGE ANNUAL PRICES

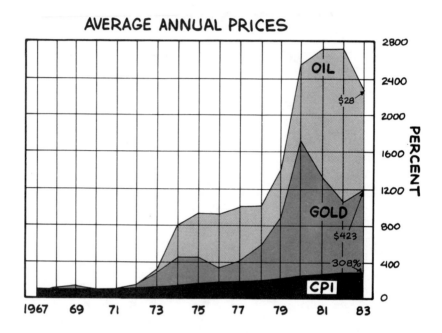

The $28 per barrel price of oil today makes sense like the price of diamonds makes sense. It makes sense when the producer has enough of a monopoly to enforce his price on the world. So it made sense when **OPEC** could dictate the world oil price. Now they produce less than 38% of the needs of the Free World and only 12% of the consumption of the United States. The lion has lost its teeth.

Now it is only a matter of time until the animals of the forest find out that the lion has lost its teeth and begin to treat him with impunity. What held the price of world oil to the $28 level in 1984 was the continuing war between Iran and Iraq and the threat to the Persian Gulf. Even without the normal production of Iran and Iraq, the price of oil was high, but if the war would finish that would draw another 5 million barrels of oil surplus on the market. If they continue their mutual destruction, the world could still wait it out at $28 a barrel.

If the Persian Gulf oil should be cut off, of course, we would see an upward movement of the price of oil company stocks. They might even once again become the darlings of the New York Stock Exchange.

The Near Term Price of Oil

One thing is certain, the present price is wrong. If Persian Gulf production is seriously jeopardized for a lengthy period of time, the price will be higher. If the war is settled in any reasonable time, the price will be lower and much lower.

Without the Persian Gulf hostilities, the price of oil should probably be under $20 per barrel. A serious shootin' war might take it temporarily to $35 a barrel. (Principal oil reserves of the world are shown below.)

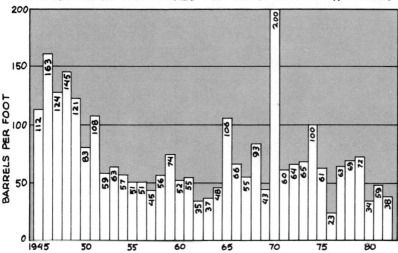

NEW RESERVES DISCOVERED PER EXPLORATORY FT, DRILLED

It would take a rash person to take a gamble on this one. Fooling around with oil company investments is a dangerous game. If you find out that the hostilities have been put into the background, you can sell the oil companies short. If the war escalates, you'll soon be paying more for gasoline and it will put a crimp in the standard of living in the western world. Because of this, an enormous and cooperative effort will eventually be made to quell the military disturbances in the Middle East. It appears that Russia and the United States are both anxious to do that. And that pretty well means it will happen.

221

Probably the most important point to remember from this discussion is that under normal conditions the price of oil would be a good deal less than the present $26.

However, it's important to bear in mind that we are running out of oil gradually and that by the 1990s oil will commence to get the attention of an endangered species and the price will gradually start to rise. By 1995, it will be well known that we have to rely for the bulk of our energy on other sources.

A very careful study by Conoco, Inc., makes the following projections.

Oil's preeminence will fall from its current level of 50% of all non-communist energy to slightly over 40%. That includes an estimated growth of 1% per year in petroleum consumption through the year 2000.

In order to meet this target, the OPEC production will have to be capable of 29 million barrels per day instead of the 18 million barrels per day of the present, and that supposes that the U.S. oil demand will only increase by 1/2 of 1% per year from today's 15 million barrels daily, and its production would fall from 8.7 mb/d in 1984 to 7 mb/d in the year 2000.

That means substantially increased dependence on imported oil. Today we buy 4 million barrels daily from abroad. That will have to jump to 7.5 million barrels daily by the year 2000. Imports are anticipated at slightly in excess of one-third of the U.S. demand.

There is doubt in some quarters that all this is going to come about as projected. The non-communist world is using 45 million barrels per day. That's all being drawn from established reserves. The preceding graph illustrates how the discovery rate is falling, as compared to our return per exploratory foot prior to 1950. Oil is getting scarcer and to find a given amount is continually requiring increased effort. This will go on. It would be foolhardy to suggest a price for the year 2000. But for the present, one thing is certain: the current price of oil is much too high.

Summary

The graph on Page 220 shows that the overall average commodity price has increased 300% since 1967. Gold has gone up dramatically. That is an increase of 1208% since 1967. But oil's increase stands at 2240% of its 1967 price.

The investor must therefore keep two situations in mind. In the long term, reserves of oil will be more important and more costly than they are today. In a few years it will be apparent around the world that the oil supply is petering out. In the meantime, we have a glut of oil and this is likely to last for a few years. Predicated on the near term, the price of $28 a barrel is much too high. Also, the advent of Mexico on the world scene, together with the oil giant at Prudhoe Bay, has weakened the power of OPEC to the point where it now produces more like one-third of the world's oil, and Saudi Arabia alone has to keep in shut-in capacity of at least 7 mb/d in order not to flood the markets.

How these conflicting assessments will work out in the marketplace is a complication that makes oil investments risky. All future events in the world of oil must be evaluated against this background: short-term oil glut, long-term shortage of increasing severity as the years pass.

It's fair to say that it's only a question of a decade or two until we must satisfy most of our energy needs by other means.

The termination of the Age of Petroleum will produce a **ROLLOVER** *in the world, the results of which are quite impossible to foresee. A lot will depend on what we use for a substitute and how we are able to harness it.*

XXII

THIS DOG WON'T HUNT

In the late 1970s, nuclear energy was the shining hope for the future. As the world's oil reserves ran down, they would gradually be replaced by almost unlimited nuclear sources. Plants were planned and commissioned with great expectations. Then the whole dream collapsed.

It started with the accident at Three Mile Island where, for a time, a disastrous meltdown was feared and none of the experts knew what to do about it. By a hair, we escaped a horror that would have killed and maimed more people than the total industrial accidents of all time. A meltdown of the core could have resulted in masses of cloud formations – clouds of death loaded with nuclear fallout and the precipitation of nuclear droplets over an intensely populated area. But the fallout from Three Mile Island went much further than its nuclear components. It brought the industry to a standstill and it uncovered two fatal flaws, each one of which by itself was enough to kill the nuclear dream. The flaws were WHOLLY UNACCEPTABLE COST AND UNACCEPTABLE RISKS.

Nuclear power was more expensive than any other kind of power, so high in fact that in many cases it was prohibitive; so bad that billion-dollar losses resulted in the form of the abandoned, partially completed plants scattered across the country.

The other flaw was the virtual impossibility of safely handling the waste from the operating plants and the insoluble conundrum of what to do with the atomic corpses – that is, the operating plants when they die. And the answers to these questions are no nearer than in the beginning. Some cling to the hope of nuclear power still, but we'd be better off if we abandoned every unfinished plant and never built another. And we may be close to that now. Here are the factors that prohibit the growth of nuclear power as a meaningful component in the energy of the future.

Delay of Years
Overruns
Uncertain Interest Payments
Per-Kilowatt Cost

*   *   *   *

My disillusionment with nuclear power happened in about five minutes back in 1977. While leafing through the Los Angeles Times I was brought up short by a story entitled "PILOT NUCLEAR PLANT BEING DISMANTLED." I'll paraphrase the story. Read it against the background knowledge that the towers of **modern** plants are 500 feet high. Here's the story:

It's like a tall silo, 30 feet high, buried in the ground. Its walls are 5 inches of steel and around this steel is 5 feet of concrete. The inside of this silo is so radioactive that if a man were to jump in, he would be burned to death in seconds. So it is filled with water.

But it has to be dismantled. It cost $13 million to build in the 1950s. It will take $6 million and two years to get rid of it only **temporarily**.

A huge machine has bared the upper portions of the silo and by **remote control** with a powerful torch, it is cutting out pieces of steel about 4 feet square. No one dare approach the demolition. Even the crane that is being used by remote control will have to be cut up into pieces and disposed of like the nuclear reactor itself. The temporary expedient will be to immerse every piece in a lot of water and then take the water away. The water can later be evaporated, but then no one is quite sure where to bury the deadly remains. The radioactivity will last for thousands of years.

NUCLEAR PLANTS DIE. That had never occurred to me before. Suddenly, I began to envision the number of great cranes and huge saws that would be needed to slice up a full-fledged nuclear plant. If it would cost half the original construction price just to cut this pigmy into parcels, what would it cost to cut up a regular commercial plant when the core died? How many enormous cranes would be processed? Where would you build such a big pool of water as to contain this plant? What would you do with the trucks? Would you have to throw them in the water, too, after the massive chunks had been disposed of? And then how many other implements would you need to saw up the cranes that had been used on the job and also throw those chunks into the water? And then what? Forever?

The process described above will be the fate of every worn-out nuclear plant in the United States. There are 81 plants. They will all wear out. Each one of them carries with it a death sentence reaching into the centuries.

What's worse, it's not even known if the big plants today could be disposed of at all. They are at least 100 times larger than the pigmy. Their walls are so thick and so high that there is no technology known to man which could adequately slice them into chunks for interment — **even if a burial ground existed**.

One suggestion is simply to weld the whole thing shut with heavy steel and put guards around it for a hundred years until some of the radioactivity has worn off. Actually, that's no answer at all. Another suggested answer is to bury the whole thing. But nobody knows how this could be done. It had been a possibility until recently, for it had been thought after a few hundred years the plant would be safe enough if buried. But now there is reason to believe that it would not be safe for several thousand years, and radioactivity would continue to seep out of the earth into the atmosphere. One isotope, Nickel-59, which is produced in the reactors, would require 100,000 years to decay. Carbon-14 would require 65,000 years.

Immediately prior to reading this eye-opener, in MFE of October 13, 1977, I had recommended the purchase of uranium. I fully thought it would be the world energy replacement for oil. Now, almost immediately afterward, I was hit with the concept of immense nuclear corpses — deadly and eternal. My MFE of November 4, 1977 was headlined **NUCLEAR PLANTS ARE DYING — GENETICS OF ETERNAL DEATH — URANIUM — NOT A SALVATION — BUT A DAMNATION!**

The news of the demolition of that 30-foot silo prompted me to write in the next MFE, November 4, 1977:

> "My recommendation of the purchase of uranium mining stocks was naive. The disposal of nuclear reactor plants, when worn out, came as a **surprise** to me. When you think of the great numbers of plants constructed on the huge scale of today, you can see clearly that if nuclear power is going to be a good investment, no investment in

the world will matter; there won't be a world — for us to know.

"So the investment advice as far as uranium is concerned is hereby not only withdrawn but reversed."

I believe MFE subscribers all cleared out of uranium investments around that time or soon after.

We have never touched a uranium or nuclear investment since or any utility that relied upon nuclear power.

The true facts about nuclear power only evolved gradually over the next two or three years, and that recommendation saved MFE subscribers a lot of money.

The sad fact is that even today the government does not face the full realization of this CURSE that has been brought on mankind.

Most amazing of all is the fact that no one seems to have bothered to add the dismantlement cost to the construction cost. I don't know of any laws that assign a responsibility for dismantlement when the plant dies, or any laws as to how dismantlement is to be carried out or even a suggestion as to where the burial ground will be. But we have been told that Three Mile Island may never operate again, and it might cost $1 billion to wrap it up if it doesn't.

Without reckoning burial or destruction costs (methods unknown), the London Financial Times gives this scale in reckoning electric power generation costs:

Uranium 40 Coal 20 Oil 15

But even in ignorance of these hidden costs, growing uncertainty about waste disposal has begun to paralyze the industry. Since 1974, orders for nearly 200 nuclear stations have been canceled or postponed. In 1978 only two new orders were announced.

Worldwide, more than 20 nations have installed them. The United States has 81 plants in operation and 48 in progress.

It's hard to believe that people, who are not insane, could go on with this without having a remote idea as to how to handle the Frankenstein when it's all over.

It's kind of like a cat starting up a 100-foot pole. Not knowing how to get down, he keeps on climbing. If, at the top, no one rescues him, he's a dead cat. As we build more plants, we climb higher on the nuclear pole. We assume, in each case, that in 30 years someone will know how to rescue us.

But the atom is the stuff of CREATION, and when it is split, man may never be able to destroy the results.

Still our government leaders urge us up the pole.

227

From the London Financial Times: "The French Government has said unequivocally that the accident will not impede its own plans to continue ordering 5,000 MW of PWR capacity a year, to apply one half of its electricity by 1985."

In the United States, James Schlesinger said: "We have no alternative if we are going to maintain energy production. . ."

How readily we lay our unsolvable problems at the doorsteps of our children and grandchildren!

Overall Nuclear Waste

Quite apart from the dismantlement and burial costs of these massive nuclear corpses is the unremitting and ongoing waste generated by their operation during their lifetime. Currently the operational waste is accumulating in great pools of water which are building up fast. And now the problem is, what do you do with the water?

Demonstrating the impoverishment in the way of practical solutions, listen to this Buck Rogers scheme. It was published in the **South African Weekly** March 1971, entitled *HIGH- FLYING RUBBISH*:

"A West German engineer has come up with a high-flying idea to get rid of nuclear waste. He says dangerous atomic rubbish should be rocketed into space.

"Dietrich Koelle, of the giant arms firm Messerschmitt—Boelkow—Blohm, in Munich, says that by 1990 West German nuclear power plants will be producing $4500M^3$ of highly radio active waste each year.

"Because no one one wants a nuclear 'dump' near his home, regardless of stringent safety measures, the best way to dispose of the stuff would be to shoot it right out of our solar system.

"Koelle is currently working on a study that foresees returnable, re-usable transporters unloading smaller, waste-packed rockets in space and then turning for home.

"The small rockets would carry lead-sealed containers each holding up to 30 tons of waste to a point close to the planet Jupiter before unloading them in turn and 'boomeranging' back for a soft landing on earth.

"Jupiter would then take over and boost the containers out of our solar system into free space on a journey that would last several thousand years before they hit anything.

" 'But by then the waste would have lost its radioactivity,' says Koelle. 'The containers would be no more dangerous than meteorites of the same size.' "

Glass Encasement Scheme

I have had a great deal of criticism for my stand against nuclear power. Recently someone wrote me that it had all been solved by burying waste enclosed in a new type of glass that soaks up surrounding water like a sponge. Well, we can wisely bring a little geology into that, too.

Nuclear burial grounds are most apt to be tucked away far from populations, if for no other reason than that populations won't stand for them. The result is the burials are most likely to take place in remote mountains, **which are exactly the most prone to earth movements.** Glass may not let the poisonous fluid out, but earth movements can crush the glass with impunity.

For the glass method to work, the cemeteries would have to be in areas of known quiescence. We would have to be confident that these areas would remain quiescent for tens of thousands of years. Only there could we dump our glass-enclosed wastes and glass-enclosed chunks of concrete lead and diced automatic cranes which had been used to cut these plants into pieces. Deep, deep ocean is suggested. There again we're uncertain. The whole world is uncomfortable with that.

The Gold Encasement Scheme

A scientist of considerable stature comes up with the following solution:

"Nuclear wastes can be stored safely by only one method. **Canisters buried 600 feet enclosed in steel and encased in gold.**

"Goesta Wranglen, foremost corrosion expert in Sweden, professor at the Royal Institute of Technology, Stockholm, president of the International Society of Electro-chemistry, categorically states that the most intricate plan yet devised to hold nuclear wastes is unsafe. The plan is this. Solidification of the nuclear wastes in glass; the glass encased in a welded steel cylinder; the steel enclosed in copper. The canisters to be buried in a hole to be dug 500 feet deep. The Commission admits that the radioactivity would begin to escape in 100,000 years. Wranglen says: 'No good.'

"Even though the ground water is stagnant at that level under normal conditions, the radiation emanating from the canister would heat the ground water to a temperature of around 100 to 150 degrees centigrade. This would cause it to rise to ground level. Radiation would increase the oxygen content much higher than ordinary hot water. Localized corrosion under these conditions can easily occur in even stagnant water – possibly even in a few months. Wranglen warns that the radiation would begin to arise to the earth's surface at the very best in 100 years – might even become very dangerous in 10 years. The answer?

"Gold is the only material which will withstand the attack of radiolysis in surrounding water over thousands of years, resisting all corrosion.

" 'It may seem drastic,' says Wranglen, 'to recommend encapsulating the canisters in pure gold – but only the best in this case is good enough.' He readily admitted great quantities of gold would be required."

The Naked Truth – No Known Answer

A few years ago, Time Magazine presented some serious food for thought to the general public.

"Still unsettled–and unsettling– is the question of how the United States can safely dispose of garbage from nuclear operations. Spent fuel and other wastes remain radioactive for thousands of years. At present a lot of such waste is stored under water in 'swimming pools' at plant sites, but nuclear plants are running out of pool space. Some may have to be shut down as early at 1983 unless a more permanent method of disposal is found." (Nuclear plants are built to operate for about 30 to 35 years.)

The state of Washington somehow got itself picked as a cemetery for much of this waste and, in time, the name Hanford, Washington, may become much better known than Seattle. Washington residents were chilled to read the following in the Spokane Spokesman-Review about five years ago. It was news to them. By now, they seem to have forgotten it. But here it is as they gave it. The problem hasn't moved an inch:

"The problem of what to do with nuclear waste remains unsolved, much to the consternation of the people in Eastern Washington where 70% of the nation's nuclear garbage is stored. A news dispatch from Olympia, Washington, says that 47 million gallons of high-level radioactive wastes are stored in a 570 square mile reservation at Hanford.

"They are staying there and accumulating there because first of all no one knows where to move them. Secondly, no one knows how to move them.

"Frank Standerfer, U.S. Department of Energy, said officials are not sure it will be feasible to move the wastes.

The extracting, processing and shipping will cost billions of dollars. The crews could be exposed to the radioactivity, and some of it might be released into the environment. He says the decisions will be postponed at least until the mid-1980s.

"Meanwhile the greatest concern is the storage tanks. In 1973 one of the tanks began leaking and the dangerous waste seeped 90 feet underground, within 115 feet of the water table. Had it reached the water table, the results could have been disastrous in many areas. After that they started making double steel-wall tanks encased in jackets of concrete."

Hanford may be stuck.

Stuff of Creation

The following is reprinted from an issue of MFE in 1977 and remains up to date:

"While the plants are in operation, they discharge rods of spent fuel. These spent rods contain plutonium. As a waste product they are absolute dynamite.

"At a congressional hearing in mid-October, it was revealed that there is even now **a tremendous backlog of spent fuel**. The utilities are starting to run out of storage space for the discharged fuel from some 67 operating nuclear reactors. What they are doing now is removing the spent rods and simply dumping them in water. That, of course, is the most temporary end solution. Congress learned that there was some 3,000 tons of this highly potent garbage at the end of 1976. **It is estimated that by the end of 1983 there will be 13,000 tons of virtual black death.**"

Now that it's 1984, nobody talks about it. Certainly, the utility industry is in no hurry to make any news announcements about the brim-full pools of water without a place to go.

Nobody has yet dared figure out what the problem will be by the year 2000 — or what can be done about the rising accumulations of all that deadly water.

"There are no volunteers among the communities of the various 48 states to be host to the waste. The best they've come up with is that the spent fuel will be buried in underground geologic formations.

"That makes it a little fancier when you say 'geologic formations.' Of course it's geologic formations. What else is at depth underground?

"James Schlesinger says that probably all of this fuel will

have to be 'reprocessed' to solve the problem of waste. The only thing is no one knows just how to reprocess.

"The atom is the stuff of the creation of the universe. We have broken the atoms apart. The spent remains are not apt to disappear harmlessly."

*　　　*　　　*　　　*

There is always the happy possibility that we will someday develop clean nuclear energy, or learn how to harness effectively the power of the sun. These are a long time away, and will only be possible then with an enormous commitment of money for research. For the present, the Three Mile Island accident may prove to be the blessing of the nuclear age. It has alerted and alarmed the world. Yet the world's politicians take these inexplicable positions – that construction of nuclear plants must go on, no matter what. And that is in spite of the unthinkable – a meltdown.

Our only real and practical salvation lies in coal. Only coal affords us the chance for independent survival. It is plentiful in China, Russia, Western Europe and especially in the United States. Are we prepared to spend what it costs to do it now?

"Meltdown" – a Volcano in Reverse

Even before the accident at Three Mile Island in April, 1979, contracts for new nuclear plants had dived. Without talking about it in public, the experts had begun to realize the danger of the accumulating wastes and the lack of any solution as to what they would do with the dead plants 30 to 35 years after their birth. The close scrape with "meltdown" at Three Mile Island dramatized the potential for disaster that lies latent in every nuclear plant. It may be most unlikely, but Three Mile Island proved that it **could** happen. Only good luck saved scores of thousands from death and perhaps millions from atomic pollution. Thus a fourth factor was added to the case against atomic plants. The disadvantages are these:

1. Ruinous cost overruns making nuclear power uneconomical.

2. The problem of disposal of unending accumulation of wastes.

3. The problem of disposal of dead plants.

4. The danger of meltdown.

"Meltdown could be disaster." That's as much as our press coverage, the government, and the Nuclear Regulatory Commission have told us. The real meaning of meltdown is beyond anyone's visualization. To understand as much as possible we need to consider the volcano.

The volcano erupts as a result of heat rising from below. The meltdown eruption would result from heat **sinking** deeper and deeper into the earth's crust.

Simply described, volcanoes happen when molten rock at temperatures of 1800 to 2700 degrees Celsius, rises surfaceward encountering water in sub-surface formations. Phenomenal pressures (8000 lbs. psi) build as the molten magma rises. Super-heated steam produces the explosion that propels the earth's crust skyward. The gaping hole which results then becomes a funnel for the magma which bursts above the surface of the earth, sometimes in great waves. As it solidifies when falling, it may build a cone or mountain, as the excess lava flows down the sides.

This of course all follows the steam. The huge avalanche of clouds is comprised of the volcanic gases, which are however about 98% water. Nevertheless they carry with them, in the case of a volcano, fantastic amounts of solid material reduced to ash. (In 1902 such a cloud traveling at an enormous speed covered the French island of Martinique, wiping out the 30,000 inhabitants of St. Pierre in a matter of seconds. This ash naturally carried no radioactivity.)

To keep ourselves rational, we ought to recognize that this was unusual; the greatest steam phenomenon in history. I use it to illustrate the principle of how a volcano operates. A great deal depends on the amount of ground water which the rising magma encounters, and at what depth such water is encountered.

Meltdown reverses the volcanic process and its results are therefore largely conjectural. However, there are a number of certainties. None of them are nice.

The meltdown means that the nuclear heat which was to have been drawn over the course of 30 years, to satisfy needs for electric power, is suddenly concentrated in an uncontrollable mass sinking into the earth, like a red hot coal sinks into a snow drift.

The faster this core sinks into the water table, the more water rushes from the sides into the hole, falling downward to encounter the rising super-heated steam, being flung hundreds of feet into the atmosphere. All of this steam carries the radioactivity from the sinking nuclear core.

Try to imagine a hole — for example, 10 feet in diameter — descending into the earth, unstoppable. The water table extends for endless miles on all sides of the hole, and the deeper the hole gets, the more water rushes into the hole because of the increasing length of the bore hole admitting it.

The supply of water to make steam is all but infinite. The only limiting factor is the final exhaustion of the nuclear core. How deep would it go? How big would those clouds be? How far would they extend? No one can remotely guess.

Ground water and waterbearing formations to 20,000 feet leave me to conclude that billions of gallons of water would be converted into a continuously increasing jet of steam, decreasing only as the core finally became overwhelmed with descending or ascending water. I have no way even to guess the mass of such clouds. But the rising cloud of steam would never stop until the core was dead and could heat no more.

The rising steam would unavoidably — under such great pressure — pick up some of the earth's crust (in the manner of a volcano) as it erupted and drop these materials indiscriminately as the clouds of steam moved on.

No one can really know how much solid radioactive material would thus be scattered over the countryside, rivers, cities, oceans. But even if no solid material erupted with the steam, the steam itself would become condensed and would descend in droplets over hundreds or perhaps thousands of miles.

Much would depend on the nature of the geologic formations below the plant, a thick and porous and therefore profuse water table, or a thin water table, and whether near the surface or deep. In Spokane, Washington, the whole city is supplied by wells at depths of over 1,000 feet. Palm Springs, California, is supplied by wells of even greater depth.

But the surface water does not limit the conversion of the meltdown core into steam. There is no vacuum in nature. Sedimentary beds are all porous, some more than others. When oil wells are called dry, they are not really dry. They are dry as far as oil is concerned. But when they are tested they often flow salt water.

The earth's temperature increases about 2 degrees per hundred feet. So at 1,000 feet it increases 20 degrees and at 10,000 feet — 200 degrees. The increase in temperature is less important than the increase in the pressure. When the melted hole reaches 2,000, 3,000 or 20,000 feet, as it certainly would unless it had been exhausted at shallower depths — it would be sure somewhere to encounter the salt water of the deep sediments.

The deeper the hole became, the more water would rush in, to be expelled violently through the flume upwards to the surface made by the descent of the melting core.

The point I make is that one should not in such an event be comforted by assurances from authorities that the ground water table was thin, and that the danger would soon be over. The melting core could not be exhausted until its heat had been spent.

We are told by government, the utility companies, and zealous nuclear scientists: "What the hell — you have to take **some** chances!"

Yes, but you don't have to take this kind of chance.

Maybe you live next door to a gas plant, or to an oil-fired boiler, or to a refinery. You take **some** chance. There could be an accident, or fire. When we talk about a meltdown in a nuclear plant, chance is hardly the word. We are talking about an unimaginable disaster — if it should ever happen.

No one can stop a volcano. No combination of experts could stop the descent of the core. Nothing in God's world could stop the resulting steam — nor the primordial power of its thrust.

No accident may ever happen. But if you get enough nuclear plants — and we now know such an accident CAN happen — then we may conclude that sooner or later there's very high risk of a meltdown somewhere. **Then the world would demand the closure of all plants — at a time when our dependence on them would have become fatal.**

It narrows down to this — we are not taking a chance, we are taking a certainty. Ultimately, that certainty may not affect us directly. It may reflect on us indirectly, remotely, instantly, or not at all. We do know we are tempting fate. When fate is tempted enough it will respond. Ten years, 10 months, 10 days. **It will happen!**

The nuclear champions have hinted that Three Mile Island may have been sabotaged by an anti-nuclear group to fuel their campaign dramatically.

This is no defense at all. It is the scariest thing I have heard. If the anti-nuclear group could bring about conditions threatening a meltdown, then why couldn't any other saboteur? **What these people are really saying is that nuclear plants are subject to sabotage and to terrorists.**

Who wants to take the responsibility for the lives of perhaps an entire city by the comforting assurance that **sabotage** is difficult and "most unlikely"! But that's the best assurance we can get.

The fact to remember is this: For a time the Three Mile Island reactor was completely out of control. Technicians were baffled, dumbfounded and helpless.

Now the nuclear proponents are asking: *"What are you kicking about – it didn't happen"!*

That's Russian roulette. How often can you win?

Sabotage

Recently, I came across the following newspaper story:

"(AP) – The FBI is investigating what might be the first case of attempted sabotage at a U.S. nuclear power plant, an official of Virginia Electric Power Company said.

"Inspectors discovered that a caustic white crystalline substance had been dumped into 62 of 64 new, non-radioactive fuel elements stored for use later.

"Luckily the fuel elements were not damaged, but we have to conclude that was more the result of the naivete of the possible saboteurs than of good management.

"The company's vice president said: *'We are told we have the best security system of any nuclear plant in the country.' "*

For the best, this isn't much comfort.

Implicit in the existence of all nuclear plants is their vulnerability to sabotage, mechanical failure, human error and outright negligence. The more plants there are, the sooner the first accident will happen. Then what do you do with the existing plants when the world public rebels? How do you get rid of them, when to destroy them is in itself dangerous?

*   *   *   *

An Industry in Disarray

Here's a June 1984 update by John Myers of MFE on the condition of the nuclear industry.

NUCLEAR INDUSTRY LEADS UTILITIES DOWN
FINANCIAL DISASTERS PROLIFERATE

"Not only is nuclear power finished, but it may drag participating utilities down with it. Reagan's China deal which would permit Westinghouse, General Electric and Combustion Engineering to build a total of 10 plants over the next 15 years, may look good on the surface, but it sits against a nuclear background that seems to worsen year by year and even month by month.

"The great nuclear hope of a dozen years ago has wilted on the vine; a hundred plants worth an estimated $15 billion have been canceled. Nuclear experts expect this figure to hit $40 billion by the end of the decade.

"But the real problems are not with the canceled plants as much as with those in progress. The utility companies are in up to their necks. **Currently 50 utilities are trying to bring on line some 40 nuclear plants. That represents about an $80 billion investment for the utility sector which only has $100 billion equity. New commitments could rise $45 billion by 1987; or to 150% of the industry's total equity!**

"The problems and failures keep rolling in.

"In Ohio, Cleveland Electric Illuminating Co. recently announced that it may cancel its 43% completed Nuclear Unit 2. The reasons: cost overruns, and difficult financing.

"In Michigan, state officials are trying to convince Consumers Power Company to abandon its Midland nuclear project. CPC has already invested **$3.4 billion** into the project which holds two partially completed reactors. The state wants to cancel the project because of a surplus of energy.

"Consumers Power, the driving force behind the plants, is spending $50 million a month on the project, and is expected to run out of funds by mid-summer. At best Consumers can only hope to complete one of the plants, cancel the other, charge off $1.11 billion in costs and raise electricity rates by more than 60% in the next six years.

"A multi-billion dollar loser is shaping up in New Hampshire, where the Public Service Company, which is now fighting off bankruptcy, has suspended payments on the construction of its Seabrook nuclear project. PSC, which holds a 35.6% stake in Seabrook, has laid off 5,200 of the 6,200 workers at Unit 1. Other participating utilities are fighting to keep Unit 2 on track, but financing is very uncertain. The project has already cost $3.5 billion, with an estimated $2.8 billion more needed just to finish Unit 1.

"All this distress follows the Washington Public Power Supply System's May, 1983 default on $2.25 billion on bonds after its cancellation of plants No. 4 and No. 5. In many respects **WPPSS**, or 'Whoops,' typifies the problems facing nuclear power. Original estimates of $4 billion for the five-plant project grew to $22 billion at latest estimate.

"Unit No. 2, the sole survivor of the project, only began to produce electricity in mid-1984. Total cost for the unit — $3.2 billion or six times more than the original estimate.

"Conditions are, in fact, so bad that uncompleted nuclear plants are actually being converted to coal! Said one nuclear spokesman, 'It's like trying to take a 747 jetliner and putting internal combustion engines in it.'

"Austin, Texas, proposed the conversion plan after trying to sell its 16% stake in the nuclear project. Two of the plants were to have been completed in 1980 and 1982 at a cost of $1 billion. Today the first unit is less than half complete while the second is about a third complete and total cost is estimated at $4.5 billion, 350% above the original estimate.

"The Texas proposal comes after Cincinnati Gas & Electric Co. and its two partners announced plans to convert its 97% complete Zimmer nuclear power project to coal. Their decision came after years of delay and more than 400% in cost overruns which totaled $1.7 billion.

"Bailout by even billions of foreign contracts seems unlikely.

"But regardless of what happens internationally, the U.S. utility sector is in sad shape. Unanticipated conservation and big spending have sent the utilities reeling. According to Business Week (May 21), 'There is more bad news yet to come – and that may well include some Chapter 11 bankruptcies.'

"Douglas C. Bauer, senior vice president for EEI, is more ominous in his assessment. 'The U.S. electric industry is in the midst of its greatest historical transition.' He and others argue that the risks involved in a large nuclear plant are too big for any one company to sustain.

"The net investment result will be a general retardation of the utilities along with weakening bond prices, as higher interest rates are used to attract much-needed capital."

In the beginning, I said "This dog won't hunt." And it is in his chromosomes and in his genes that he won't hunt – never hunt. In time, an accident like Three Mile Island – due to sabotage, failure of parts, or human error – will come to its conclusion. A global furor is likely to close all atomic plants and result in a huge energy crisis. One that will make the 1973 and 1978 shocks seem mild.

Although the public in the United States has almost put a stop to the construction of new plants, the plants already in existence will probably have to keep going. To stop the nuclear plants around Chicago would cut off half the electricity. Much the same applies to New England and parts of the southeastern United States. A city like Chicago would cease to exist as an organized community.

Nevertheless the brakes will be put on the nuclear industry's future throughout the United States. Yet there is a solution to the energy problem, and it lies right at our feet.

XXIII

ROLLOVER ON COAL

Coal used to be the main source of power, heat, and light. It fueled our factories, our transportation, our homes. The general use of petroleum, begun less than 100 years ago, pushed coal into the background. But the New Boy's polish is gone, and coal re-emerges as the principal source of energy for the 21st century.

The abundance of coal and the future of coal is a little-realized fact. Coal's bad image as a pollutant has, by bad press, become ingrained. Few realize that coal represents our energy salvation for the next several decades at least. Nuclear power will be dead. Oil will be exhausted. Solar, wind and thermal energy will be subsidiary helpers. But none of them alone or combined could anywhere nearly satisfy our energy demands. And without satisfaction of those energy demands our society would drop back maybe as far as the Middle Ages. The great secret of our advanced social order has been the abundance of our energy. If we have to go back to what our muscles will do we are looking on pretty primitive times. Perhaps coal can do it all and with the development of new processes now for removing the sulfur, "clean coal" will become commonplace in a decade. With our enormous, almost unimaginable resources of coal, energy may become once again as cheap as it was when petroleum was in its heyday.

There are just a few facts that give coal a stature not yet even imagined by the general public who will be using it, or using the electric power derived from it. These blockbuster facts are as follow:

Coal resources are virtually unlimited. A ton of coal contains the energy equivalent of four barrels of oil. The available U.S. coal amounts to the energy equivalent of 900 billion barrels of oil.

Coal in the United States alone far surpasses the total energy of all the oil in the world.

The coal energy in the United States amounts to more than five times the total oil energy in Saudi Arabia.

Coal is cheaper. A ton of coal, on the average, may cost $30 more or less. Its equivalent, which is four barrels of oil, costs $112. There's more than enough margin to handle the extra processing of coal necessary for "clean burning."

Coal is scattered generously around the world, including huge quantities in China, the Soviet Union and Australia. It's also abundant in parts of Europe, Canada, and various countries throughout the world.

Coal is safe from any cartel; there's too much of it and it's too widely distributed.

The technology for the "clean burning" of coal is already here. Its position as a plausible source for large quantities of liquid petroleum is already established. First, on a commercial basis in Germany during World War II, it supplied the German war machine with more than half of its gasoline. Currently, petroleum from coal is very high on the agenda in South Africa. The technology in use there could see South Africa through a petroleum blackout, if necessary.

The greatest objection about coal is something altogether different, not pollution, cost, transportation, or distribution. The danger posed by coal is the same as that posed by petroleum, they affect the climate of the world. It is reckoned that the carbon dioxide in the atmosphere has increased by about 15% in 100 years. No one knows at what point the accumulating carbon dioxide would change the world's climate but we do know that it would change. It is a very dangerous limit to toy with. Once the climate is changed, there will never be a way to get the carbon dioxide out of the earth's atmosphere again. Studies on this subject are continuing, but it may be a long time before we have specific answers. As the years go by, we are more and more vulnerable to an irreversible change that could make human habitation on this planet much more difficult.

We have this danger whether we use oil or coal or natural gas — any of the fossil fuels. The cleanest power in any kind of volume is hydroelectric where we harness the power of moving

241

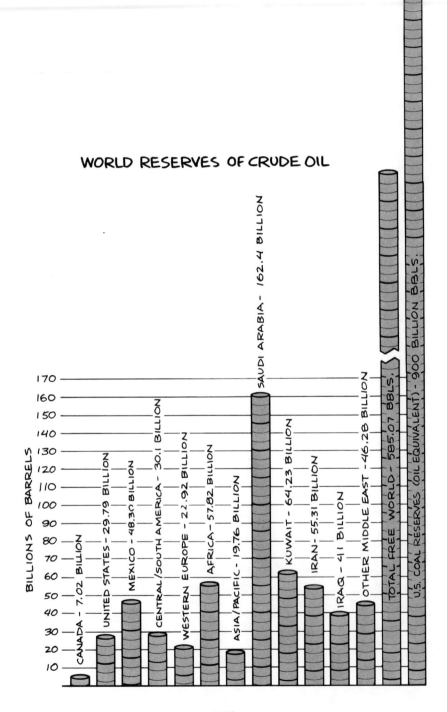

WORLD RESERVES OF CRUDE OIL

BILLIONS OF BARRELS

CANADA - 7.02 BILLION
UNITED STATES - 29.79 BILLION
MEXICO - 48.30 BILLION
CENTRAL/SOUTH AMERICA - 30.1 BILLION
WESTERN EUROPE - 22.92 BILLION
AFRICA - 57.82 BILLION
ASIA/PACIFIC - 19.76 BILLION
SAUDI ARABIA - 162.4 BILLION
KUWAIT - 64.23 BILLION
IRAN - 55.31 BILLION
IRAQ - 41 BILLION
OTHER MIDDLE EAST - 46.28 BILLION
TOTAL FREE WORLD - 585.07 BBLS.
U.S. COAL RESERVES (OIL EQUIVALENT) - 900 BILLION BBLS.

water. That supplies only about 5% of our electrical needs. For the foreseeable future into the 21st century, we will have to rely on the fossil fuels. And as the 21st century is ushered in, we will rely more and more on coal and less and less on oil. There is no question in the long view that the petroleum stored in the earth's crust has been largely tapped.

*   *   *   *

To get a quick picture of where we stand at present, please refer to the graph on Page 242. This shows you the oil reserves of the various countries of the world, and then the last column shows you the oil equivalent of the available coal in the United States. Now if this coal reserve graph were extended according to the scale, it would be 30 inches high, 20 inches off the page. (See graph.)

So we do have a comforting conclusion. We will not run out of energy. When the flow of oil dwindles, the flow of coal-generated electricity will increase. We have ample usable reserves of fossil energy — especially coal — to last us some hundreds of years.

We have a short-term danger in the fact that enlarged hostilities in the Middle East could foreseeably cut off the flow of Middle East oil — at least for a limited time. If that happened, many countries would immediately find themselves in a very serious position. Japan, for example, has practically no energy of its own. Western Europe is highly dependent (40%) on Middle East oil, and the North Sea oil will be well on its way to exhaustion in another 10 to 15 years. All we have to do to remedy that problem is to proceed at a faster pace with the industrialization of the petroleum-making process from feedstocks of coal.

*   *   *   *

As for the other possible sources of energy, the talk is heavy in proportion to the performance.

You must consider that when you have admitted we are nearing the end of the petroleum phase of our economy, and when you have understood that nuclear wastes, at this stage in our technology, are impossible to live with, you have to come down by deduction to the fact that only one fuel can move us from the end of the present century into the early decades of the 21st century. We would hope that by then there could be a technological breakthrough either in solar power, nuclear fission, or some as yet unimaginable way to handle atomic waste. Meanwhile here is a quick look at our other alternatives.

243

Canada Oil Sands

A lot of oil here; 220 billion barrels classed as available, more than Saudi Arabia; including deposits at depth — a trillion barrels or more.

The product, though, is a heavy tar-like substance. Actually the oil sands can be considered a mineral deposit; 85% sand by volume, 90% sand by weight.

We must mine about two tons of residue for every barrel of oil.

To get one million barrels of oil a day, we must dredge, heat and treat two million tons of sand. And we have an additional problem:

The treated sand takes up more space than the compacted sand we mined. Where are we going to put this extra sand as time goes on, and as we mine billions of tons of sand? The disposal problem in itself is incredible.

Also imagine the number of bulldozers it will take to mine two million tons — 100,000 — tons every hour of a 20-hour day. How long would it take and how much would it cost to make the machinery? That's for one million barrels of oil daily. If the United States were to continue to supply half its pretroleum needs (which it won't) we still need to mine enough for 10 million barrels of oil a day — or nearly one million tons of sand every hour — 17,000 tons of sand a minute.

A nine-company effort planned to produce 140,000 barrels daily by 1986 and cost $5 billion, no doubt underestimated. Then came the oil glut and now we would be lucky to see any important commercial oil at all by 1986, let alone 140,000 barrels per day. The Alaska pipeline alone delivers over a million barrels per day — 5% of U.S. needs, so you can see how unimportant the oil sands are. They offer no real answer at all. Neither do the huge oil sands deposits of Venezuela or Russia or anywhere else; or the oil shales of Colorado.

Compared to coal, oil sands are a poor source. When you mine a ton of coal, you get a ton (less ash) of concentrated energy. The sulphur can be scrubbed out and even sold. The carbon dioxide gas can be piped into existing but badly depleted oil fields to raise gas pressure to raise more oil to the surface; or it can be injected into countless exhausted natural gas reservoirs.

When you mine a ton of oil sands, you get **one-tenth** of a ton of energy. Do we have any choice?

Alcohol

Here again the crucial consideration is **volume**. How many tons of wood, wheat, or garbage to make a ton of oil?

What we are speaking of is vegetation — **current vegetation**. That is, the required tonnage must be produced each year.

We reach desperately for new ideas. Alcohol is an excellent fuel. It can be made efficiently from wood, grain, or almost any organic matter. Agreed. But how much?

Alcohol proponents say we could get 61 gallons per acre of wheat. That's less than a dollar per gallon if you allow for processing. But if we leave it in the form of wheat and if the land produces 35 bushels per acre, our income would be $120 to $140, much more than we would get for the alcohol.

I have heard it said that artichokes will yield four times as much oil per acre. I wonder how much artichoke acreage we have, because at six barrels per acre, we would need 150,000 acres of artichokes for a million barrels a day. And what are the world's people going to eat when we convert huge land masses into growing vegetation to be turned into oil?

Another study claims that 19 billion cubic feet of wood residues in Canada would produce 800 million barrels of fuel alcohol. I wonder how we are going to gather, load, transport and handle 19 billion cubic feet of supplies and residues. Add those costs and the processing costs and the 800 million barrels of fuel alcohol, even if the claim is true — recedes into dreamland.

Once again when you introduce the concept of **volume** your answer disappears.

A help, sure — an answer, no.

Think of the genesis of coal and oil.

The alcohol proponents rely on one year's vegetation for one year's supply. But coal and oil are the result of hundreds of millions of years of accumulated vegetable and animal matter — that is to say, sea life — dead and buried by nature and stewed into petroleum with the escaping gases becoming the natural gas of today, trapped in impervious geological formations overlaying the porous sedimentary reservoirs.

Our coal is decayed vegetation of an abundance unimaginable on earth today. The dense forests of the Carboniferous era of some 500 million years, grew, decayed, and fell one upon the other. Then nature, by piling thousands of feet of rock overburden deposited by the sea, compressed the vegetation like no pressure we could ever produce, heated it, aged it and bequeathed it to our modern world, where the vegetation of the land mass is mainly consumed as food in the

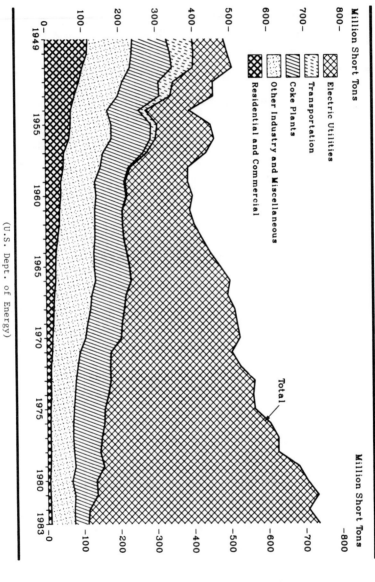

Coal Consumption by End-Use Sector

(U.S. Dept. of Energy)

246

form of small plants. Only a small percentage of our land mass is in forests which are needed to produce our shelter.

And we suppose that year by year we can use **current** vegetable growth to match nature's hoard?

We forget that we are drawing from a bank which nature took hundreds of millions of years to produce, and in less than a hundred years we have nearly exhausted the full essence arising from the most prolific sea life imaginable.

Alcohol — yes. It will produce energy and quite a bit — **if you are thinking in limited terms.** But in terms of a percentage of our needs — as an answer — alcohol is no answer at all.

Solar Power

I believe the point is made. I shall not try to calculate the hundreds or thousands of acres of photoelectric cells needed to even approach a significant fraction of our needs.

Solar power will heat swimming pools, and homes in the sunny states. It will help and as it helps it will lessen the shortage. In the 21st century solar contributions may be very significant. But for the next five to 10 years, its contribution will be small.

Wind Power

Windy areas could become virtually self-sufficient. But constantly windy areas are a very small percentage of our total area, and because of the wind, sparsely populated.

U.S. Windpower Incorporated of Massachusetts planned the biggest wind-energy system so far at Pacheco Pass, about 100 miles south of San Francisco.

The $75 million project will produce enough power for 1,000 people — the equivalent of 175,000 barrels of oil a year. It would consist of 23 bladed windmills, each with three 45-foot whirling blades sitting on towers 150 feet high. Each tower would have three generators.

If successful, the company would set up several hundred more windmills in the west where the winds blow constantly around 20 to 30 miles an hour.

A quick calculation tells me that if it requires $75 million to serve 1,000 people, it ought to cost $75 billion for only one million people.

Again, the answer is the same. The wind can be a helper, but not an answer.

Nuclear Fusion

Very promising for the next century. Fusion may very well solve humanity's energy problem forever. No radioactivity as in fission (atomic splitting). The United States is spending

$500 million on two fusion projects and a group of countries including Russia plan cooperation to produce a $25 billion project to actually begin producing energy some time in the 1990s. This possibly could be a long-lasting answer to the energy needs of the world. But it is far too early to count on that and it may be that we never can.

Shale Oil

Like the oil sands, this is a mining venture. One ton yields about two barrels of oil. There are two catches, too — **volume and production.**

1. Each barrel of oil produced requires two barrels of water for processing. So, even one million barrels of oil a day would require two million barrels of water. This possibility is non-existent in dry Colorado, Utah and Wyoming.

2. Like the oil sands the resulting volume of shale is larger than the volume mined, creating a huge disposal problem when you start talking about excess shale from one-half to one million tons every 24 hours.

The idea of cooking the oil out of the shale **in place** is undeveloped and may well be impractical. Certainly it amounts to no answer at all over our critical period, the next 10 years. And why we would go to all this trouble when we can mine a ton of coal and get nearly a ton of instantly available energy, is hard to answer.

*   *   *   *

From the above, it is evident that coal will enjoy a reincarnation in the early part of the next century. The revival of coal is already underway. The chart on Page 246 shows the increased usage of coal in recent years, according to a world coal study involving 80 people from 16 major coal-producing and consuming countries. Chances are this work may look conservative when viewed with hindsight some years down the line.

At any rate, a **ROLLOVER** in the number one source of energy in the early 21st century is in store.

XXIV

ROLLOVER OF
INFLATION

It is very hard to question the mores by which we were reared. Having spent half a lifetime under a certain set of beliefs and practices we are very apt to accept them as if they were written in stone. How can we question what we have seen by our experience? If certain events of history are brought forth to challenge our beliefs we are prone to throw out those events as peculiarities of bygone days. Our experiences show us that these events are old-fashioned. We conclude they cannot stand up in the modern world.

If someone suggests that our present beliefs should be submerged in form of such old-fashioned notions, we are apt to be outraged. After all isn't the password **PROGRESS**? Are we going back to the obsolescence of the past? Once the deflationary monster, for example, was something to be feared. Meantime we've gotten rid of small pox, scarlet fever, tuberculosis, **DEFLATION.** We have learned how to deal with all these things and never again will they scourge the earth.

So it is quite natural that people over 40 categorize deflation along with small pox or even the "black death" of the Middle Ages. It won't be seen again. We have learned how to handle it.

This is all to the good providing it is true, extremely dangerous if it happens to be false.

In the minds of these people two magicians are blocking deflation. They are, (1) the Federal Reserve, and (2) the U.S. Government. And these two great powers can even change the course of the economy. If there are a million more jobs this year the president of the United States claims he made them. If interest rates go down the Fed is given the credit for it. These magicians are being very careful to do nothing to disturb this blind but unfounded faith.

But it remains the truth, although the youngsters don't know it — we can no more banish an economic depression with its attendant deflation than Arthur of Camelot could banish snow until December. Of course such laws could be passed. The trouble is, if the economy is sick, it is sick. And these two magicians are not even good doctors. Rather than get the fever down they change the calibration on the thermometer.

They pretend that the banks are sound but they have never been so unsound. They pretend the great recovery is on track and it is going to get better, but it is an artificial recovery in the first place and it is not going to get better. They know that the last deflation hit them out of the blue without any advance notice during the greatest developing prosperity in the world. President Hoover became famous mostly for his great slogan, "Two chickens in every pot."

Even after the stock market had suffered the worst tumble it had ever seen, the investors, principally on Wall Street, would not believe still that there could be a pot with only one chicken, much less a pot without any chicken. So after the terrible tumble they dived in to buy more because they figured this was just a shake out for the faint-hearted.

Older people know that you don't have to have official warning to be hit by a depression. Unlike inflation it does not build up bit by bit by bit. It strikes like a thunderbolt. That's when people realize that they have over-extended, and that all their debtors are over-extended; that they are supporting a farce. Everyone seems to get wise at once. Everyone gets worried about the money he has lent out.

Will Rogers spoke for our nation when he said, **"I'm not so much concerned with the return on my money as with the return *OF* my money."**

All seem to be concerned about the return of their money, and surely that means a contraction all across the land. And surely a contraction means there is less money moving around, less money available, less money at risk — in other words a full-blown **DEFLATION IS SETTING IN — AND NO ONE IS GOING TO BE ABLE TO TURN IT AROUND.**

A stampeding herd of cattle can't be turned around by the greatest cowboy that ever lived or by cowboy Paul Volcker if he rides 24 hours a day. Suddenly printing up some money will

250

just make people more scared than before. And that's what the Fed is scared to death about right now in 1985.

Except for a short-term influence, the Federal Reserve does not control interest rates. That should be obvious. The last thing the Fed wants to see is high interest rates and a collapse in recovery. If they control rates, why would they allow this to happen? The truth is that the interest rates are the function of two or three different things.

One is that lenders will say to themselves, "Well, there is so much inflation and it may even be more next year so I have to have a fair interest rate as a return on my money, and to this I must add inflation."

Another reason for high interest rates is a desperation on the part of debtors to stay in business and their willingness to pay the high price for scarce liquidity. As the liquidity shrinks the price the debtors will pay goes up — until somebody says, "Why, these debtors can't pay anything and so we've got to stop lending them money."

Finally, the borrowing grinds down from a stream to a trickle mainly because people are afraid to go out on a limb to borrow money for new ventures, or to expand business, or on the other hand the people who do have cash, and would like to lend it, can't find worthy borrowers. They have to wonder if every borrower is going to go bankrupt.

Deflation is more like a contagion than anything else. What doctors are able to stop a contagion?

About the only way the authorities have of keeping the situation remotely in hand is to make the public believe that everything is sound, that the banks are sound, the economy is going to grow and to go ahead, there is no danger about losing your job, your house. We have to paint an even brighter picture of how great the future is going to be. As soon as people begin to say "horse manure" the money doctors are finished. People are very suspicious about the banks although the media is doing its best to keep them misinformed, ignorant and gullible.

The following story is drawn from MFE and constituted our best effort to show people how they are deliberately being misled by the media.

THE GOVERNMENT IS TRYING TO FOOL THE PEOPLE
THE BANKS ARE TRYING TO FOOL THE PEOPLE
THE PRESS IS TRYING TO FOOL THE PEOPLE

Deception is rampant. The banking crisis is so bad that collapse has nearly happened three times. In May, 1984, the U.S. government was forced to place full faith and credit behind every deposit in every American bank — **as it is presently understood.** That means billion dollar deposits of foreign sheiks or institutions, multi-million dollars of certificates of deposit across the country. But the significance here lies not so much in the size of the obligation as the fact that the government had to make it an **emergency** measure to stop a worldwide deluge of withdrawals from American banks, and widespread failures of the big money banks in New York.

The misrepresentation of the condition of these banks goes to the highest quarters of government. For example: Mr. Isaac of the FDIC and the currency comptroller himself, who announced only days before the fall of Continental that it was financially sound. It was a most unusual step, according to reports, but he took it to stop the panic. If a lie from the government would stop the panic — why not?

People learned long ago not to trust the government. But they did not learn until lately of the deception by banks through use of misleading accounting systems.

Perhaps the banks could be forgiven; they were doing it to save their necks. But the popular press cannot be forgiven. Let it be said of the Wall Street Journal that in the last year or so they have certainly taken pains in many cases to show what lies behind the figures. This cannot be said of Time and BusinessWeek.

I have chosen to publish a table from BusinessWeek of June 16, 1984, and right alongside it the table from a Myers Finance & Energy newsletter dated June 8, 1984. Its value here is a contrast with BusinessWeek, and the resulting unavoidable conclusion that the BusinessWeek table is a deliberate attempt to mislead the readership into believing the Latin American debt is, after all, only a small piece of the pie.

Take, as an example, the first bank named in the table, Manufacturers Hanover. If you add the debts of Mexico, Argentina, Brazil and Venezuela you come to a total of $6,430 million dollars.

In the Myers table the figures are slightly different but the total is close to the same. It is $6,094 million dollars.

Now the important point is what do the two publications do, given those figures.

BusinessWeek uses this huge debt as a percentage of assets. The Myers table uses it as a percentage of net worth.

AND, WOW, WHAT A DIFFERENCE!

THE MAJOR U.S. LENDERS TO LATIN AMERICA

	Outstanding loans (Dec. 31, 1983)* Millions of dollars				Percent of total assets
	Mexico	Brazil	Argentina	Venezuela	
Manufacturers Hanover	$1,915	$2,130	$1,321	$1,084	10.0%
Citicorp	2,900	4,700	1,090	1,500	7.6
Chase Manhattan	1,553	2,560	775	1,226	7.5
Chemical N.Y.	1,414	1,276	370	776	7.5
J.P. Morgan	1,174	1,785	741	454	7.2
Bankers Trust N.Y.	1,286	743	230**	436	6.7
BankAmerica	2,741	2,484	300**	1,614	5.9
Wells Fargo	655	568	100**	279	5.9
Continental Illinois	699	476	383	436	4.7
First Chicago	870	689	NA	NA	4.3

*Excluding local currency loans   **Estimated   NA=not available

DATA: KEEFE, BRUYETTE & WOODS INC.

(Different data sources have resulted in slightly different totals)

Ten Most Vulnerable Banks							
Bank	Mexico ($ Mil)	Brazil ($ Mil)	Venezuela ($ Mil)	Argentina ($ Mil)	Total ($ Mil)	Net Worth ($ Mil)	% of Net Worth
Man. Hanover	1,730	2,014	1,100	1,250	6,094	2,780	219
Chase Manhattan	1,687	2,362	1,012	800	5,861	2,760	212
Citicorp	3,270	4,360	1,090	1,100	9,820	4,833	203
Chemical	1,500	1,300	-0-	375	3,175	1,946	163
Morgan Guaranty	1,082	1,688	543	800	4,113	2,715	151
BankAmerica	2,500	2,300	2,000	300	7,100	4,595	155
Bankers Trust	875	875	475	275	2,500	1,560	160
Continental Ill.	695	490	463	400	2,048	1,705	120
Security Pacific	525	490	-0-	-0-	1,015	1,488	68
First Interstate	680	474	-0-	-0-	1,154	1,803	64
TOTAL	14,544	16,353	6,683	5,300	42,880	26,185	164

MYERS FINANCE & ENERGY

Time and BusinessWeek know very well that the average reader does not understand the meaning of the assets of a bank compared to its net worth. Most people just assume that assets mean what you are worth — what you have — your farm, your car, your money in the bank, etc. It means to most readers solid worth. And in most cases it means the same as net equity.

Now let's look at the picture given of Manufacturers Hanover Trust in BusinessWeek. Those four countries owe it over $6,000 million. The very next table in BusinessWeek shows that as 10% of its assets. Meaning what? **No big deal!** What are you worried about? That's what this story says.

But a bank's assets include its loans. So its assets include the $6,000 million it has loaned to those countries. Manufacturers Hanover could instantly increase those assets by another couple of billion dollars if it could fund another loan, let's say to Argentina. Then it could advertise even bigger assets. The percentage of its questionable loans to the assets would be even smaller.

But are the assets — assets? That's what this is all about. The assets are completely uninformative unless we know what the assets are and can rate the value of the assets. If the loans are no good then $6,000 million drops from the assets and must be charged the equity.

AND THERE IS THE CATCH!

The equity of Manufacturers Hanover as you will see in the Myers table is $2,780 million. That's all the whole shooting match is worth and that is less than half the loans to the South American countries alone. In other words Manufacturers Hanover has lent to these countries twice as much as the value of every brick, stone, and pencil in its organization. Those assets that BusinessWeek serves up on a platter without explanation simply don't cut any ice in the situation. What they do is to slip one over on the reader. Without any explanation, the effect of the table is to say these banks are pretty well off. "After all, even in spite of the huge loans to the South American countries, that is a measly tenth of it all. How could the bank go broke?"

That's what they want you to believe. They don't go so far as to say that and get themselves on a legal hook where they could be brought before the law for misinformation. But just as surely as if they had said so, they have given their readers the impression that the banks are really well-heeled.

Otherwise, why don't they talk about equity? But not a mention of that.

If you look at the Myers table you see the net worth of $2,780 million (and the loan to Brazil alone at $2,014 million) — so if Brazil defaulted, the assets of Manufacturers Hanover would only be $766 million. We haven't included here at all the other bad loans, such as Argentina or any bad loans at home.

Look at Continental Illinois — now defunct. In the June, 1984, BusinessWeek, Continental Illinois' loans to these four countries is only 4.7% of its assets. But what about its equity, the money it actually had of its own. After all, it can't go using depositors' money to cover bad loans. It must take its equity to cover its bad loans. If it goes broke that means the equity is all used up and the next step must be to use depositor money. **But then the government must step in, stop the operations of the bank and put in money from the Federal Deposit Insurance Corporation to save the depositors.** Meanwhile all the shareholders of Continental Illinois would be busted.

But if you look at the table in BusinessWeek, June 16, 1984, Continental Illinois seems to look pretty well off especially in relation to Latin America — and they don't say anything about Continental's position with other loans which really did them in, such as $2 billion bad loans from the Penn Square Bank.

The result from studying the table by BusinessWeek is to ask the question: "What are all these gloomers and doomers talking about? The bad loans in South America are only a small portion of the total assets of this enormously wealthy bank."

Perhaps when this is all over, there will be a congressional inquiry into the way that Time and BusinessWeek and other magazines treated the illiquidity of the U.S. banks during the crisis.

*　　*　　*　　*

To fully understand what they are doing we need to go a little further.

For example, Citicorp has run up loans to the point where its equity, everything that it owns, every building, every cent, every share is 5% of the total money loaned.

Once the requirement was 15%. But many of the banks have much less.

To bring the picture home clearly and shockingly let's get into banking ourselves:

Suppose you and I start up a bank with $50 thousand capital. We solicit deposits, and let's say we are very successful in getting deposits into our bank. Of course the only way we are going to make any money is to loan out these deposits. Let's assume we get deposits for $1 million. Now we loan out this $1 million in various places. So far the only net worth we have is the original $50 thousand we put in. It's just 5% of our total loan, a situation similar to Citicorp.

Now let's say one of these loans for $100 thousand goes sour. It defaults. We can declare we have assets of a million (our total loans). It doesn't make a spoonful of difference. We have lost $100 thousand by a bad loan and we only have $50 thousand to meet that loss.

Now we have to do one of two things. First of all we lose all of our equity; we give that up. We have $50 thousand in excess claims against us by our depositors: Either we go broke and the depositors lose $50,000 dollars, or the FDIC comes in and closes us down and they get some bank to take us over by means of putting up what we had lost, the $50,000. We walk away broke.

So with a million dollars in assets our real core of wealth was small.

Because Citicorp has such a big name people seem to go along with this without getting excited. To the Latin American countries alone Citicorp has lent twice as much as its net worth. If these countries should all default Citicorp would be broke twice over. It would have a minus zero value on the stock market of many dollars per share. If any one of them defaulted or went broke Citicorp would be in a very serious position, because its net worth is only about $5,000 million and a default by Brazil alone would knock $4,300 million of the net worth. Citicorp would be virtually finished.

But to look at the charts that are being published by the public media you would never guess — never in God's world — that these banks are skating on this enormously thin ice. You can only guess this if you watch the panic-stricken efforts by the government, and its bureaucrats, who are trying desperately to paper over the seriousness of the whole banking structure.

*   *   *   *

It seems like the previous tricks are not going to work much longer. There has been a stern letter from the Fed, for one thing. What they have been doing demonstrates more positively than any other factor why the banks are a house of cards.

Let's say $100 million is due Citicorp in interest on its loans to Argentina. Argentina can't pay. Up to recently the bank would lend the debtor the $100 million. The debtor would then pay the $100 million to the bank and increase the debt of the debtor by $100 million.

At that point, behold **MAGIC**. The assets are increased $100 million – and the earnings are up $100 million. And not a dime more of solid value!

*   *   *   *

All of this credit pyramid is just fine, as long as the credit front remains quiet. It could go on and on, but there's coming a day when the **call** is made and the bank can't deliver.

The Indians are Coming

I am a captain in a frontier army and I have 10,000 rounds of ammunition. Captain Smith, some miles away, has requested ammunition from headquarters, but they do not have it, and I lent Smith 5,000 rounds of ammunition. My entry on the books shows me with assets of 10,000 rounds of ammunition, 5,000 on hand and 5,000 lent to Captain Smith.

In the night I am awakened by the general who says Indians may attack in a day or so; prepare. I am not worried. In my inventory I still list a positive 5,000 rounds of ammunition – 5,000 with Captain Smith and 5,000 on hand. I report my ammunition assets to the general as 10,000 rounds.

The next night I am awakened again and the general says an attack is underway. Prepare to meet it. I say, "I only have on hand 5,000 rounds of ammunition." The general says, "Your inventory shows you have 10,000 rounds." I say, "I know. I do have them, but they are owed to me. They were to have been repaid to me by Captain Smith yesterday."

"Why didn't you require him then to pay you earlier?" asks the general. I reply, "He could not pay; so I rescheduled time of payment, but I will get the ammunition tonight."

Urgently I send scouts to get the 5,000 rounds of ammunition from Captain Smith. But I am informed that Captain Smith has already shot the 5,000 rounds at other Indians and he is unable to pay me as agreed, since the shipment he expected had not come in. He now wants to reschedule the debt.

My problem is the Indians are coming. The 5,000 rounds Captain Smith has fired have used up their explosive power at his end of the line. The fact that my inventory shows 10,000 rounds does me no good at all. If the Indians were not coming, I could keep it on the books for weeks and months and everything would look copacetic to the generals who examine my inventory. But now I have to go to the general and declare ammunition bankruptcy. That could be avoided until the chips

257

came down. But when the chips came down, the 5,000 rounds of ammunition had to be written off. Their explosive power had been used by Captain Smith; and it could not again be used by me. I had to have new ammunition. Now we must retreat or face annihilation.

*   *   *   *

Let us take a small example of an unpaid debt. Let us take the $2.5 billion that Poland was to have paid by the end of 1981; a debt that has been rescheduled. And now it is plain that all of the explosive power of that $2.5 billion has been used up by Poland. It is spent. The fact that we keep it on our books as inventory is all very well, until it is needed.

We have just one little problem. If you listen, you can hear the war whoops and the drums. **THE INDIANS ARE COMING!**

Of course this still hasn't answered the argument of those who say the minute the government gets in trouble the Fed will just print more money and that will blow up the money supply and that will start a new wave of inflation which will trigger another wave of inflation which will make the money worthless and which will make gold about $5,000 an ounce. So let's look at that one.

In the first place the Fed cannot give money away. It cannot give money to banks. It can create money in only one of two ways:

The first way it creates money is by buying Treasury obligations. This means the Fed creates a credit for the government and issues the government currency or its equivalent. But remember that when the government goes to spend this money it can only come with the approval of Congress. The very linchpin of the American system is that the money power lies with the Congress and every department of government must get its money from Congress. Even the president must get his budget from Congress. Congress are the elected representatives of the people across the land and these representatives are quite sensitive to the hue and cry at home. In past years they have not had to worry too much what the Fed has been doing. But let the Fed create money by buying government securities to be used in bailing out foreign countries at the cost of the taxpayers and just watch what happens when this news is out.

In any case the fact is the Fed just can't up and print billions of dollars — just like that. That answer is just too pat.

258

The only other way the Fed creates money is by people borrowing it. If you go to the bank and borrow a thousand dollars and if the Fed is in a mood for extending credit that the bank itself cannot supply, a thousand dollars is placed in your account, and the money supply is increased by a thousand dollars at once. The Fed perhaps has supplied the liquidity. Now it is up to you to pay the bank. If you don't pay the bank, the bank must pay the Fed. The Fed is not giving any money to the banks, not even a dollar. It is not empowered to give money to banks.

However, this can be an enormous source of inflation if the population is in the mood to borrow, to expand, to spend, and if the Fed is in the mood to grant credit to the banks. Through borrowing, the money supply is greatly increased, and through borrowing inflation is accordingly advanced.

But don't give heed nor mind to the vast array of money preachers across the land who constantly keep shouting, "Whenever there is a need for money the Fed will print it." The Fed cannot print up debts for the taxpayers of the United States without reference to Congress via the Treasury.

Reserve Currency of the World

Another reason that inflation cannot race as fast as many of the so-called experts maintain is the fact that the U.S. dollar is the reserve currency of the world. The supply of U.S. dollars not only affects money in the United States but all around the world. So in fact any inflation in the United States has a cushion all around the world.

Most reserves of foreign countries are kept in dollars. If the dollar is inflated so are the reserves of those other countries. So this provides an enormous extra cushion for any inflation that takes place in the states; the effect is not confined to the United States, it is spread around the whole world. And that is the exact difference between the inflation in the States and the classical cases that they will ask you to look at, such as previous inflations in Germany and France and elsewhere. Those inflations were for a single nation which was a small potato in the whole world.

The developing countries depend on the U.S. dollar to buy oil; they have to pay dollars for it. Nearly all purchases in international trade are calculated in dollars and people in Italy who want to buy Japanese cars have to pay for them in dollars. They can't earn enough from the Japanese yen, so they pay for them in dollars.

259

Most of the copper, nickel, iron, zinc, wood, in fact all commodities, are paid for in dollars.

You can't buy oil with gold. You must first convert the gold to dollars. You can't buy copper with oil; you first sell your oil and then pay for the copper in dollars. The net result:

Inflation of the American dollar is inflation of the world.

So you can stand a lot of that distributed all around the world until you get runaway inflation in the United States, and therefore around the world. When I say runaway inflation I am talking about inflation of maybe 100% to 1,000% in one year. Nothing like that is going to happen because we have the world as a cushion.

Still, 100% in a year would be bad enough, but there is absolutely nothing in the cards anywhere that would support the belief that we are going to see 100% inflation in any year.

Inflation will proceed to its limit until the crowd gets scared. The crowd got scared in 1982 and we fell to a full-blown recession that promised to develop into a depression. We came out of it mostly by propaganda and concerted effort by financial institutions and big financial interests whose names never appear in the newspapers. We got a phony recovery started which really wasn't justified at all, considering the enormous overhanging debt, the inability of the Third World countries to feed their people or even to pay off any interest on their loans. But we got it going. It lasted maybe two years, but the days are numbered.

Now it has become common knowledge that the Third World countries cannot pay off their debt. Some $700 billion dollars around the world is owed and no one knows when it is coming back. The likelihood is that it will be treated like the foreign debt before the last depression. That came partially as a repudiation of debt by the same South American countries who are on the verge of repudiation now and by the fact that Germany defaulted on its huge war debt. The defaults came largely for the reason that it was impossible for these countries to pay this debt. And the adage that you cannot take blood out of a stone applied then, and it applies now. No matter how much propaganda comes out of the banks, the government; no matter how much reasurrance they give you about the soundness of the economy and the financial structure — still no blood seeps out of a stone.

And that is the situation we are in today.

The Fed cannot cure the situation by printing money. And they just can't print money and give it to those countries and say go pay the banks. Nor can they just print up money and give it to the banks and say, "We take over those foreign loans and now here is your money."

Since that can't be done, and since there is a growing concern that a crisis of illiquidity is threatening the world, where is this hyper-inflation, fathered by the Fed, to come from? It just isn't coming.*

But not very many people will dispute that this whole mess is going to end up in either (a) inflation, or (b)deflation. I have repeatedly stated this and it can be taken as an axiom.

"A debt will always be paid either by the one who borrowed it, or by the one who lent it."

So this trillion dollars owed by the government of the United States domestically, some $5 trillion owed in the whole United States, adds up to within a trillion dollars or so of the U.S. total net worth plus the nearly trillion dollars owed around the world that won't be coming back. This immense load inundates the world with credit and a monster built out of

---

*There is a strong argument that the Fed could do this as a result of the 1980 Bill PL 96-221, which gives the Fed authority to buy foreign loans. In some quarters, this is taken to mean that, if Citibank had a $10 billion loan from the Argentines, the Fed could buy this Argentine loan from Citibank. I don't agree that this will happen for two reasons. Firstly, it was explained to me that the Fed always carries balances of currency of foreign countries for international exchange purposes and sometimes considerable sums. This money earns no interest. If the Fed can use it to buy an interest-paying loan, it would be so authorized but **only to the extent that it has the funds on hand for other purposes**.

Secondly, and in any case, I do not believe for one moment that Congress or the public of the United States would stand still for the Fed to buy up a $10 billion loan of the Argentines at Citibank, or any such other loan, and I do believe that the 1980 law is subservient to the much greater law that the money power and the spending power lies with the Congress of the United States and that the only money that can be spent is the money authorized by Congress.

I think, therefore, that the 1980 law is valid up to the point where it would conflict with the power of any U.S. agency to make authorized expenditures.

illiquidity is taking shape very fast. Somehow trillions of dollars of this debt have got to come off. The interest by itself is choking the whole financial structure of the world.

There are two ways to reduce this horrendous and impossible debt. One is reducing the value of the debt by inflation. And we have just discussed how that is most unlikely if not impossible. The second is by deflation; that is the destruction of money through bankruptcy. If the equity of Continental Illinois is gone and the bank went broke, then those $2 billion which the owners of Continental Illinois had considered their own are now lost. They have to go toward paying off depositors and if they don't have enough to pay off the depositors then the federal government has to come in and pay off the depositors. But that doesn't make for inflation. That doesn't put any more money in the money stream. It scares the pants off of everybody, makes everybody more careful, and more restrictive in handling money.

Every scare worsens the liquidity situation by reducing confidence.

I see nothing that has happened in the last year or so which could possibly be interpreted as the nucleus of a new wave of inflation.

Inflation has shrunk from 12% to about 4% or 5%, and this has been called disinflation. It's a new word. In truth disinflation is deflation. We are deflating the amount of money resulting from ongoing inflation. Now for some strange reason people seem to think when disinflation has dropped from 10% to 4% to 2% to 0% — that's the end of the matter. It seems somehow not to occur to anyone that disinflation could go through 0, that is to 2% deflation, 4% deflation, 10% deflation.

Well, what would that deflation mean? That would mean lower wages of 2%, 4%, 10%, lower prices all around, lower interest rates, fewer new homes, smaller cars and fewer cars, and a whole and serious contraction in the living standard. And that is getting us very close to a definition of a depression. Lower wages.

* * * *

Thinking people pretty well agree that we are approaching a monetary and therefore an economic climax. They don't know whether it will be an inflation or a deflation, or when it will come. But one of the very reasons it causes them to agree is the fact that the monumental debt is increasing by leaps and unstoppable bounds by the mere function of interest. Interest is now working like a fast-growing parasite. Its expansion is exponential. For example, the interest on the federal debt is now over $100 billion when only a few years ago the total budget deficit was thought to be horrendous if it reached $100 billion. Every year the interest rate is greater and our federal debt becomes greater, and the debt of the country becomes greater, and the foreign debt becomes greater — and all these unexponential bases get bigger. Obviously the parasite will kill the host. Obviously there has to be a climax.

My reason for believing it will be deflationary is the very reason that causes all observers to agree there will be a climax. The inflationary route would only bring interest rates higher and higher, hasten the development of the exponential curve into the stratosphere and bring the whole world civilization to ruin. And once that inflation got started again it's not likely that any power on earth could stop it. Since the reason pushing us into this climax is principally interest, it seems like common sense to believe that the climax would not take the inflation route — because that wouldn't be producing the climax — that would just be producing an immeasurably worse climate, for that climax still to come.

I think it can be called a truism that for this social order to survive in any form — the interest rates will have to come down. I think it is a truism that only in a period of deflation will the interest rates come down.

And therefore I think it is next door to a truism to say that the climax will be worldwide **DEFLATION**.

The meaning of that is, the depression will be the worst in history because now it includes the whole world due to the enormous influence of the United States and the role of the U.S. dollar throughout the world. There will be few bastions of prosperity to fall back on. The meaning of that is enormous social unrest, probably rioting, and consequently very strong government measures to control the population. We shall be lucky if we get away without a dictatorship.

I have mentioned that here and there in this book. But only now probably can it all be put together to demonstrate INEVITABILITY of the denouement of the earthshaking courses as they all fall into single focus, as with the glass that can concentrate the light rays to the point where they start a fire.

Surely this means the ROLLOVER OF INFLATION, the subject of this chapter.

Yet there is a complacency around the world and even though thousands, maybe millions, can tell the storm is in the air, few of them can really believe that it will happen.

Every religion has a story about the great flood. And inherent in the story is the idea that none of them knew when it would happen — none except maybe Noah. I once wrote a little parable on that.

THE DAY THEY FLOATED THE ARK
Starring
Mr. Knowa   Mr. Whena
Mr. Doubta   Mr. Dumbo

While Knowa and his sons are hammering the last nails into the completed ark, his neighbours gather around.

Mr. Whena: Friend Knowa, it is a beautiful morning. The birds are singing in the trees, the dust is blowing along the trail. I know you say there is going to be a great flood that will sweep us all away. Sometimes I half believe you. But when?

Mr. Knowa: I cannot tell you the day of the flood. I do not know whether it is tomorrow, next month, or next year. But I can tell you, if you do not build yourself a ship, you will surely drown. And you cannot build yourself a ship overnight.

Mr. Whena: Yes, but you have been saying for two years that there is going to be a flood. Several times you have scared me to death. But always the sun shone again, and it turned out to be no more than an ordinary rain. I do believe that you had a vision and that there will be a flood. Meanwhile, others are reaping crops and making money. As long as the weather looks this good, I am not about to miss these profits to get ready YET for your flood.

Mr. Dumbo: The whole thing is silly. It is inconceivable that all this land should be covered by water. Has it ever happened before, Mr. Knowa? No, never. And since it has never happened before, it cannot happen now. And even if the Lord did say there was going to be a flood, I say the Lord is wrong.

It cannot happen, because it would be such a disaster — the Lord couldn't let it happen.

Mr. Doubta: I do not agree with Mr. Dumbo, that because it never happened before, it can never happen. But I doubt that it will happen in our lifetime. At least I am sure that if such a flood is to come, the water will rise very gradually, and we will have plenty of time to see what is happening. In other words, the water will rise a little more each month and each year, and then we will all start to build our ships.

Mr. Knowa: Since I do not know exactly when the flood is coming, I cannot argue with you. But my position is this: I know the flood is coming. I know it takes me two years to build my ship. Thus I lose two years of crops. But, if at the end of that time the flood has not come, my ship is ready, and I shall return to growing crops. It costs me nothing because my ship is ready. You, on the other hand, will still have to take out two years' revenue from your crops to build your ships, and you run a risk which I do not run. Because you do not **know** that the flood will not come in six months.

So, if the flood comes in six months, my family and I and all our species will be saved — and you will all drown. You will have reaped this harvest in vain, because you will never get the chance to build your ships. But if the flood does not come for four years, I will still reap my grain for two years, and you will lose those two years building your ships.

The difference between you and me is that you gamble, and I don't.

Mr. Whena: But I do not like to be an alarmist. Before I let my crop go, I must have a better idea as to when. I see these pretty nice profits right now, and last year I started my ship, and failed to fallow my land, and lost money because of you. And I do not intend to lose any more. When **I know when**, then I will go back to building my ship.

Mr. Dumbo: Every day it doesn't rain, the crowd laughs at you. Everyone knows that such a wild thing has never happened before, and we are on very sound ground for that reason to say it will not happen at all.

(They all begin to laugh at Knowa, and Mr. Dumbo laughs the loudest.)

Mr. Knowa: He who laughs last, laughs best.

That night the sky grew inky black, and the rain commenced to fall, first in torrents, then in a veritable deluge, 'til by morning all the water holes were filled, and the valleys were rushing torrents. And by afternoon the ark began to lift, and Mr. Dumbo, Mr. Whena and Mr. Doubta and their families were racing around frantically trying to build some small rafts. And they dropped their hammers in the water and could not find them, and their nails were washed away, and they began to swim, and the ark rose. And a smile broke on Knowa's face, and as the ark sailed away on the waves you could hear the roar of his laughter above the din of the torrents and the wind. Knowa was the last one heard to laugh.

And that is the origin of that wise old saying —"He who laughs last, laughs best!"

*   *   *   *

If Noah lived today, there is a precaution he would take, and I have to bring it to your attention.

Monarch of All

This will shock you. But you have to put your brain to it. Who has cash — I mean currency — I mean money?

Do you have cash? Count it. Does your banker have cash other than the small currencies? Ask him to count his cash.

The banks themselves carry very little cash.

Does your car dealer have cash?

If the banks should be closed (God forbid) for a week, who would have cash?

Would the man with currency in his pocket be able to get a bargain?

*   *   *   *

This nation spurns cash. The moment somebody gets a chunk of money, he can't wait to get over to the bank fast enough to put the money in some money market fund, some stock enterprise, some IRA, some scheme or corporate treasuries — anything but cash.

All of this money goes into the institutions. It is immediately sent swirling out the back door in the form of loans to waiting borrowers. But loans have been widely unsound and billions are lost. Banks continue to go belly up.

We have had two close calls with panics within a few months of each other. Even the Federal Deposit Insurance Corporation trembles on the brink of depleted funds. Failure of 40 banks in Ohio sent waves of fear to all savings and loans and all uninsured institutions to the point where, before the end of 1985, Congress will be forced to put a guarantee under depositor accounts. The savings and loan deposit insurance (FSLIC) is admittedly now broke.

Guarantee indeed. When?

The volume of currency in the United States compared to the volume of recorded money is infinitesimally small. Under a banking panic, nobody would want to take checks from anybody — even one bank from another.

"When?" When you can get it. Do you ever read the fine print posted up in your bank? Look at it. Here's what it says:

The "depositor" may at any time be required by the bank to give notice in writing of an intended withdrawal not less than 30 days nor more than six months before such withdrawal is made. If it is not made within five days after the expiration of such withdrawal notice, withdrawal rights pursuant thereto shall be considered waived and a new notice shall be required.

There must be a reason. The **reason** for this provision signifies recognition of the unpalatable proposition: Demand could exceed the supply of money; and then the demand would have to be curbed.

This is a warning. Banks do not have to pay you out your cash even if they are not broke.

In view of the above, even if you have a Treasury bill, you are not assured of cash. You are assured it will be credited to your account in a surviving bank. But if there is a run on cash, cash will be rationed.

The credit build-up is so overwhelming, it is like a mighty mountain reeling on its base. Don't let someone tell you it can't happen. Look at the growing deficits and the failing institutions.

I don't have trouble envisioning the man with assets of a million dollars and his friend with assets of ten thousand dollars going down to the bank together to get their weekly allotment of $500 cash — until things could be straightened up. Guaranteed sure. When?

The Treasury literally could not make currency fast enough to satisfy the national need. They could only promise cash available as soon as possible.

*   *   *   *

Currency is an absolute necessity for everyday life. It cannot be bypassed. Gold can be bypassed; silver can be bypassed; bonds and CD's and Treasury bills can be bypassed — but currency cannot.

Who has bank accounts? — everybody. Market funds, CD's, IRA's, real estate bonds, you've seen all these — notes of all kinds — all debt. **EVERYBODY**.

Who has cash?

NOBODY.

Does this tell you something? Well, it tells me something. People will be brought to sell gold coins or anything else to get currency — **CASH**. If you have $100,000 real cash, you may be able to get $500,000 worth of value for it.

I'm not going to write a book about this, but just remember: In the last crash, gold was money of last resort; saved gold coins were very valuable. What is the money of last resort today? Gold? Not at all. Currency — cash.

Gold has a fluctuating (and unknown) value.

Here is the most shocking message I have for you: —

If you have $5,000 liquid money, you should have $1,000 in a safety box and maybe more or all later on. If you are wealthy use your own multiplier.

Take it or leave it. I believe that the biggest run of the 20th century will be on cash.

When?

When the glue gives way. The whole system is now stuck together by fragile glue. No one can tell just when the glue will give.

*   *   *   *

The deflation is on its way. The date is not known. But if you wait to get ready until it starts to rain, it's not likely you will have time to build anything more than a rowboat. The time to get ready for the world rollover is the time when the dust still swirls along the road.

In the next and final chapter we will talk about the ROLLOVER itself.

XXV

WORLD ROLLOVER

Any one of the many subjects discussed here could, itself, be handled without threatening our social order as we have known it for 100 years and more. Anything, that is, except the debt problem. The debt problem is a manifestation of all the problems and it acts as a barometer of sorts to the condition of the world order wherein the timing gears have gotten out of line.

The debt problem projects many pictures across the screen. It shows the widening divergence between the haves and the have-nots and particularly in the Western Hemisphere, between the northern half and the southern half.

It shows that technology has gone wild with abundance in the industrialized world but that backward populations, growing like weeds, are unable to get a handle on the technology that brought the west out of the Middle Ages into the computerized present.

In the debt problem we have a reflection of the energy problem. Energy, by itself, could have been handled, of course. The price revolt by OPEC was a disturbing feature but a swift advance in coal technology, stepped by oil exploration at home, plus enormous conservation, could have stamped out the energy problems without any serious long term effects.

As it was, the energy problem, by siphoning off hundreds of billions of dollars into the OPEC countries, brought on a world revolution in the capital markets. Excess billions sent to the Western countries, especially the American banks, produced a momentous banking problem. How to deal with all this money?

The banks are blamed for being greedy. That's not altogether justified. Here suddenly hundreds of millions of dollars were coming into deposit. The banks had to do something with it. They can't pay out interest on money sitting in a vault, completely inactive. Money has to be active. Where are they going to find a likely spot to put this money to produce activity and new goods and new value? Certainly not into their own economies. We were already battling surpluses to the point where the government had to store up cheese later to give it away, and the same with butter, and had to pay the farmers for not growing any crops. We didn't need more dams. We didn't need more factories. We already had factories over capacity of 25%. Where were the banks to find a stopping place for this money.

Obviously in the undeveloped countries. That's where the industry needed to be built. The banks jumped at the chance. Here was money coming in like manna from heaven and here was a debt market that could absorb it all, and here were juicy interest rates like they have never seen before and the banks dished the money out as fast — or faster than it came in. They lent it to Brazil, Argentina, Peru, Hungary — all around the world.

But they hadn't seen the joker. The joker was that these countries did not know how to handle the money to bring forth an industrial revolution of their own. They spent it on airports where no planes landed; on great docks where no ships came to rest. They spent it on new capitals like Brazilia, they spent it on gold and Cadillacs for dictators, harems and palaces. They sent it to Switzerland in the name of the new rich rulers — rich on oil money that had been funneled through American banks.

Then it turned out the banks had made a terrible mistake. They expected this oil money to not only continue but to increase at a hefty rate. The projections in 1980 were that $35 oil, by 1985, would be $50 or $60 a barrel and that from there on the inevitable direction was up. They were wrong. They were all wrong. All the economists, all the banks, Wall Street, the governments, the whole shooting match was wrong. Instead of a worsening oil shortage, steep inflation and preposterous prices — we got an oil glut. Conservation in the western countries, smaller cars, cutting back everywhere, substitution of coal for oil, the coming on a stream of fields like the North Sea, Prudhoe Bay and Mexico — all of these together added up to an oil glut like we had never dreamed. The oil price dropped. The outlook became down instead of up while the glamorized oil loans wilted and the bankruptcies multiplied, and the great volumes of new money from the Middle East failed to appear from the debtors and even OPEC countries began drawing some of the money they had put into the American banks.

Even that would have been all right if the gambling on the Third World had worked. But it didn't. Instead, the banks reaping modest capital repayments on schedule, plus handsome interest payments, found that the big debtors had run on evil days. Even Mexico with its great new oil fields had planned far beyond the prospects of reality. So had they all. So the American banks found out that they couldn't collect the oil money that had flooded in and for which they were responsible. The result turned out to be a disaster for American banks, for some found their loans had mushroomed so much that their equity by now only amounted to 3% to 5% of their total loans. Desperately they tried to control the sudden situation, to keep the public from getting nervous about it, but all the time the tension was building and the truth was emerging.

Meanwhile the outlook for employment was changing quite drastically. Although unemployment had eased somewhat in 1984 it was obvious this was a temporary phenomenon. Unless the rest of the world could move into prosperity the United States could not stay in prosperity. Moreover — even under normal conditions — the United States is headed into a period where robots will be doing the work of men. The smokestack industries would be cutting blue collar workers back to the bone. Many unions began agreeing to take lower wages.

That was the most important sign. When even unions write new contracts for less than the old ones, then, as the Indian would say, you can expect water to run uphill.

Today we are in the very beginning stages of a huge ROLLOVER across the world. The kind of factories we use will employ fewer workers, and because of the shrinkage of employment there will be a fall in production and a fall in consumption. Generally a sinking economy cannot be rescued by men, politicians, economists or bankers. The world economy is too big for any of them. They are like jack rabbits pushing on an elephant. The elephant will not change his direction one iota. The forces of social evolution can be duly entered in our history books as they have been in ages long past. No one seizure can be given credit for the fall of Rome. No leader could be called to task for the fall because each was merely following a pattern in which he was being pushed by the natural evolution of social man.

271

When men found out how to domesticate animals the evolutionary changes took place that could not be attributed to any of their leaders. When they learned to handle explosives, changes took place that could not be credited to any leader. When industrial man discovered power in coal and the results of that in the form of the steam engine, and all of the devices that led to the ascendancy of England, they could not be credited to England's leaders, nor to England's thinkers. They were a part of the inevitable social revolution of man.

No group of Republicans can keep the recovery on track. It will advance or decline according to the worldwide forces of the evolution of our economy — that is to say, social man.

The leaders are children — they follow; they don't lead. Most any leader will do as well as any other leader. No new leader in Russia has changed the outlook of Communism for half a century and more. No leader in the western world has changed it very much. Possibly the only leader who single-handedly interrupted the orderly progress of the social world was Adolf Hitler. He was like a bomb thrown into the middle of it. But his influence soon passed away and the social evolution of man and his inventions continued and the changes continued as they had continued from the days of transition from cave dwellers to herdsmen, from herdsmen to farmers, from farmers to serfs, from serfs to workers, from workers to owners, from owners to financial giants, and the corporations they created.

It is all evolution of the human race coming toward its destiny on this planet ignoring the futilities of those who think they are shaping the world.

When this happens you run into a new climate, an era of storms and cyclones, of new precedents, of uncontemplated events. We run into a time where the conventional signposts no longer mean anything. The factors on which you have been able to predict certain events have lost their significance. Only the very broadest view will give you a hint of what is coming. I hope that in this book I have been able to cover enough of the panorama to bear witness to the fact that many elements are now in tandem changing the world, its money, **its mores, our way of life, our freedoms or lack of freedoms.** It's all coming together at a focal point in the last two decades of the 20th century.

To us who are watching it, it will seem very slow, a year or so at a time, small changes that will hardly be noticed. But add the changes one on another for five or six years and the great difference will be seen. In 10 years I expect a complete ROLLOVER in our ideas of our modern society.

During that time we will suffer quite a bit. We are likely to have to endure a dictatorship for a while. The American people are, however, very resourceful, and deserve to hope that they will finally come back into order after the dramatic convulsions that are coming forth to meet us.

The very fact that most of the people believe in inflation because that has been the way to play it in the past, is in itself a pretty good sign that that is not the way it is going to go now. Did you ever see most of the people right, when only a few were wrong? No, if you look back you will see that most of the people are wrong and only a few of the people are right. And by mere fact that 90% of the population fears inflation I would myself say it is most unlikely. These people buy things because they think the dollar will be inflated and they can borrow and pay back with cheap dollars and thus prove to themselves how smart they are. Things instead of money, they say. But I am saying that I believe that money is going to become extremely scarce and a better slogan would be, "Money instead of things." Buy the things afterward.

I do not see how the U.S. dollar can depreciate to the point of a nullity. I only see it getting stronger, because when you come right down to it, what other currency would you think would be stronger? What union of currencies would you think would work together in harmony and be stronger?

And if the United States is the strongest currency, it is not going to be told by other countries, one by one that the United States must use gold. It may be that gold will never again be used officially as money. Or it may be that in time it will be adopted again. But for the present there exists no viable reason to think that gold would change the world ROLLOVER **one iota.** We are in the world ROLLOVER wave; we will have to roll with the wave. It is not seen by many. But that is not strange. Great changes are not often foreseen by very many. I might mention a few practicalities which by now are self-evident.

Interest rates will increase as we advance toward a great liquidity climax. At that time the stock market will be in shambles, building will have declined drastically; new car sales will be way down, and unemployment will be way up.

But following that climax the interest rates will begin to fall. They will fall seriously. Not many people will want to expand, and the liquid people will not want to risk money, and certainly will not want to borrow money. The illiquid people will be desperate for money but they, the creditor people, will not be able to find worthy borrowers. They will turn down most of the people who want money, and most of the people who want money will turn out to be would-be borrowers.

So the interest rates will become very low.

So if you have money tied up in U.S. Treasury notes up to say five to seven years, you should be sitting pretty well. The U.S. government will not go down unless we think the whole world is going to capsize in one sudden swoop. If it does not go down it has to remain the dominant power in the world, its Treasury obligations will remain the best security in the world.

It's kind of obvious from the entire conversation that we should own our own home if possible. Everyone should feel secure in this home. Also it is clear we will be vulnerable to great social unrest for some time. You have to deal with thoughts of that in your own way, but the least I can say is that you should increase your thoughts about personal and family security, and take what measures you think might be appropiate.

In such periods as I envision you could have times when stores are closed, or transporation by truckers is shut down, or planes don't fly, or in certian instances banks are closed. You should be prepared for all of these as temporary events.

It all means that you should have a fair nest egg tucked away and that should amount to cold cash in your possession, or in a place equal to being in your own possession. For instance, some people are afraid of having money in safety deposits or in banks. I don't think they should be afraid of losing it but they may have to be afraid of sometime not being able to get in there for a week or so — or who knows. I think that any family, where possible, should have enough spare cash tucked away to last for a month, and if at times some of that cash is called upon then it should be replenished when possible for the next crisis that may arise.

There will, of course, be an end to all these troubles that are coming. Civilization isn't going to fold up and die. It is going to advance to a much higher scale. It's the higher scale that scares me. I fear genetics, I fear the expansion of great state power by above. I fear restricted choice of people to have their own children in whatever numbers they choose, and to send them to whatever schools they choose. I feel all those personal liberties that we now enjoy may come in jeopardy in this new high-phased, highfalutin society that is going to grow out of the technology of the present day.

Unfortunately that is not the end of it. The technology of the present day will produce more technology for the next day. In all of history I think the most unfortunate development since man found his first shelter in caves was the splitting of the atom. It may be that civilization will someday end with that.

I don't believe that will happen in your normal lifetime. I don't believe the traumatic times approaching need to be traumatic for you if you foresee them and I believe that life can still be enjoyed. And I believe intelligence properly applied can make the next 20 years the most interesting period of your entire life. If you are very young you have great excitement before you.

In the meantime, I'm sorry to tell you, you must get ready for a storm. And that is not altogether without its pleasures. Let me paint you a picture of the inner pleasures of security that this afforded me when I was a child on the farm.

*   *   *   *

Among my earliest memories are memories of *the storm*. It was a small frame house of perhaps 500 square feet and it sat alone (so it seemed to me) on a vast and endless plain. Far beyond my known horizons lay a town. And in that town you could — if you had money — buy coal and lamp oil, sugar, even some preserves. The town was a reality only when the weather was right. It was a long day's journey. We were as far from the town, in time, as Los Angeles from London.

When the deep winter set in, then the storms came, the town might as well have been London. Anything you needed from the town must have been laid in store long before *the storm*. You knew *the storm* would come. And you took it for granted. And you laid in the store of goods, with such resources of money as you had.

Long, long before any sign of snow we were getting ready for *the storm*. The early frosts brought us to our knees, plucking potatoes from the soil, pouring buckets of red spuds into sacks, and storing these in the dark cellar. There was canning of beans and beets; and even peaches — if we could afford them from the town. As the frosty mornings moved in, and long before the daylight, I could hear the rattle of the wagon as my father set out for the mine to lay in the winter's store of coal.

When it was all done, it was a pretty safe feeling. There was oil for the lamps, sacks of flour and sugar, dried prunes and raisins. The chicken house had been thatched. The hens were comfortable on the straw. The cows were in the nearby pasture. The barn was ready. When it was all done we read by the evening lamp. And we didn't worry. We knew *the storm* would come. We didn't have to know **what day**. And we didn't worry.

When, at length, the sky grew black in mid-afternoon and the wind began to whistle 'round the eaves and the temperature started to drop we were almost glad. The snow fell. The winds howled. The darkness settled, and the drifts piled high. So high, sometimes, that a boy could not see over them. Even when it went to 20 degrees below, 40 degrees below, and the chill factor stood at 90 degrees so that three minutes would freeze your nose off, we made our quick trips, as necessary, to the well and the barn. The warm milk was in the pails. The pot-bellied stove glowed its heat. And as *the storm* increased in fury, my father would say: "Let her come. We were here first." He would say it on the third day, and if need be, say it on the tenth day: "Let her come. We were here first."

The storm always blew out. And the sun shone again. And eventually there was spring.

*   *   *   *

Had we not known *the storm* was coming, of course, we should have perished.

I feel very strongly that we have had all the signals we could ask for in predicting the monetary and economic storm. Already the skies in the north are black, and the winds are rising. The temperature is dropping. This may be a preliminary storm, or it might be **the big one**. On the farm we didn't worry if *the storm* came a little later than we expected. The important thing was to be ready for it. It came when it came. Why should we wish it before it came? Or why should we conclude that because it had not yet arrived, it would not happen at all?

We are now entering the period of winter. If we are ready for it, we need not fret, nor hope that it will happen tomorrow, nor hope that it will happen sooner or later. We have no control. Our situation is simply this: To the best of our financial and economic ability we have stocked our cellar, boarded up our house, and we might as well relax. "Let her come. We were here first."

This book is concerned with a universal ROLLOVER. That means the end of an era of permissiveness, the end of an era of the spoilage of people, the end of an era of credit and waste, the end of an era of something for nothing, the end of an era to buy now and pay later, the end of an era of dependence on someone else.

End of an Era of Inflation

Americans aged 40 years and younger have become so

accustomed to the idea that the country owes them at least a living that the withdrawal of this presumed privilege could result in widespread rioting across the nation. Empty bellies produce inflamed minds.

One thing is certain. You will see the collapse of this inflation and that will mean the end of the era you have known. But you and your country can still be saved. The storm **can** be weathered. The **ROLLOVER** will come.

APPENDIX

Trendlines are notorious indicators. They are used by millions of people and almost everyone closely connected with the market. They are subject to interpretation. If the price of a stock is in a decline for over a period of six months, we're talking about a six-month trendline and, depending on the fundamentals, that picture is subject to changes which we cannot foresee and, being on the outside, do not know about.

But if you have a trendline for a year, that is more solid; for two years even more solid; for five years very solid; for 10 or 15 years you have an ocean tide. It's not a guarantee, of course, but if broken it makes the old trendline very suspect, and as an investor **you would be well advised to abandon your previous positions based on the direction of that long, long trendline. Something is very much amiss.**

Presented here is a trendline of inflation from 1948 to 1984. The net message of the trendline is that inflation on the average has been proceeding at the rate of about 5% for more than three decades.

Inflation dropped back to touch the rising trendline in late 1964, again in 1972 and nearly touched it again in 1976. **But never was the trendline broken.** After the contact, inflation roared ahead again and, as you can see from the graph, exceeded 10% in 1979 and actually reached 15% in 1980. Throughout this subsequent period one had to wonder whether the fall of inflation would once again merely touch the trendline and bounce off and go into a new superinflation.

However, it did not.

In 1981 the inflation hesitated at the trendline, but in hardly any time at all began sinking again.

279

It is clear from the graph that a very definite break in the inflation trendline occurred in 1982 and 1983. It's unmistakable and it's a violation of a trend of 36 years. **That has to carry great meaning.**

The inflation rose to some extent in 1983 but it did not rise to reach the previous level of the trendline. It continued to operate below the trendline, and now inflation has commenced to fall once again.

It means that a whole era of inflation has gone out of style. Those who call for superinflation and ruinous inflation ought to be badly shaken in their boots by the fracturing of this trendline. If indeed inflation were in the cards, the falling inflation as seen in the right-hand portion of this graph, would have bounced once again off the trendline and we should now be at around 10% inflation.

Obviously, and fundamentally, things have changed. The disinflation has persisted in spite of the Iran/Iraq war and in spite of government benefits continuing, and in spite of the widespread almost universal expectation that we would soon be facing a renewed inflation, more rabid than ever before.

Gold, too, has paid attention to this trendline and it has dropped several hundred dollars since 1980.

The downward trend of inflation and the falling price of gold promise to remain in tandem. Unless we get a big reversal in the inflationary picture in the world, you can look for the price of gold to continue to fall with shrinking inflation.

A trendline of a third of a century has been violated. We'd better pay attention.